America's
Concentration
Camps

AMERICA'S CONCENTRATION CAMPS *Allan R. Bosworth*

Introduction by Roger Baldwin

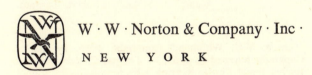 W · W · Norton & Company · Inc ·

NEW YORK

To the past and present members of the Japanese American Citizens League. Through precept and example and their wholehearted devotion to an ideal, they could teach other Americans a great deal about Americanism.

Introduction

Although this story of racist hysteria and abuse of government power took place twenty-five years ago during World War II, its significance is far greater than that of a piece of history. This significance lies in the fact that the law today provides for what might be a repetition of the same violations of citizens' rights under the fears of war, as the author points out in his concluding pages.

It is no unwarranted speculation. In order not to be caught again improvising measures for security in wartime or a national emergency declared by the President, Congress has thoughtfully provided that next time camps will be ready for the immediate internment of all persons, aliens and citizens alike, whom the FBI and other intelligence agencies suspect of sympathy with whatever enemy then confronts us.

It may seem incredible that native-born American citizens could be thus arrested and herded without trial into internment camps; but that is exactly what happened to tens of thousands of Americans of Japanese ancestry on the Pacific Coast in the last world war. As the then director of the American Civil Liberties Union, which is dedicated to defending the rights of all Americans, I was at once involved in the legal and practical problems raised by what the Commanding General in San Francisco called "military necessity," and what we of the ACLU regarded as constitutional issues.

Captain Bosworth, a former San Francisco journalist who was then serving in the Navy Intelligence, saw the issues as we did. The Navy could see no military necessity for the internment and opposed the Army's action. Captain Bosworth has now added to the literature on the episode a fresh look backed by interviews and research, enlivened by personal stories of the evacuees that give a vivid impression of official folly and its cost in human suffering.

From the start, the evacuation and later internment of over 100,000 people was a tragic and confused affair. As I look back on it after all these years, with my memory refreshed by these pages, I am impressed most by a fact that at the time seemed irrelevant to the abuses. It was the loyalty of the Japanese Americans to the United States and their uncomplaining patience under the most extreme adversity that seem so remarkable, and Captain Bosworth emphasizes them. Here was a minority only one generation away from Japan, among whom, aliens and citizens alike, there was not one single instance of sabotage or espionage, despite all the charges and suspicions.

Here was a minority interned in concentration camps under the most austere conditions. But their young men demanded the right to

6

serve in the armed forces as equals of other American youth. In
Europe they distinguished themselves on the field of battle, emerging
the most decorated regiment in American army history; and in the
Pacific they rendered unique services as soldiers and interpreters.

I suppose it is the irony of their loyalty in the face of distrust,
abuse, and racial hostility that moves us most in this unhappy story.
In Hawaii, closest to the enemy, the Japanese were not interned. The
Hawaiians knew their Japanese and trusted them. So did the U. S.
military forces. They scorned the words of the commanding general
on the Pacific Coast to whom "A Jap's a Jap," enemy or citizen, and
who demanded the evacuation that not even the FBI or the Navy
thought necessary. But it received the approval of all the higher
departments of government. The President issued the necessary executive order; Congress approved; and the Supreme Court, bowing to
the Army's finding of necessity, validated the removal.

But perhaps the most striking of ironies was the fact that no evacuation was even suggested for the Germans and Italians, aliens or citizens, on the Atlantic Coast where submarines and defense installations were far more numerous, and the dangers of espionage and
sabotage apparently greater. Only racism can explain the discrimination.

Captain Bosworth gives us the precise record of this sad and tragic
dislocation of a whole people from their homes, their internment in
idleness in desert barracks, the stories of bewildered families, of government stupidities, of a government bureaucracy trying to make the
best of a bad job in servicing the camps.

When the government prepared, toward the end of the war, after
dangers from Japan had passed, to dismantle the camps, most of the
inmates were fearful of returning home to face hostility and uncertainty, goods and homes had been seized, and recovery would take
time. Even the President was quite aware of the prospect of trouble;
he ordered "nothing sudden, and in not too great quantities." But
they went back to the coast by the end of the war, all but some
thousands of the younger people who had gone east to make new
homes. And eventually they got back their homes. The vast property damages of over $100 million were paid off at about 10 percent.

Some good came of the tragedy. Besides the easier assimilation of
the many who left the west coast, citizenship for alien orientals (who
were previously ineligible for citizenship) was won—largely through
the efforts of the Japanese American Citizens League, a still-lively organization, which even before the war represented the hopes for
equality of the whole Japanese minority. Equality, with a few minor
survivals of discriminatory legislation, has been won. Three Japanese
Americans sit in Congress, one a senator. In every profession and
occupation our citizens of Japanese ancestry distinguish themselves.

Japan is now a friend and ally. Suspicion and hate were quickly
dissipated as the world political picture changed, illustrating the folly

of enmity between peoples. Probably no immigrant minority in America has made so striking an adjustment as the Japanese, and that, despite the most callous collective treatment ever accorded a racial minority by our government.

But it could be repeated. The laws and the machinery are ready for another day, another war, another emergency, another minority, as Captain Bosworth suggests. Maybe suicidal wars are out and a world order is taking shape, so that we may not have to face another such horror. But it did happen once. It should be the profound concern of every public-minded American to see that it does not ever happen again—whatever the challenge to our national security.

—Roger Baldwin
Director, 1917–1950
American Civil Liberties Union

Acknowledgments

A book such as this one naturally owes much to a great many people, some of whom actively assisted in the research of historical facts, others of whom generously shared personal memoirs. All were exceedingly kind. The writing has taken a considerable time, my records are poor, and my memory is treacherous. I apologize, beforehand, if some names have been omitted from the list which appears below.

I am very deeply indebted to Mike Masaoka, Washington representative of the Japanese American Citizens League, and to his secretary, Mary Toda. In Washington, I also owe thanks to John Y. Yoshino of the Department of Commerce, Bureau of Public Roads, and to his wife, Mary Louise Yoshino. Key K. Kobayashi of the Library of Congress and Mr. and Mrs. George Suzuki of the Washington area supplied important help. Admiral Arthur H. McCollum, U.S. Navy (retired), who was once my commanding officer, exhibited the Navy's spirit of loyalty up and loyalty down by coming to my aid. Far out in Japan, James Kipling Cooper of the Copley News Service did the same: he also had served with me in the Navy.

Laura McDaniel of La Grange, Ill., gave me some leads. Mrs. Donna H. Traxler and Mrs. Edna Curcio of the Army's pictorial section in the Pentagon helped with photos. So did James Moore and others in the National Archives.

I greatly appreciate the assistance of Dr. Joseph D. Sasaki of Ann Arbor, Michigan, and that of Mary Frances Stewart and Alice and Richard Winn of Sacramento, California.

My acknowledgments include famous names. Eugene V. Rostow, Dean of the Yale Law School, kindly permitted me to draw upon his scholarly observations concerning the constitutionality of the Evacuation. Jacobus ten Broek of the University of California, author of a definitive work on the Evacuation, did the same. Colonel Karl R. Bendetsen, U.S. Army (retired), graciously granted an interview which cleared up a number of things.

I am grateful for the assistance of Gordon Shoemaker of The Homestead, Hot Springs, Virginia. Similar help was rendered by Margot Coley, Director of Public Relations at The Greenbrier, White Sulphur Springs, West Virginia, and by officials of the Grove Park Inn, Asheville, North Carolina.

Special debts are owed to Harry Honda and the entire staff of the *Pacific Citizen,* to Mas Satow, and other officials of the Japanese American Citizens League.

Raymond Best, of Carmichael, California, had the courage to explain and defend his status as Director of the Tule Lake Relocation Center in California. He did this well, and I honor him, and am inclined to believe that in some accounts he was grievously abused.

My literary mentor, Marie Rodell, provided her usual excellent professional counsel. Merrill Pollack, my editor, deserves a vast amount of credit for cutting out the "gee whiz" and over-emotional passages in this work, and keeping it strictly objective. Their help was exceptional, in that both Mrs. Rodell and Mr. Pollack themselves succumbed to emotion a few times while reading it.

Finally, when all had been reduced to a complicated mass of penciled and confused manuscript, Mrs. Ruby Smith did a superb job of restoring order with a clean typed copy. To her, my warmest thanks.

—Allan R. Bosworth

America's Concentration Camps

Wide open and unguarded stand our gates,
Named of the four winds, North, South, East and West;
Portals that lead to an enchanted land . . .
Here, it is written, Toil shall have its wage
And Honor honor, and the humblest man
Stand level with the highest in the law.

—Thomas Bailey Aldrich

One

From little towns in a far land we
came,
To save our honour and a world
aflame.
By little towns in a far land we
sleep;
And trust that world we won for
you to keep.

—Rudyard Kipling, *Epitaphs of the War.*

I

By the summer of 1944, the Americans of the 100th Infantry
Battalion and the 442nd Regimental Combat Team had come
a long and rugged way from the mud of Mississippi and had
even longer to go. They moved steadily northward from Na-
ples to keep their rendezvous with fame and death.

If any troops ever had an excessive amount of that intangi-
ble thing called *esprit de corps,* it was the men of the 100th
and the 442nd. Their motto was "Go for Broke," which is a
Hawaiian crapshooter's term for "shoot the works." The
442nd did that on many occasions. Practically none of the
GI's complained, because they were finally where they wanted
to be—in the war. At Cassino there was a little griping, not
about the fighting, which was hard indeed, but because for
three days there was nothing to eat but C rations. The cooks
were AWOL, their field kitchens abandoned. But they had not
deserted (no man assigned to the 442nd ever did desert, a record unmatched by any other American military outfit). Every
one of them was up in the front line serving as a rifleman, an
ammunition carrier, or at least a litter bearer.[1]

The Americans of the 442nd advanced fifty miles in four
days, liberating eleven towns. One war correspondent, John

13

Lardner, reported that he was astounded when the whole outfit made a night march of four miles over rocky and terraced
uphill farm land, with each man carrying a case of rations or a
forty-five-pound can of water. The 442nd was tough physically and morally. "They did it," Lardner wrote, "breezing." [2]

They were in the line four weeks without a break, getting
only two hours sleep a night, spending the rest of the time
whipping elite, battle-hardened Nazi SS and Jaeger troops.
They cleaned up every sector assigned to them in Italy, and on
September 27, 1944, they embarked aboard the transports
Thurston, Dickman, Chase, and *Henrico* and sailed to Mar-
seille. From there they went on to their crowning glory in the
French Vosges, where they rescued the "Lost Battalion"—
some three hundred Texans of the 36th Division who had
been surrounded for a week. When the 442nd began its attack, it took the "Go for Broke" outfit only thirty-five minutes
to smash a Nazi stronghold that had defied other Allied forces
for five weeks. The 442nd suffered 60 percent casualties in
this fight—a greater number of dead and wounded than the
number of troops saved. In many companies, only thirty or
forty men answered roll call after this mission. The normal
strength of a company was two hundred men.

Before the batteries died in the radios of the beleaguered
Texans, they got off one final message: "442nd patrols in
sight. We love them!" And they did—to the extent that in
characteristic Texas fashion an immediate move was begun to
make all the 442nd "honorary citizens" of the Lone Star State.
(The war got in the way of this gesture, and it took a while.
But six years later, by Governor's proclamation, all members
of the Regimental Combat Team were made honorary citizens
of Texas.)

II

A great deal of the brave and bloody fighting that rescued the
Lost Battalion took place on October 27. By then, the entire

Nation was proud of the fighting unit. Honors and awards piled up along with the casualties. A final tally of the honors, at the end of the war, showed:

7 major campaigns in Europe
7 Presidential Unit Citations
9,486 casualties
18,143 individual decorations, including:
    1 Congressional Medal of Honor
   52 Distinguished Service Crosses
    1 Distinguished Service Medal
 560 Silver Stars, with 28 Oak Leaf Clusters in lieu of second Silver Star awards
  22 Legion of Merit Medals
     Approximately 4,000 Bronze Star awards, with about 1,200 Oak Leaf Clusters representing second Bronze Stars
  15 Soldier's Medals
  12 French Croix de Guerre, with two Palms representing second awards
    2 Italian Crosses for Military Merit
    2 Italian Medals for Military Valor [3]

These statistics are impressive, because the 442nd was a rather small outfit. Its exact strength at any given time is difficult to determine. It had no historian attached to its staff; records were destroyed by fire and explosion in the field; there were necessarily many replacements. On November 18, 1944, after the bloody fighting to save the Lost Battalion, 382 replacements came in—and these brought the outfit to about half its strength. On the following day, when the 442nd was pulled out of the line and ordered back to Nice, 1,800 of its men were in hospitals, and 140 had been killed in the previous twenty-five days of action.

Official Army figures said later that the casualties were 314 percent of the unit's original strength.

If that sounds impossible, consider soldiers like Allen H. Okamoto, who went through four battles, was wounded three times, and therefore was officially counted as three casualties.[4] There were many like him. The battle flags of the 442nd showed where and how well its members had fought; the muster rolls revealed how gallantly they died, and the Pentagon records revealed that this was the most decorated unit in the United States Army, in all its history.

Back in the United States, fondly known as CONUS (Continental U.S.) and ZI, or the Zone of the Interior, the Army had been sending spit-and-polish teams to present posthumous awards to the families of these fallen heroes. Color guards turned out. Military ceremony was observed as the DSC's and Silver Stars, Bronze Stars and Purple Hearts were pinned on mothers' blouses.

The parents of the dead heroes, or the wives and brothers and sisters, could not go to Washington or even to the nearest Army base to accept these honors. They were under machine-gun guard, behind barbed wire and searchlight watch towers; they were being detained in the tar-paper barracks of ten dreary camps called Wartime Relocation Centers.

Virtual prisoners of war, many of the mothers were in those camps for as long as four years, or many months after their sons had died for America. Neither the Gold Star mothers, nor any of the rest of a total of more than 110,000 people, had been charged with any crime. None had any kind of hearing. None had a day in court.

But they had names like Okamoto. They had names like Muranaga . . .

PFC Kiyoshi K. Muranaga's company had been stalled in difficult terrain and was suffering heavy casualties from the fire of an 88-millimeter gun. Muranaga went out voluntarily, single-handed, with a mortar. The Germans withdrew the gun after his third well-placed shot. But their last round killed Muranaga.

They had names like Nakamura . . .

PFC William K. Nakamura, fighting at Hill 140 on the Fourth of July, crawled within fifteen yards of a machine gun that had pinned down his platoon and killed the entire crew with hand grenades. He repeated this performance in a later action, at the cost of his own life.

They had names like Masuda . . .

Staff Sergeant Kazuo Masuda, a truck gardener from Santa Ana, California, ran uphill for twenty-five yards through heavy enemy fire, twisting and sidestepping like a fullback, carrying a 60-millimeter mortar tube, a supply of ammunition, and a spare helmet. He filled the helmet with dirt, used it for his mortar mount, and wrapped his legs around the weapon to steady it. Masuda fired the mortar for twelve hours, twice returning to his own lines through continuous artillery fire for more ammunition. He turned back two enemy attacks. Later, on an Arno River patrol, Sergeant Masuda died holding off the Nazis so the rest of his patrol could reach safety.

And they had names like Munemori . . .

PFC Sadao Munemori's outfit was pinned down by heavy enemy fire. Munemori volunteered to go into action with hand grenades. He knocked out two machine-gun nests. He was rejoining his comrades in a shell crater when an activated grenade caromed off his helmet. Munemori instantly rose in a withering hail of bullets, and dived to smother the grenade with his own body just before it exploded. He was blown in half. He was awarded the Congressional Medal of Honor, and is buried in Los Angeles. At this writing, Munemori's mother still lives in Long Beach. For what it may be worth, Munemori was a good Buddhist.[5]

III

The names—Muranaga, Nakamura, Masuda, Munemori— suggest the men were foreign, but they had been born American citizens; their parents were Japanese who had come to this country twenty and forty and sixty years before.

Altogether, 33,000 Japanese Americans, more than half of them from the continental United States and the rest from Hawaii, served in World War II. They were divided almost equally between Europe and the Pacific.[6] Most Americans are not aware of the presence of these troops in the Pacific. The 442nd, with its colorful "Go for Broke" motto, was much better publicized: early in 1951 Metro-Goldwyn-Mayer produced a motion picture under that title. The 442nd's personnel were virtually all Japanese Americans. It was, except for its commissioned officers, a segregated unit, and, as such, more readily identifiable in terms of publicity.

On the other hand, the thousands of Japanese Americans who fought in the Pacific theater suffered some loss of identity because they served alongside thousand upon thousands of ordinary GI Joes. Mainly they did combat intelligence work, served as interpreters, and constantly ran the risk of being shot at by their own troops because they looked like the enemy. General Charles Willoughby, Chief of Staff for Intelligence to General Douglas MacArthur, expressed the belief that the use of these Japanese Americans shortened the Pacific war by at least two years and saved hundreds of thousands of American casualties.

No matter where these Americans were fighting, the fact remains that their parents, wives, and younger brothers and sisters were, for practical purposes, prisoners behind barbed wire. It was not supposed to happen in America, a nation made up of immigrants, but it did. Seventy thousand of the more than 110,000 people who were uprooted from their homes and herded behind barbed wire in 1942 were U.S. citizens. These were the *Nisei* (pronounced *Nee*-say), or second generation. They had attended American schools and knew nothing but America; they liked hot dogs and football games and jazz, and were whizzes at playing baseball. Not one in ten could really speak Japanese. Their language was pure American, filled with colloquialisms and West Coast accents.

Their parents were *Issei* (pronounced *Ee*-say), or "first generation in America." These were the early settlers, with a genuine pioneer spirit. They had come to a strange land—where it seemed every man's hand was against them—and they did well. Many of them were farmers who loved flowers and knew how to grow strawberries two inches long. They worked cheerfully from dawn until dark, and their names were never written on police blotters. Actually, since school dropouts had never been known in Japan, practically all of them had a high school education, and quite a few had attended college. Their educational average therefore was higher than the average of many people in this country.

It has been said that they did not lend themselves to assimilation. Their neighbors on the West Coast were hostile toward the Japanese émigrés from the very beginning; assimilation was never encouraged. They had very little chance to intermingle. The sociological meaning of "assimilation" is the merging of cultural traits from previously distinct cultural groups, not involving biological amalgamation. There is a considerable difference between this and "intermingling." The West Coast Japanese actually assimilated a great deal of the American culture, while at the same time understandably—and desirably—cherishing and retaining some of their own folkways.

Any doubts about the Nisei certainly should have been ended by the patriotic sacrifices of the 442nd Regimental Combat Team and by the Nisei who fought and died in Burma and other parts of the Pacific. The attitude of the people in the Relocation camps should have counted for something. But as late as February, 1945—which was pretty late in the scheme of things—an Oklahoma Congressman named Jed Johnson reportedly made an "extension of remarks" suggesting a piece of Hitlerian legislation to take care of the Japanese in the Relocation Centers. This was to the effect that Congress should make an appropriation to sterlize the whole outfit.[7]

Few people today know who Sadao Munemori was, but many can tell you that Sergeant Alvin York, a Tennessee hillbilly, captured a whole passel of Germans, single-handed, in World War I. Kenny Yasui's feat in World War II was not so well-publicized, possibly because it happened on the India-Burma front. Kenny became known as "Baby York" because he personally captured sixteen Japanese. He posed as a Japanese colonel, ordered the men to stack their arms, and then marched them off to commands he had learned as a student in Tokyo.[8]

Kenny Yasui was a Nisei. He also was what was known as a *Kibei* (pronounced *Kee*-bay), which means "returned to America." There were several thousand Kibei in this country at the time of the war, who had been at least partially educated in Japan. A great deal of suspicion was attached to them individually and as a group.

Probably ninety-nine percent of this suspicion was unjustified. Sending one's son back to the homeland to wear the old school tie was nothing new among immigrants to America, and the Issei had reasons for doing this which went beyond the bounds of mere sentiment. Not many jobs were open to their children; they stood a better chance of employment with Japanese firms on the West Coast if they could speak Japanese.

IV

The Evacuation of the people of Japanese blood from the West Coast was a remarkable event in American history. It had an unsavory precedent. In the 1830's, our Government moved another minority group out of its homes. These were the American Indians—Choctaws, Cherokees, Chickasaws, and Creeks—who had been living in the South since long before the white man came.

With the Seminoles in Florida (who were not affected), they were known as the Five Civilized Tribes. Under treaties made with the United States, they had been granted the right to maintain a system of tribal governments, but the states of Georgia, Alabama, and Mississippi passed legislation outlawing such governments and putting the Indian nations under state jurisdiction. The Indians appealed to President

Jackson. Jackson said that the federal government was power-less to abide by the old treaties, and he began negotiating for new ones under which the four tribes would consent to re-moval west of the Mississippi River.

As a result, Congress passed the Indian Removal Bill in 1830. The bill did not authorize the eviction of any Indian but empowered the President to initiate land "exchanges" with the tribes. The Nations did not want to remove west of the Missis-sippi, or anywhere else, but each of the three states adopted another law which prevented any court from accepting the tes-timony of an Indian against a white man, and life for the Indi-ans became progressively worse. This measure virtually sanc-tioned crooked land deals, fraudulent certification of land ti-tles, and much other shady business. Only a white man could administer the estate of an Indian who died, and the seizure of properties became a very lucrative practice. Squatters, land speculators, and bootleggers moved in—and the federal gov-ernment continued to insist that it had no more control over these opportunists than it had over the state legislators. One by one, the leaders of the four tribes despaired and weakened.

Removal began in November, 1831, with the first party of four thousand Choctaws setting out for "exchange" land they had chosen in western Arkansas. It was a desperately cold winter; the Mississippi River was choked with ice at Vicks-burg, and the migrants were ill-equipped and poorly clad. Re-moval went on. For five successive summers, although Vicks-burg had cholera epidemics, the people were forced to pass through that area.

The Creeks had five years, under the removal treaty, in which to select their "exchange" land. They delayed for four of those five years, but in 1836 the Secretary of War ordered the Army to move the whole tribe at once, as a "military mea-sure." The Creeks walked westward in a double file hand-cuffed and chained together.

The Cherokees, most civilized of all five tribes, kept fighting and finally took their case to the U.S. Supreme Court. The court found that the State of Georgia had violated the Constitution and Chief Justice John Marshall scathingly denounced its actions. But then President Jackson effectively nullified the judicial decision by simply refusing to enforce it: federal forces, he said, were too feeble.

In 1838 and 1839, the Cherokees also were removed by force—the last of some fifty thousand people driven from a country that had been theirs for untold centuries before the white man came. The Cherokees were guilty of no crime; they were in the unfortunate situation of owning land their new neighbors coveted. William Brandon, in the American Heritage *Book of Indians,* says the Cherokees were dispossessed with the excuse of a false treaty and that nearly one-fourth of them died on the hard journey to what later would be known as the "Cherokee Strip" in Indian Territory. And there would come a time, of course, when even the Cherokee Strip would be thrown open, very dramatically, to the white homesteader . . . so that the Indian had neither justice nor peace.

Eviction—Evacuation—and the covetous glance at the land of a neighbor were to be repeated more than a hundred years later.

Few people know anything today about the Indian Removal of the 1830's. It seems obvious that America has done its best to forget the whole thing; the episode has been glossed over in school history texts. For that matter, relatively few people today know anything about the Evacuation of the West Coast Japanese in 1942, which, in the minds of many, constituted a shocking violation of civil rights on a mass scale. The words of Section One of the Fourteenth Amendment to the Constitution, declared in force July 26, 1868, are plain:

All persons born or naturalized in the United States . . . are citizens of the United States and of the States wherein they reside. No State shall make or enforce any law which shall abridge [their] privileges and immunities . . . [nor] deprive life, liberty, or prop-

erty, *without due process of law;* nor deny to any person . . .
the equal protection of the laws [italics supplied].

The civil rights movement is on the march today as never
before, but in 1942 martial law was *not* declared on the West
Coast, and the civil statutes were still in force. Yet, a few
months after the war began, seventy thousand American citizens were deprived of their liberty without due process of law;
they were certainly denied the equal protection of the laws,
and they were deprived of their property in many cases without just or adequate compensation.

The things that happened in 1942 had the quality of nightmare: they began in fear and continued in hysteria. Virtually
no one analyzed what was going on or understood its full, ominous significance; the few people who objected did not protest
loudly enough when they argued that the cause of the Japanese Americans was the cause of every citizen. It still is today,
for the constitutionality of the Evacuation was later upheld
by the U.S. Supreme Court in one of the strangest and most
ambiguous decisions ever handed down by that tribunal.

Because of that extremely dangerous decision, no minority
group in this country is really safe, today, from federal search,
seizure, and impoundment. *Nobody* is safe, under certain conditions, from unexpected detention and incarceration.

Two

Oh, what was your name in the
    States?
Was it Thompson or Johnson or
    Bates?
Did you murder your wife
And flee for your life?
Say, what *was* your name in the
    States?

—A limerick from the Gold Rush days.

I

In the sixteenth and seventeenth centuries, Spain's Franciscan friars left their sandaled footprints on the beaches of California, along with place names that ring like cathedral bells. But they were not the first strangers to come to that Pacific shore, and 1965 archaeological discoveries near Acapulco in Mexico prove that Asiatics were in the western hemisphere as much as two thousand years before Columbus.

The Mexicans found pottery which exactly matched pottery found on the Japanese island of Kyushu and was known to antedate the Christian era by two or three thousand years. However, one should not leap to the conclusion that these artifacts—in either case—were Japanese. They could have been Chinese, since it is known that the Chinese, long ago, invaded the southern Japanese islands.

Richard F. Pourade, a distinguished San Diego historian, cites ancient Chinese literature which tells of visits to the land of Fusang, "on the other side of the ocean." The land described here is California. Pourade points out that the clumsiest of ships could have sailed from China to the California coast without ever being long out of the sight of land. And of

24

course there was a time when people could walk, dry shod, across Bering Straits, from Siberia to Alaska.

The Chinese were never notable colonists, but Pourade thinks it strange that the Japanese did not take more interest in the lands touched by the Pacific. In August, 1610—a decade before the voyage of the Mayflower—a Japanese ship visited the Mexican port of Acapulco, bringing twenty-three Japanese merchants. There was another voyage in 1613.

But for a quirk of history, then, the sandals of the Franciscan friars might well have been preceded by the marks of wooden Japanese geta, and Monterey today could easily have had the Japanese name Matsuyama, Pine Mountain. Three hundred years ago, when British colonists had no more than a foothold on the Atlantic coast of America, Japan was a powerful, warlike, and highly advanced nation. At that time, however, it was embarking upon a course of withdrawal. The Tokugawa Shogunate had observed Spanish missionary efforts in Southeast Asia and was determined that Japan would not be corrupted by such teachings: it shut the country's gates upon the outside world in a way that made Russia's Iron Curtain which, of course, came much later, look like a mosquito netting.[1]

The isolation lasted more than two hundred years. A United States naval officer, Commodore Matthew Calbraith Perry, ended it in 1853 when he sailed his "black ships" into Tokyo Bay and negotiated a commercial and diplomatic treaty virtually at gunpoint. Perry accomplished this beautifully, with just the right show of force and a considerable display of pomp and circumstance. He excited the Japanese by showing American trade goods and running a steam train on a Yokohama beach. He had an interpreter named Manjiro Nakahama, known for many years in this country as "John Mungo," who had been rescued from an uninhabited island in 1841 by the New Bedford whaleship *John Howland*. One of the owners of that vessel was Warren Delano—grandfather of Franklin Delano Roosevelt.[2]

Perry opened Japan to the outside world, and—with such things as his steam locomotive—touched off an industrial revolution in that country the like of which has never been seen anywhere. Japan, a mediaeval nation in 1853, was a highly industrial country before 1900. She earned the name of imitator and copycat. But Japan was not so much imitating as she was "adapting." She took what she needed, or liked, and then set about improving it.

II

The first Japanese in this country, for the most part, were scattered castaways on the West Coast; many were shipwrecked sailors who had been put ashore in Hawaii and came on to the mainland. What there was of immigration, in those days, began gradually.

A Dutch adventurer named Schnell, married to a Japanese and reportedly a Japanese citizen, established a tea and silk plantation near Placerville, California, in 1869. He smuggled a dozen farmers out of Japan, and, the story goes, when he went back there to get more tea plants, he was executed. The last tea plant died a few years ago, and now the only monument to the colony is a tombstone in El Dorado County marked IN MEMORY OF OKEI, DIED 1871, AGED 19 YEARS (A JAPANESE GIRL). Okei is believed to have been the first Japanese woman in America.[3]

But she may not have been. Records kept by Chinese brothel owners in the hard-rock mining camp of Denver during the 1860's list "pleasure girls" named Ohana, Oyuki, Osumi, and so on. These were undoubtedly Japanese girls, smuggled in from China in the shiploads of coolies coming to work in the mines.[4] What we call the "white slave trade" was flourishing. A shapely, petite, dainty Japanese girl was no doubt a great attraction.

Official U.S. Bureau of the Census figures show that (not

including Hawaii or Alaska) there were only 55 Japanese in this country in 1870, and only 148 in 1880. When the Chinese Exclusion Act was passed in 1882, Japanese were in demand to replace the Chinese as laborers, and in 1890 there were 2,039 Japanese in the United States. In 1900, there were 12,268 arrivals.[5] By 1910, America was home—if not exactly haven—to 72,157 Japanese.

Long before 1910, the bugaboo of the "Yellow Peril" had been conveniently transferred from the banned Chinese to the later arrived sons of Nippon, and the voice of bigotry was loud and shrill along the western slope.

The discovery of gold in Sutter's Creek touched off one of the most adventurous and significant migrations in American history. Men came from the South, where the blacks were still slaves. They came from Texas, the proud new state with such a glorious and violent history. They came up from the Mexican War still singing the incongruously gentle "Green Grow the Lilacs." They sweated across the Isthmus of Panama from all over the East. Bearded men came from Pike County in such numbers that they were called "Pikes."

Digging for gold was a tough and competitive business. California in the forties and fifties was a frontier: it attracted the tough and the ugly, and never mind what a man's name was back in the States. Racial prejudices were simple. The early settlers were dedicated to what a government inspector said in 1858 was the "great cause of civilization, which, in the natural course of things, must exterminate Indians." Many of the Missourians and other inlanders had never before seen a "foreigner," and the color of a man's skin was important. A Scandinavian, arrived yesterday, could say he was "American," and be accepted. Indians, the most American of all, had no rights. Neither did the swarthy Mexicans, who were called "Greasers."

Then the Chinese came . . . and violence found a new outlet.

Everything that later befell the Japanese Americans had its

origin in what happened to the Chinese. In 1857, a newspaper, the *Shasta* [California] *Republican,* said that

hundreds of Chinamen have been slaughtered in cold blood during
the last five years by desperadoes that infest our state. [Yet] we
have heard of but two or three instances where the guilty parties
have been brought to justice.[6]

Small wonder, since California had passed a state law pro-
hibiting Chinese from testifying in cases that involved whites.

In 1862, the Californians got back to the redskins with a
vengeance. They attacked Indian Island in Humboldt Bay,
after dark, and killed more than two hundred people, mostly
women and children. While the Indians indulged in occasional
livestock thefts and other depredations, the incident that
sparked this foray has not been recorded. The American
Heritage *Book of Indians* quotes an old-timer, Kingsley, who
told how Sacramento Valley ranchers found a steer wounded
by Indians, trailed the redskins with dogs, trapped them in a
cave, and killed

about thirty. . . . In the cave . . . were some Indian children.
Kingsley could not bear to kill these children with his 56-caliber
Spencer rifle. "It tore them up so bad." So he did it with his 38-
caliber Smith and Wesson revolver.

At the presidio town of Los Angeles, a white man was shot
in a tong war. A mob stormed the Chinese section, killed six
people, and hanged fifteen others, including women and children, from handy awnings and lampposts.[7]

An orgy of anti-Chinese violence swept San Francisco in
1877. Tacoma's Chinese quarter was burned that year.[8] Members of "anti-coolie" clubs drove Chinese out of some fifteen California towns.[9] Discrimination was no longer a hit-or-
miss affair: It was organized. Politicians saw advantages in
this. The Workingman's Party of California rose to power
with its slogan, "The Chinese Must Go!"

Writing in the 1880's, California historian Hubert Howe
Bancroft said that in Pacific Coast annals

there is no fouler blot than the outrages perpetrated . . . upon
Indians, Mexicans and Chinese. . . . As a progressive people, we
reveal a race prejudice intolerable to civilization; as Christians we
are made to blush beside the heathen Asiatic; as just and humane
men we slaughter the innocent and vie with red-handed savages in
deeds of atrocity.[10]

For thirty years—ever since Gold Rush days—the California workingman had been fighting the Chinese in every way
possible. The California politicians were keenly attuned to the
labor vote, and no party platform was complete without a
strong anti-Chinese plank. The Democrats, who had been
against both the Negro and the Chinese since the Civil War,
took the lead in demanding Chinese exclusion: the Republicans followed suit, but not so vigorously. Discrimination,
which had begun at the grass roots with miners' antipathy
toward the Chinese, moved on up through the labor organizations and into municipal, county, and state governments, until
it was no longer confined to any group but was general practice. A large number of discriminatory laws were passed at
every level. In 1876, the California Legislature printed ten
thousand copies of a memorial to Congress, entitled, "An Address to the People of the United States on the Evils of Chinese
Immigration." These were mailed to governors, Congressmen,
and newspaper editors all over the country.

Finally the Golden State turned to Washington. In 1882,
with the sympathetic support of Southern Congressmen and
Senators, the West Coast legislators put over the Chinese Exclusion Act. This effectively halted Chinese immigration, but
in their eagerness the lawmakers slipped up. They failed to apply the ban to the Japanese.

Many of the Chinese returned to China, although no move
was made to oust those already here. Others moved inland or
all the way across the continent, away from the discrimination
of the West Coast. With the Chinese labor supply thus cut off,
many of the big employers—farmers, railroads, and others—
quickly turned to Japanese as substitutes. There was a great
difference between the two groups: Chinese coolies were

largely illiterate, the Japanese had been pretty well educated. The Chinese had been laborers, cooks, and laundrymen. They washed the miners' shirts but contributed little to America in a cultural way, other than giving us the term "Chinaman's chance." This applied to any prospecting the Chinese might do. If any gold turned up, the Americans took over.

The Japanese inherited the soiled and tattered mantle of their predecessors. In the long run, they had little more than a Chinaman's chance, themselves.

III

Japanese immigration began as a trickle in the 1880's and quickly fell into a pattern. San Francisco was the main port of entry. Few of the émigrés were older than thirty, and they came alone; the older ones usually left their families behind. Many were teen-age boys, striking out in a new world with no knowledge of the language and with only a few dollars in their pockets. They were met at the docks by hotel keepers who acted as employment agents, on commission, for all who wanted laborers.

The Chinese who had come to America during the Gold Rush days were growing old when the Chinese Exclusion Act was passed, and many of them were moving on to other parts of the nation to set up laundries and chop-suey houses. There was a shortage in the pick-and-shovel, stoop-and-squat labor supply. Railroads were expanding throughout the West and the Northwest. The first passenger train from Omaha had whistled into Cheyenne on November 14, 1867; the tracks still had to be laid to Portland, to Seattle, and all up and down the coast.

Japanese immigrants became "gandydancers": they put down the rails. Before long, the North Pacific had a crew of three hundred Issei in North Platte, Nebraska—near the geographical center of the United States—harvesting ice from ponds in winter, icing refrigerator cars in summer to keep vegetables and fruit from spoiling before reaching the Chicago and New York markets.[11]

Later, the Japanese went much farther east. Kotaro Suto, a gardener and landscape architect, went to Miami Beach in 1916, when he was thirty-three years old, and found a job working on the luxurious estate of Carl Fisher

Miami Beach was a sandy peninsula then. Suto had a very green thumb with hibiscus and all other flowering shrubs, as well as with grass and trees. But he was not content with beautifying the Carl Fisher gardens. On his own time he went out and worked along the roads that were being built into Miami Beach, and many an owner of a new home would wake one morning to find that roses or trees had been planted on his property.

"Papa" Suto, as he eventually became known, kept no count of these endeavors and made no charge for them. But almost everything he planted, due to some magic powers given only a few, thrived marvelously.

When World War II came, there were stories in Miami Beach that somebody had seen Mr. Suto hide "secret papers" in his trunk. Bill Baggs, editor of the *Miami News,* tells what happened then and afterwards:

Intelligence people knocked on the door one evening. Papa invited them in and they found the papers in the trunk. The papers were crisp new U.S. Savings Bonds. Papa was growing old in the 1950's, and he talked with friends of his concern for Masa, his wife. If he should die, she should be near relatives and her only relatives were back in Japan.

We all cried when he and Masa left. In a few months, we all laughed. Papa wrote a letter and said he was homesick and he was coming back to Miami.

In 1963, Papa Suto died. But the things he had planted so skillfully lived on as his memorial of forty-six years in Miami Beach. And on October 8, 1965, another memorial was put on a placque in the Miami Beach Conservatory, along with pictures of what he had done.

You knew, [Bill Baggs wrote] that the landscapes were not the only things better because of him. No. The soul of many persons was better because Papa Suto passed this way and stayed with us for a time.[12]

The Issei were the only ones who knew how to build dikes in San Francisco Bay so that salt could be harvested.[13] California farmers at first gladly hired the Issei as replacements for the Chinese. The new immigrants brought an ancient heritage of knowledge and skill gained from tilling the inhospitable soil of their volcanic islands, and this earth was virgin. They remembered the tiny, terraced plots of Japan, looked out over the vast California fields—and saw a lot of land being wasted. Gradually, after saving a little money, they began buying or leasing land of their own. It was usually submarginal, because they could afford no other kind. They took railroad land, and began draining and improving marshy portions of the Sacramento River delta.

After a few years of back-breaking labor, the Japanese made their little farms fruitful. There was a sudden cry of economic competition from their neighbors. It was a period when union labor was rising to political power in California, and the unions were filled with racists who saw a threat to white supremacy. The cry of "Yellow Peril" was raised.

(It has been generally believed that the West Coast, particularly California, impoverished our language with this epithet. But Barbara W. Tuchman in *The Zimmermann Telegram* quotes the London *Spectator* of December 11, 1897, as saying that Kaiser Wilhelm coined the phrase *Die gelbe Gefahr,* and was the first to use it in a public speech).

The real Yellow Peril faced by the West Coast around the turn of the century was to be found principally in yellow journalism, which was rampant and thriving. On the seventeenth of March, 1900, when San Francisco's large and boisterous Irish population was holding St. Patrick's Day parades, the editor of a paper called *Organized Labor* wrote vitriolically:

Chinatown with its reeking filth and dirt, its gambling dens and obscene slave pens, its coolie labor and bloodthirsty tongs, is a menace to the community; but the snivelling Japanese, who swarms along the streets and cringingly offers his paltry service for a suit of clothes and a front seat in our public schools, is a far greater danger to the laboring portion of society than all the opium-soaked pigtails who have ever blotted the fair name of this beautiful city.[14]

The newspapers were not alone in such attacks. A whole school of American literature denigrated the Oriental throughout the last half of the last century—and, indeed, through almost half of this one. The Chinese was usually portrayed as a wily, inscrutable heathen, a crook and a cheat, and Bret Harte's "heathen Chinee" was not so peculiar as "Plain Language from Truthful James" said. Lesser writers in the seventies and eighties ground out such thrillers as "The Chinese Invasion," "Last Days of the Republic," and "The Short and True History of the Taking of California and Oregon in the Year A.D. 1899"—this one in 1882. After the Japanese became the target, Wallace Irwin wrote his purportedly humorous *Collier's* magazine series about Hashimura Togo, in "Letters of a Japanese Schoolboy." Irwin later ran a serial called "Seed of the Sun" in *The Saturday Evening Post*, at the same time Peter B. Kyne's "Pride of Palomar" was appearing in *Cosmpolitan*. Both were racist in theme.

W. A. Swanberg, in his biography *Citizen Hearst,* recalled that while William Randolph Hearst was trying to keep the country out of World War I, he

began by waving the yellow peril in the face of America, warning that the Japanese would stab us in the back the moment we became involved in Europe. The *New York American* featured under the heading, "Japan's Plans to Invade and Conquer the United States," a "translation" of a book published in Japan, titled *The War Between Japan and America.* It was declared to have been sponsored by high Japanese officials and was said to have sold more than a million copies. (*New York American,* September 26–

October 3, 1915.) It told how Japan would ally with Mexico in an invasion that also would include the destruction of the Panama Canal.

The Japanese consul-general, who had never heard of the book, cabled home for information. He learned that the original book had been written by a Japanese newspaperman *to exploit the measures against Japanese in California* [italics supplied].

It was a flimsy effort that sold only a few thousand copies, had no official support, and was ignored by the intelligent public. Its true title was *The Dream Story of the War Between Japan and the United States.* In it there was no mention whatever of the Panama Canal. The "translation" for the Hearst press was no translation at all but included many inventions calculated to inspire fear. It was, in short, a fake.

In 1920, California's American Legion sponsored, principally on the West Coast, a luridly anti-Japanese film, *Shadows in the West,* to support its drive for a law forbidding aliens to own land.[15] In the 1930's Peter Lorre was portraying a Japanese character in *Mr. Moto* films, . . . but by 1938 feeling was running so high against Japan that the series was abandoned.

IV

Propaganda, politics, and pressure groups had replaced the cruder forms of vigilantism. The lie—or at least the wild exaggeration—was a principal weapon. In 1906, Japanese children were excluded from the San Francisco schools in what has been called a tactic to divert public attention from a notorious scandal involving Abe Ruef, political boss (later convicted of bribery) and Mayor Eugene E. Schmitz.[16] During this incident, a California Congressman went on record as saying, "It would be easy to marshal an army of *50,000 Japanese veterans* at any point in California in 48 hours [italics supplied]."

(ITEM: In 1910, the total Japanese population in the entire United States, including women and children, was 72,157.)

A press release of that most active of all anti-Japanese groups, the California Joint Immigration Committee, on March 2, 1935, quoted a charge before a Congressional group that "there are 500,000 [sic] armed Japanese in the United States." (This quotation has been attributed to a speech made by W. Almont Gates, in Buffalo, away back in 1909.)

(ITEM: In 1940, five years after the Joint Immigration Committee dusted off these ancient statistics, the total number of people of Japanese blood in this country was 126,947.)

A more subtle manipulation of the official U.S. Census figures had to do with the population yet unborn. The Japanese, it was said, were out to conquer America by sheer fecundity. . . .

The first immigrants came to this country alone. Later, those who were married sent for their families. Single men received photographs of eligible Japanese girls through the ancient system of *nakodo,* or "marriage go-betweens." The young women who came to America under this arrangement were "picture brides." It was a system not at all peculiar to the Japanese; European immigrants practiced it, too.

Discriminatory legislation was passed. The Ozawa case, decided by the Supreme Court in 1923, held that since the Founding Fathers did not contemplate Japanese in this country, alien Japanese were not eligible for naturalization. California, ten years earlier, had passed the Alien Land Law, preventing them from making further purchases of land. After World War I, with an election year coming up, California politicians and race baiters found they had failed to plug a loophole in this law: Issei parents were acquiring land in the names of their Nisei children, who were citizens.

It was found, also, that the Japanese were "breeding like rabbits." The demand for a law to stop immigration entirely was accompanied by claims that the Emperor had "ordered" Japanese wives in California to have a baby every year. In

January, 1921, John S. Chambers, the California State Controller (he just happened to be chairman of the Japanese Exclusion League) published a magazine article saying: "Their
rate of birth is between three and four times that of our own
race. . . . At this rate, in ten years there will be 150,000
Japanese born here, and by 1949 they will outnumber the
white people."[17]

(ITEM: At the end of Mr. Chambers' ten year period, there
were only 68,357 children of Japanese ancestry in America.
And the 1940 Census revealed that the birth rate among California Japanese was 15.8 per thousand, while that of the total
population was 16.1 per thousand.)

V.S. McClatchy, wealthy owner of newspapers in Sacramento and Fresno who dropped out of active newspaper management to devote all his time to the chairmanship of the
Joint Immigration Committee, reportedly had told the Senate
Committee on Immigration (in 1919) that the Japanese birth
rate was *five* times that of the whites.

A former missionary and admittedly enthusiastic (and
rather erratic) Japanophile, Dr. Sidney L. Gulick, wrote a
magazine piece attempting to prove that the Japanese birth
rate was low. In a two year period, he said, 182 babies had
been born to 524 Japanese picture brides. He asked how many
American brides would become mothers within two years
after their marriage? [18]

It was also pointed out that the white birth rate in California was low because so much of the population was made up
of older people who had retired there. The California Committee of Justice said,

Only 2.2 percent of California's total population is Japanese. . . .
We should not be placed in the ridiculous position of 97.8 percent
of our population being in fear of 2.2 percent.

But readers remember the sensational. The racists had succeeded in frightening many citizens, and the hysteria vine

flourished like the green bay tree, with the result that the Japanese Exclusion Act was passed in 1924. It was designed to prevent any more Japanese from entering this country. It had one effect that often goes unnoticed. The Issei, already middle aged, or approaching middle age, were just beginning to rear families. Unlike the members of other ethnic groups, who were still coming to this country while young, the Japanese were shut off. Seventeen years later, at the time of Pearl Harbor, an interesting and significant age gap had occurred. The Issei were nearly all fifty, sixty, or older: their children, the Nisei, for the most part, still had not come of age. At the time of the Evacuation more than 40,000 Issei parents—who were not American citizens—had to be guided by youngsters of seventeen, eighteen, and nineteen—who were.

V

A detailed account of Japanese troubles on the West Coast would overflow a five-foot shelf. It is enough to say that in the spring of 1942, West Coast officials and the West Coast public had been conditioned for the drastic step of the Evacuation, whether the Japanese were ready for it, or not.

It is not possible to say how much the West Coast attitudes contributed to the attack on Pearl Harbor and Tokyo's embarkation upon war in general. It is inarguable, however, that the Japanese were a proud and very capable race, with an ancient culture, and that the time was long past when one nation could insult another nation with impunity. Indeed, some of the discriminatory acts on the West Coast had threatened to bring on war much earlier. The 1906 San Francisco segregated school law, for instance, aroused great resentment in Tokyo, and was called "a wicked absurdity" by President Theodore Roosevelt in his annual message to Congress. Thomas A. Bailey quoted the President as telling his son, Kermit,

The infernal fools in California . . . insult the Japanese recklessly, and in the event of war it will be the Nation as a whole that will pay the consequences.[19]

The school measure led directly to the Gentlemen's Agreement of 1907, by which the U.S. government limited emigration from Japan. This stirred up ill feeling because similarly limited quotas were not applied to European nations. California acted independently in 1913, with its Alien Land Law; Washington and Oregon followed suit. The *Hartford* [Connecticut] *Times* editorialized that "of the two it might be cheaper to go to war with California than with Japan." [20]

In 1923, Californians formed a Congressional Steering Committee, opened a Washington office under V.S. McClatchy, and were active in obtaining passage of the Exclusion Act, which shut off immigration entirely. Again Japan felt insulted; again there was talk of war.

Much of this was probably emotional. Japan did not want to lose her people and made emigration difficult. But having the gates closed to Japanese was another matter. It called for face saving.

When war finally came, the pressure groups in California had been generally inactive for a decade, but they had not been disbanded. The following list includes some of the organizations that gave varying degrees of support to the campaign to evacuate or permanently get rid of the Japanese. Some were common to the entire West Coast. The names are not in any way presented in the order of their importance:

Political Groups: These included office holders and office seekers, municipal, county, state, and federal. In California, 1942 was election year.

Oriental Exclusion League: In 1908, this group had claimed 110,000 members. It was exceptionally active in 1924.

Joint Immigration Committee: The McClatchy organization which supplanted the Oriental Exclusion League. Formed "temporarily" in 1923, it was active until at least 1941. It had been made up originally of representatives from the American Legion, the State Grange, the Federation of Labor, and the Native Sons of the Golden West.

Labor Unions: Various and many.

Native Sons and Daughters of the Golden West: a social order, a lodge, a transplanted people's attempt to create a blue-blooded aristocracy out of the mere fact of California birth. It brought loud guffaws from those not eligible, and an irreverent wag wrote:

"The miners came in Forty Nine,
The whores in Fifty One;
The two soon got together,
And produced the Native Son."

The American Legion: The veterans who had fought to save Democracy got off the track and dealt Democracy some hard blows. The Legion canceled charters of Posts made up of Japanese Americans who also fought for this country in 1917. Individual Legion Councils and Posts on the West Coast submitted more than thirty resolutions aimed at evacuating the Japanese. About half of these were worded so similarly as to suggest a directed pattern. Seconding many of the Legion's policies were some units of:

United Spanish War Veterans: who forgot that seven Japanese went down with the Maine and have their names inscribed at Arlington.

Disabled American Veterans: who would soon see hundreds of Nisei being disabled in Italy, France, and the Pacific . . .

Military Order of the Purple Heart: which later would have to acknowledge that the highest percentage of Purple Hearts ever won by any U.S. Army outfit was won by the Nisei of the 442nd Regimental Combat Team . .

Veterans of Foreign Wars: who overlooked the fact that a considerable number of Nisei were already eligible to join their group.

There were others:

The Associated Farmers: composed of the big and corporate farmers, this group was especially active in the Central California Valley near Fresno and around Salinas.

California Farm Bureau Federation: which may owe its origin to the fact that in 1940 Japanese operated 5,135 farms in California, covering 226,094 acres. The average farm was valued at $16,300; the Japanese farms, usually much smaller, were valued at an average $12,800. They grew 42 percent of the state's commercial truck crops.

Western Growers' Protective Association: which apparently

protected only Caucasians.

Grower-Shipper Vegetable Association of Central California:
which did the same.

Los Angeles Chamber of Commerce: One of the most successful promotional enterprises in the world, it ultimately allowed racial bias to enter a program that had very ably plugged climate, economic growth, the movie industry, and the Los Angeles Harbor.

Clubs: Many and various. It is not meant to suggest that they
were following any line laid down by their national organizations,
but local groups of Lions Clubs, Elks Clubs, and—in California—
Townsend Clubs went on record against the Japanese. Later, there
were a number of "Ban the Japs Committees," "Anti-Japanese
Leagues," "California Preservation League," "American Leagues,"
and the like. The "American Leagues" had nothing to do
with baseball, but were designed to keep the Japanese from
coming back to California at the end of the Evacuation. Most bit-
terly active of all in this fight were the various Japanese Exclusion
Leagues, formed all up and down the West Coast. With a membership consisting principally of farmers, these groups fought to keep
the Japanese from returning and claiming their former lands.

Three

We have fought new wars and
   won them. In the French
   field
There are bones of Texarkana
   and Little Falls,
Aliens, our own; in the low-lying
   Belgian ground;
In the cold sea of the English; in
   dark-faced islands.
Men speak of them well or ill;
   they themselves are silent.

—Stephen Vincent Benét, *Ode to Walt Whitman*.

I

People living on the Atlantic seaboard in 1941 had for some time been accustomed to news of ships being sunk by Nazi submarines. But war came to the West Coast as a terrible shock, and it signified many things, large and small, after the shock subsided. It had a singular nearness. It was a chill and foreboding wind off the wide Pacific, laden with rumors and bringing nothing but bad news: Guam taken, Hong Kong seized, Wake Island fighting valiantly under hopeless siege, Manila and Cavite fallen, Bataan under attack, . . . and so on, endlessly.

War was a cultivated and well-loved voice saying "Yesterday, December 7, 1941, a date which will live in infamy. . . ." It was a sudden shrinking of distances. Honolulu had been too far away for a short vacation cruise, but now it seemed no farther than Catalina Island or the Farallons. People drove restively along the beaches and apprehensively watched sea and sky: the more imaginative fancied they saw periscopes and thought they could smell bomb smoke and bat-

41

tleships burning.

War was an anxious scanning of the latest casualty reports and sitting tensely on the edge of a chair to hear the next radio news bulletin. It was gas rationing and belt tightening, and the discovery that sugar is a strategic material. It was housewives lining up for ration coupons, and their sons standing in queues outside recruiting stations; it was Daddy taking back the old tire he had given the children for a swing.

It was all these things—multiplied by shame, uncertainty and dread—to the more than 110,000 West Coast residents of Japanese ancestry.

About two thirds of them were in their late teens and early twenties.

Sam Yoshimura was ten. He was riding his bike that Sunday morning in the small California community of Florin, and another Nisei lad ran out of his house to shout:

"Sam! Hey, Sam! The Japs have attacked Pearl Harbor!"

Sam Yoshimura didn't know what a pearl harbor was, but he sensed something dread and ominous about the news. He knew the word "Japs" was unkind and ugly and had to do with his father's people across the sea, but he didn't quite see how it applied to himself. When Sam repeated the pledge of allegiance to the flag, at school, he felt no different than other American boys.

Now he turned and pedaled soberly back home, not knowing what was in store for himself and his family, but somehow suspecting. He vowed that when he was big enough, he'd join the Army and fight "the Japs." [1]

John Kimata was fourteen, and lived in South Pasadena. On Monday, December 8th, he played hookey from school because he was fearful of what his classmates would say. When he went back Tuesday, nobody treated him any differently. It took time, in South Pasadena and some other places, for the hate fuse to sputter and burn. Eventually, one evening, rocks and eggs were thrown at John Kimata's house. [2]

Sam Yoshimura and John Kimata were both too young to fight in that war. But they were not too young to be listed by an Army General, two months later, as "among the potential enemies, of Japanese extraction," on the West Coast. They would go behind barbed wire with more than 110,000 other "potential enemies." Sam would have to sell his bicycle, since nothing could be taken to the Assembly Centers that couldn't be carried by hand. . . .

Anxieties and fears increased proportionately with age and understanding. George Suzuki was home from college for the weekend. Early in the morning of December 7th, a friend telephoned him.

"George? I'm back from a hunting trip and have a lot of ammunition left. Let's drive up into the hills and have some target practice."

They went into the hills near the Federal prison at Folsom and banged away for a while with rifles, shotguns and pistols—and then they heard the news on the car radio.

Both were mature enough to know that the veritable arsenal in the car would look bad, indeed, if they were stopped. George Suzuki remembers that he and his friend were scared out of seven years' growth, and that they drove home very, very carefully.[3]

Miné Okubo, an artist living in San Francisco's East Bay, was just back from a year in Europe on an art fellowship from the University of California. She heard the news that morning and turned to her brother.

"Oh-oh!" she said. "We're in trouble!" [4]

In San Francisco, a Kibei named Shirow Uyeno, the editor of the *New World Sun,* a bilingual English-Japanese daily, had just put his paper to bed, with the front page play devoted to President Roosevelt's message to the Japanese Emperor. Telephone calls began coming in from staff members who were home listening to their radios.

"Don't joke!" Uyeno pleaded.

They were not joking. Uyeno had to stop the press and re-plate for an extra. In doing this, he translated a radio bulletin from Honolulu that said Japanese paratroops were dropping into the city. Thus, unintentionally, he helped spread false rumors.[5]

It was quite awhile before a newspaperman could get much else. . . .

Even in its first few hours, the still undeclared war in the Pacific began to disrupt the lives and fortunes of all the people of Japanese blood.

John Yoshino and his family ran a cleaning plant in Alameda. John was a quiet and studious man, older than most Nisei. Although he had an excellent reputation, by Monday he could not draw any money out of his bank account. Bank credits of all Japanese Americans had been frozen by Federal order. The Yoshinos could not pay their employees. Customers began taking their dry cleaning elsewhere. The business failed.[6]

Just south of Oakland, Yoshimi Shibata and his four brothers, who ran the Mount Eden Nursery, had begun Sunday in their usual fashion—with a careful inspection of the rose bushes in their large greenhouse. They had 80,000 rose bushes growing in pots; their gross receipts were around $60,000 a year. They were artists in the trade, and could either accelerate the blooming of their flowers for such events as Pasadena's famed Tournament of the Roses or could "blind out" the plants through a period of hibernation, and cause them to bloom on a desired date.

The news of Pearl Harbor threw a chill into the Mount Eden greenhouses even before the steam heat was shut down. The Shibata brothers did not know whether to accelerate or retard the growth of their plants. On the next day, their bank account was frozen by government order. They had to let workers go. Even worse, the FBI had picked up their wholesale distributor in Los Angeles, so they could not sell what they had on hand.

A thriving business quickly went under. The people who leased the greenhouses while the Shibatas were in an internment camp did not know how to take care of them or how to grow roses. Later, the five Shibata brothers all enlisted in the U.S. Army and fought overseas. Later still, they came back and filed a claim against Uncle Sam for $336,000.[7]

This was only a part of what they had lost, and the average rate of reimbursement on such claims (the last one was settled in October, 1965) has been estimated at approximately ten cents on the dollar.

II

In the strange and ominous quiet which followed the attack on Pearl Harbor, no voices were raised against the West Coast Japanese, but trouble came at once to a large number of the Issei, or Japanese born noncitizens. All day that Sunday heavy radio traffic was alerting Army and Navy commands from Seattle to San Diego. Plans had been made long before to cover the eventuality of hostilities with Japan: they went by such hush-hush code names as "Orange," "Orange-Red," and "Rainbow 5." Many of the dispatches only had to say, "Execute my date-time-group so-and-so" to put things on a wartime footing.

"Nat" Pieper, West Coast head of the FBI, received his share of dispatches and telephone calls in his San Francisco office, and his agents had a busy day. By nightfall they had arrested some 1,300 potentially dangerous aliens—most of them Japanese. These arrests were selective, met no resistance, and completely lacked any elements of a James Bond international spy drama, but they were highly efficient. Naval Intelligence and the FBI had long coöperated in a program to identify known or suspected enemy agents and sympathizers. Army Intelligence had been assigned the task of policing its own personnel.

This arrangement had its unfortunate aspects. Navy and

FBI men were quite sure they knew the aliens who were or might be enemy agents, while the Army did not. This statement implies inter-Service rivalries, jealousies, and occasional reluctance to share information; such things existed. But, when war came, the Army was the senior command on the West Coast, and Lieutenant General John L. DeWitt was in the saddle.

The scope of the December 7 arrests was widened to take in civic, business, professional, and religious leaders—at least for questioning. It became a major activity. During the first year of the war, more than 12,000 enemy aliens were seized; some 3,500 were released after questioning; 2,900 were paroled by the U.S. Attorney General; more than 1,000 were freed after hearings, and more than 3,600 were interned for the duration.[8]

The FBI did a magnificent job on the theory that it was better to be safe than sorry. Of the 3,600 internees, just over half were Japanese.[9]

And who turned out to be the real spies?

After all the investigations, only one Japanese—Tsutomo Obana—was sentenced to a term of two to six months on a charge of having violated the Foreign Agent's Registration Act to cover business dealings involving the Japanese government. He had attempted to register; Japanese official red tape had held him up.[10]

Obana was the only person of Japanese blood to get even a light conviction. On the other hand:

William A. Schuler, twenty-three, of German descent, was arrested at his home in Palos Verdes, California, and on June 3, 1942, was sentenced to six years in prison by a Federal Court for sending radio messages intended for the enemy.[11]

The Reverend Kurt E. B. Molzahn, a German, was sentenced to ten years in prison on August 3, 1942, after being convicted of obtaining secret West Coast military information for Japan.[12]

Dr. Otto Willumeit, Chicago head of the German-American

Bund, pleaded guilty to charges that he plotted to transmit U.S. defense secrets both to Germany and Japan. He was sentenced to five years in prison on August 21, 1942, . . . about the time most of the Japanese Americans were being moved from the Assembly Centers to the Relocation Camps.[13]

Gerhard Wilhelm Kunze, another Bund leader, was given a fifteen year prison term that same day, on charges that he had charted harbor installations, naval dispositions, and vulnerable landing places on the Pacific Coast.[14]

Dr. Wolfgang Ebell, who, earlier, reportedly had helped Kunze and others get into Mexico, was convicted of operating an "underground railroad" to assist spies in fleeing the country.[15]

Captain Fritz Wiedemann, German Consul General in San Francisco from 1939 until July, 1941, was expelled from this country for espionage activities. He went to Europe briefly. He was in Argentina by September—and in October, 1941, he was in Tokyo.[16]

The Office of War Information said that the only person who tried to signal the Japanese attackers from Hawaii was a German spy named Bernard Julius Otto Kuehn, who not only gave Japan a system of signals but had a special dormer window built in his house from which he hoped to flash them without detection. Naval Intelligence and the FBI were on the job in Hawaii, too, and Kuehn was arrested on the day before Pearl Harbor. He was convicted on February 21, 1942, and was sentenced to be shot. On October 26, 1942, his sentence was commuted to fifty years at hard labor.[17]

There were many others, but these are enough to show that German names and Nazi loyalties ran like a strong thread through the actual story of espionage on the West Coast and elsewhere. Militarily, it all made good sense. America was hurting Hitler terribly by supplying England in those dark days; anything Hitler could do to promote a Japanese-American war was smart.

Besides, a German agent made a better spy in this country

for the simple reason that he wasn't conspicuous in his looks.
The Japanese would have been too easily recognized.

III

Yosabura Hama was fifty-eight. On the morning of December
7, he opened, as usual, his general merchandise store on Terminal Island, near San Pedro, where about five hundred Japanese families lived. Because it was the base for Japanese-
owned and radio-equipped tuna fishing boats and happened to
be close to Navy facilities, the people of Terminal Island were
about to become whipping boys.

Before noon that day, Yosabura Hama was seized by the
FBI.

The island settlement dated from 1901, when some Issei
railroad workers went to San Pedro on a holiday and found
abalone under the rocks. In Japan, where it is called *awabi,*
abalone had long been a delicacy, but in 1901 it was almost
unknown in America. Some of the Issei went into business selling dried abalone, but their neighbors were hostile. They
moved to Terminal Island, built houses on piles driven in the
tideland mud, and became fishermen. By 1940, there were
about five hundred families, and their fishing boats cruised as
far as Panama.[18]

Yosabura Hama and other business leaders were seized December 7, and of course the freezing of credits and restriction
of movement paralyzed the fishing fleet. Cash money soon ran
out, businesses were collapsing, and nothing was certain,
. . . but there was relative quiet for nearly two months.

On January 29, 1942, the U.S. Attorney General ordered
enemy aliens to evacuate certain "strategic areas"; Terminal
Island was one of these. The order touched off panic in the
community.

On February 2, two things happened. There was no planned correlation between the events, but certainly their aims were mutual. On that day a swarm of FBI agents descended on Terminal Island and arrested 336 Issei on presidential warrants as potential enemy agents. This was quite a number out of five hundred families.

On that same day, California Attorney General Earl Warren called together the sheriffs and district attorneys of a majority of California counties. He told the conference it was significant that no fifth column activities and no sabotage had been reported. These efforts, he said, were probably being saved for a specific zero hour. Later, he asked county officials from Alameda to Yuba to prepare maps showing all lands owned, occupied, or controlled by Japanese, both alien and American born.[19]

On Terminal Island, meanwhile, the confusion was multiplied by vacillating and contradictory government orders. The U.S. Justice Department on February 10 informed residents they must move by February 16. Next day, they were told the area had been put under Navy control and they would be given thirty days. Less than a week later, they were ordered out in twenty-four hours. Christian churches and other groups protested, and the deadline was put off for forty-eight hours.

Then the profiteers in human misery got busy.

There were telephone calls to the Japanese. A man's voice would say, "This is just a friendly tip. I'm with the FBI. You are going to be evacuated sooner than you think."

Within an hour or two, visitors arrived to offer ridiculous prices for household possessions.

Mrs. Yosabura Hama, whose husband already had been seized, had the store's merchandise trucked to Los Angeles and auctioned. She got about $4,000 for an inventory valued at $25,000.

She sold a $250 piano for $60, practically gave away two cars, and abandoned a gas stove, her kitchen equipment, and linens.

While Yosabura Hama was interned, the store building—which he owned—was condemned and moved from the site.[20]

IV

Warren Watanabe's father, an Issei who had been in this country since the early 1900's, was a college graduate and was a representative of the Japanese Foreign Trade association in San Francisco. This well-known organization was admittedly subsidized in part by the Imperial Japanese Government, perhaps in a way no more sinister than various federal agencies in Washington promote our own foreign trade: Japan, in other words, wanted American dollars.

The senior Watanabe was arrested on December 7 and sent to Missoula, Montana, for internment. (Some of the people who were confined there called Missoula the coldest spot in the United States.) His office was padlocked, and he had no time to dispose of his personal property. His son, Warren, sold the family car, but he got less for it than he might have because it had been stored in a public garage after his father was picked up, and somebody had removed the four new tires and replaced them with badly worn ones.

Warren Watanabe was in his third year at the University of California, with nearly a straight A scholastic record. His father had no hearing, but was offered an opportunity to be repatriated to Japan and sail on the Swedish liner *Gripsholm* with the Japanese ambassadorial and consular staffs. After what happened, he saw no future in America and accepted the offer.

Warren was sent to the Relocation Center at Topaz, Utah, and later was released to continue his education—not at University of California, which was in the restricted zone, but at the University of Chicago.[21]

Mike Masaoka, reared in the Mormon Church of the Latter Day Saints in Salt Lake City, was about as American as anybody could be, and twice as sharp as most. He was early hailed as a prodigy, breezed through college, and became the under-paid secretary of the then young Japanese American Citizens League.

Mike Masaoka wrote the Japanese American creed in 1940 to inspire the Nisei to be better citizens. It was first read to the Senate by U.S. Senator Elbert D. Thomas of Utah, then Chairman of the Senate Military Affairs Committee, and was published in the Congressional Record of May 9, 1941. It was an expression of patriotism that sustained thousands of Nisei during the difficult days of the Evacuation; it was the Bible for the heroes of the 442nd Regimental Combat Team. It remains the creed of the Japanese American Citizens League today. It reads:

I am proud that I am an American citizen of Japanese ancestry, for my very background makes me appreciate more fully the wonderful advantages of this Nation. I believe in her institutions, ideals and traditions; I glory in her heritage; I boast of her history; I trust in her future. She has granted me liberties and opportunities such as no individual enjoys in this world today. She has given me an education befitting kings. She has entrusted me with the responsibilities of the franchise. She has permitted me to build a home, to earn a livelihood, to worship, think, speak and act as I please—as a free man equal to every other man.

Although some individuals may discriminate against me, I shall never become bitter or lose faith, for I know that such persons are not representative of the majority of the American people. True, I shall do all in my power to discourage such practices, but I shall do it in the American way—above board, in the open, through courts of law, by education, by proving myself to be worthy of equal treatment and consideration. I am firm in my belief that American sportsmanship and attitude of fair play will judge citizenship and patriotism on the basis of action and achievement, and not on the basis of physical characteristics.

Because I believe in America, and I trust she believes in me, and because I have received innumerable benefits from her, I pledge myself to do honor to her at all times and all places; to support her constitution; to obey her laws; to respect her flag; to defend her against all enemies, foreign and domestic; to actively assume my duties and obligations as a citizen, cheerfully and without any reservations whatsoever, in the hope that I may become a better American in a greater America.

Mike Masaoka and thousands of other Nisei kept their faith under this creed. The American government betrayed them.

Mike went to North Platte, Nebraska, on December 7, 1941, to make a talk to Japanese Americans there—the descendants of those three hundred Issei who used to ice the refrigerator cars on transcontinental express trains. The North Platte authorities said, "We are at war with Japan," and promptly threw him into jail—under no actual charge, at all.

Such arrests were common for several weeks. The Mountain States wanted none of the Japanese. After three days, Mike was finally permitted to get in touch with Utah's U.S. Senator Elbert D. Thomas (mentioned previously). Then his jailors unlocked his cell door with a begrudging but wholesome respect, and said, "Well, you must be all right, when a U.S. Senator vouches for you!"

A little later the Army in California sent Mike, his five brothers, and their widowed mother to internment camps, where Mike's faith in American ideals and benefits was put to a severe test, indeed. As a leader of the Japanese American Citizens League, he was allowed to do considerable traveling east of the military zone to help loyal Nisei resettle. He was still arrested frequently, sometimes as an enemy spy. He worked tirelessly for the right of the Nisei to bear arms in defense of their country, and this brought him a measure of fame across the Pacific. Radio Tokyo called him Japan's Number One enemy and said he would be the first American hanged when the Japanese fleet steamed into San Francisco Bay.

When enlistments were finally permitted, Mike Masaoka was the first of all the Nisei to volunteer for the 442nd Regimental Combat Team. Four of his brothers also joined up, while their mother remained in the Manzanar Relocation Center.

Ben Frank Masaoka was killed in October, 1944, in the fight to rescue the Lost Texas Battalion. Sergeant Akira Ike Masaoka was so gravely wounded that he is still a hundred percent disabled. Mike Masaoka, Private Henry Masaoka, and Private Tadashi T. Masaoka all were wounded.

Among them, the Masaoka boys collected more than thirty medals for bravery in action.[22]

Four

IN THIS SOLEMN HOUR WE
PLEDGE OUR FULLEST COOPERA-
TION TO YOU, MR. PRESIDENT,
AND TO OUR COUNTRY. THERE
CANNOT BE ANY QUESTION. THERE
MUST BE NO DOUBT. WE, IN OUR
HEARTS, KNOW WE ARE AMERI-
CANS—LOYAL TO AMERICA. WE
MUST PROVE THAT TO ALL OF
YOU.

—Telegram from the Japanese Amerian Citizens League
to President Roosevelt on December 7, 1941.

I

Even the professional racists were stunned by the attack on Pearl Harbor. Although the leaders of many West Coast organizations had long been on record as anti-Japanese, it was a little while before they realized what a weapon had been placed in their hands.

The *San Luis Obispo* (California) *Independent,* a small mid-coast newspaper, urged evacuation of the Japanese in an editorial on December 12,[1] but the general tone of the press was one of tolerance—as it had been, for the most part, during the months preceding Pearl Harbor. The *Stockton Record,* for example, had said in August:

It must be recognized that most of the residents of Japanese blood are American citizens, a status they gained by being born here. Also, as shown by practically every list of Stockton draftees called to the colors, the young Japanese, American-born and educated, and knowing no other homeland, are accepting their patriotic responsibilities in the same spirit as other youths.

To all these Americans of Japanese background, Nippon's rampage is as distasteful as to the rest of us. Japan's acts are embarrassing to these people. They fear the reactions on themselves. They should be assured that they will be treated as they have been in the past so long as their allegiance is undivided.[2]

In September, 1941 the influential *Oakland Tribune* had carried an editorial written by Raymond Lawrence:

Most of these Japanese are American citizens, educated in our schools, familiar with no culture save ours, and as loyal to this country as are any others. [They] have supported to the full the U.S.O., defense bond campaigns, and all of the programs of defense. They are contributing man-power and ideas to this country. The Americans who permit emotions or suspicions to run away with them, may be guilty of an affront to the very philosophy and allegiance which the American-born Japanese have acquired in this democracy . . .[3]

Hal Johnson, who wrote a column for the *Berkeley Gazette,* had also said in September:

Legally they [Japanese Americans] are just as much Americans as those of us whose ancestors came to this country via the Mayflower or on some of the later boats. . . . There are 500 Japanese American young men in Camp Ord and some 25 are from Berkeley. Many of the "Japamericanese" didn't wait to see what numbers were coming up in the big "goldfish bowl"—they enlisted.[4]

Although the *San Luis Obispo Independent* repeated its stand for evacuation some seven times during the two months following the attack,[5] the press in general continued to remain fair. This eight-week period was a curious one, indeed, and subsequent events made it appear as if a time bomb had started ticking away on December 7, and was waiting to go off.

Because suddenly the attitude of the press changed. Even the conservative *San Francisco Chronicle* came dangerously close to supporting the Evacuation. On February 1, 1942, the *Chronicle* said in a front page editorial: "It is not necessary to imitate Hitler by herding whole populations, the guilty and the innocent together, into even humane concentration camps."

But on February 21, after President Roosevelt had issued Executive Order No. 9066, the *Chronicle* said "we have to be tough, even if civil rights do take a beating for a time." [6]

Another traditionally conservative daily, the *San Diego Union,* remained editorially silent on the question for six weeks after Pearl Harbor—and then published fourteen editorials between January 20 and March 16, all calling for evacuation. [7]

The initial attitude of most of the West Coast Congressmen was both tolerant and fair: indeed, three of them—John Coffee of Washington, and Bertrand Gearhart and H. Jerry Voorhis of California—praised the Japanese minority from the floor of the House, and had their remarks entered in the *Congressional Record*. All three men had Nisei constituents, Gearhart received a running fire of letters from Dr. Joseph D. Sasaki, a Fresno optometrist who was president of the Fresno chapter of the JACL and very active in promoting Americanism. [8]

Violence began two weeks after Pearl Harbor. A Nisei who had just been honorably discharged from the U.S. Army was stabbed to death in a Los Angeles street. Filipino farm workers attacked Japanese in Gilroy, California. Other incidents were responsible for seven deaths. [9]

Three weeks after Pearl Harbor, there had been no attempts at sabotage, anywhere. But now reports were rife of radio communication with the enemy. . . .

In late January, 1942, DeWitt believed that "intercepted" radio messages were related to ship sinkings. He never changed this belief, despite facts proving it wrong. In DeWitt's Final Report (June 5, 1943) he states that his

conclusion was in part based upon the interception of unauthorized radio communications which had been identified as emanating from certain areas along the coast. Of further concern to him was the fact that for a period of several weeks following December 7th, *substantially every ship leaving a West Coast port was attacked by an enemy submarine* [italics supplied].

Just how DeWitt came to these conclusions is not clear, but neither claim he made—a year later—had any basis in fact. The official Army history today says that the Japanese Sixth Fleet had ordered nine submarines to attack West Coast shipping. They arrived off the West Coast about December 17. Only four actually attacked. In eight or nine contacts, they sank two tankers and damaged one freighter. There were only two Japanese submarines off the coast in February, 1942.[10]

As for the report on unauthorized radio communications, the true story, which came out a few years later, is interesting. When James L. Fly, chairman of the Federal Communications Commission, reviewed the Commission's monitoring activities on the West Coast for the period under suspicion by the Army, he stated that in no case "was the transmission other than legitimate." He elaborated:

In the case of 760 reports of unidentified or unlawful radio signals within the evacuated area during the period in question . . . a field investigation was conducted. . . . In 641 of the cases it was found that no radio signaling at all was involved. Of the 119 cases remaining, 116 were found to involve lawful transmissions by the following stations:

United States Army Stations	21
United States Navy Stations	8
Local Police Stations	12
U.S. and Foreign Commercial Licensed Stations	65
Japanese Stations in Japanese Territory	10
	116

The final three were found to involve the very short range transmissions of the ordinary commercial type phonograph oscillator used in playing recordings for home amusement.[11]

The FCC investigations covered the entire period from December 7, 1941, to the end of the Evacuation, and the following testimony came about in 1944, when the Department of Justice was preparing the Government's case defending the constitutionality of the Evacuation before the Supreme Court.

The exact figures on those early wartime sailings from the West Coast are not available. But they were considerable, and the assertion that "substantially every ship was attacked" is absurd.

The Army's personnel and monitoring equipment, Fly said, were

entirely incapable of determining whether or not the many reports of illicit signaling were well founded. . . . Frankly, I have never seen an organization that was so hopeless to cope with radio intelligence requirements. The personnel is unskilled and untrained. Most are privates who can only read ten words a minute. They know nothing about signal identification, wave propagation and other technical subjects. . . . They take bearings with loop equipment on Japanese stations in Tokyo listed in the Berne list as such, employing their authorized call letters, and report to their commanding officers that they have fixes on Jap agents operating transmitters on the West Coast. These officers, knowing no different, pass it on to the General, and he takes their word for it. It's pathetic to say the least.[12]

While it was happening in 1941 and 1942, however, it was more than pathetic for the West Coast Japanese. It was tragic.

U.S. Attorney General Francis Biddle conferred with Secretary of War Henry L. Stimson, and the Department of Justice called for enemy aliens on the West Coast to turn in all short-wave receivers, radio transmitters, and some types of cameras, by January 5.

The stage for the assault on the West Coast Japanese was being set, now, to the accompaniment of an increasing amount of whispering in the wings. There were persistent stories of sabotage at Pearl Harbor. The rumor merchants hinted darkly that if the truth were known, every ship in the Pacific Fleet had been sent to the bottom—and so had every merchant vessel sailing from West Coast ports.

From many areas came reports of arrows marked on the land, all pointing to airports or defense plants as guides to hostile aircraft. Flowers were said to have been planted in arrow shapes; fields were partially plowed in the same design.

The story was brought from Hawaii by the first refugees, and it wasn't true there, either. The Northwest went Hawaii and California one better. The Northwest had an arrow of fire.

On December 11, Hearst's *Seattle Post-Intelligencer* ran a front page headline: FIFTH COLUMNISTS SET PLANE BEACON FIRES NEAR PT. ANGELES. The story told of flaming arrows pointing toward Seattle. But on an inside page of the same edition (there'll always be a news editor) was about a stick of type quoting the Governor's office as saying the fires were set by forestry workers burning brush, and the "arrow shape" was purely coincidental.

The time lag of nothing going on was curious and ominous. It was nerve-wracking to the Japanese, who could only wait and wonder what was going to happen to them. Patience was part of the Oriental heritage, but most of these people were Americans and did not have that much patience. They were jumpy about rumors they had heard. They had no credit. Their cash was running out.

By the end of December, hostile voices began to be heard.

One of the first was that of John B. Hughes, a well-known and highly respected commentator for the Mutual Broadcasting Company in Los Angeles. In his program, "News and Views by John B. Hughes," he opened a month-long campaign against the Japanese population and wrote letters to Attorney General Biddle urging that both Issei and Nisei be interned. His broadcasts became critical of the Department of Justice.[13]

Newspaper editors, jealous of the increasing importance of radio, would have denied that they were influenced. Nevertheless, by the time the Hughes diatribes against the Japanese had ended, most California newspapers were seeing eye-to-eye with him.

On January 21, Congressman Leland M. Ford of Santa Monica had the dubious honor of being the first Congressman to advocate a mass evacuation on the floor of the House.[14] Ford had already been busy advancing this idea to Attorney General Biddle; he had read a constituent's telegram into the *Congressional Record*. This was from film actor Leo Carillo, on January 6, asking: "Why wait until [the Japanese] pull something before we act . . . Let's get them off the coast into the interior. . . ." [15] When they read about this, Mike Masaoka and other Nisei leaders recalled wryly that on the previous Labor Day weekend Carillo had addressed a JACL district convention in Long Beach, saying he knew what it was to be persecuted and discriminated against (being Mexican) and pledging to do all he could to prevent discrimination.

A former sports writer, Henry McLemore, who wrote a syndicated column for the Hearst newspapers, grew vehement on January 29:

I am for immediate removal of every Japanese on the West Coast to a point deep in the interior. I don't mean a nice part of the interior, either. Herd 'em up, pack 'em off and give them the inside room in the badlands. Let 'em be pinched, hurt, hungry and dead up against it. . . .

Personally, I hate the Japanese. And that goes for all of them.[16]

It is probably peculiar to America, alone, that an observer of called strikes and balls at home plate should be qualified to comment upon the larger human tragedies, but McLemore had his following. Three weeks later, the highly respected Walter Lippmann was in San Francisco, and even he advocated setting aside the civil rights of citizens of Japanese ancestry. His syndicated column for February 20 was echoed next day by Earl Warren, before the Tolan Committee; it was still echoed a year later in General DeWitt's Final Report. Lippmann said:

the Pacific Coast is in imminent danger of a combined attack from within and from without. . . . It is [true] . . . that since the outbreak of the Japanese war there has been no important sabotage on the Pacific Coast. From what we know about the fifth column in Europe, this is not, as some have liked to think, a sign that there is nothing to be feared. It is a sign that the blow is well organized and that it is held back until it can be struck with maximum effect. . . . I am sure I understand fully and appreciate thoroughly the unwillingness of Washington to adopt a policy of mass evacuation and internment of all those who are technically enemy aliens. But I submit that Washington is not defining the problem on the coast correctly. . . . The Pacific Coast is officially a combat zone: some part of it may at any moment be a battlefield. Nobody's constitutional rights include the right to reside and do business on a battlefield. And nobody ought to be on a battlefield who has no good reason for being there.[17]

Other eastern columnists now joined in. Westbrook Pegler said, "to hell with habeas corpus until the danger is over." [18]

II

Lieutenant General John L. DeWitt, sixty-two, slight, wiry, and bespectacled, was Commander of the Western Theater of Operations, with headquarters at San Francisco's Presidio. The son of an Army General, he had been appointed lieutenant of infantry at the age of eighteen. In World War I, he served in France as Assistant Chief of Staff for Supply. Later, as a Brigadier, he commanded troops in the Philippines.

On January 2, after Pearl Harbor, DeWitt opened a three-day series of conferences with James Rowe, Jr., Assistant to the Attorney General. General DeWitt wanted the Justice Department to conduct spot raids in a search for contraband. He wanted Attorney General Biddle to order the registration of all enemy aliens and exclude them from prohibited zones—to be designated by the Army—around vital installations.

Identical memoranda, that is, identical copies, exchanged by DeWitt and Rowe on January 6 said:

Indications are that, should Army recommendations include areas in which there is resident a large number of enemy aliens *and evacuation will thereby be rendered necessary* [*the Attorney Gen-*

*eral] will also require the submission of detailed plans for evacua-
tion and resettlement.* The Army has expressed disinclination to
compliance on its part with such a requirement for the reason that
the Justice Department will . . . have in its possession all the information essential for planning purposes [italics supplied].

Translated, this military jargon meant that DeWitt already
was thinking about evacuating the Japanese, but he hoped the
Department of Justice would handle the job. This interchange
was not the first suggestion of some disagreement between the
War and Justice Departments. On the previous day, DeWitt
had said:

It should be stated at the outset that the Army has no wish to
undertake the conduct and control of alien enemies anywhere
within continental United States. Impressions to the contrary not-
withstanding, the Army would accept transfer of such responsibility and authority with the greatest reluctance. Its desire is only that
the Department of Justice act with expedition and effectiveness in
the discharge of its responsibilities.[19]

DeWitt's reluctance to take over the job, which (on January 6) he had thought might call for Japanese evacuation, was
matched by that of the Justice Department, which did not believe that military necessity dictated such drastic action. It
looked as if the two reluctant dragons might fight it out on
that line if it took all summer.

Three days after Pearl Harbor, a man who said he was a
Treasury agent telephoned the staff duty officer at DeWitt's
headquarters and reported that an estimated 20,000 Japanese
in the San Francisco area were organized for action.

The hysteria was working, even on the Army. It would appear that nobody checked the informant's credentials, and
even his name has been lost in the records. Nobody pointed
out that the 1940 Census showed only 5,200 persons of Japanese ancestry in San Francisco.

Instead, the Army staff worked late and feverishly into the
night to produce an evacuation plan. Next day, the West

Coast FBI chief, Nat Pieper, scoffed at the entire affair as the "wild imaginings of a discharged former FBI man." [20]

Nevertheless, General DeWitt reported the incident to the War Department, and followed it up on December 19 with a recommendation:

1. In view of the fact that the West Coast of the United States has now been designated and is functioning as an active Theater of Operations, it is recommended that action be initiated at the earliest practicable date to collect *all alien subjects fourteen years and over, of enemy nations,* and remove them to the Zone of the Interior.

2. It is also recommended that these individuals be held under restraint after removal from the Theater of Operations in order to preclude their surreptitious return.

3. Records indicate that there are approximately *40,000 of such enemy aliens* and it is believed that they constitute an immediate and potential menace to vital measures of defense [italics supplied].[21]

DeWitt's racism was showing here, if only through a *lapsus calami.* In 1942, "all alien subjects of enemy nations" on the West Coast would have included some 58,000 Italians and 23,000 Germans, as well as 40,869 Japanese. General De-Witt's use of the 40,000 figure indicates he was thinking only of the Japanese.

His later actions bore this out.

The blanket phrase, "military necessity," which covered many of DeWitt's attitudes and actions, was not of recent coinage. Abraham Lincoln used it in May, 1861, to justify suspension of *habeas corpus* in the Army's arrest of a Baltimore civilian named John Merryman, who was a Southern sympathizer. In the fight that followed, the White House and the military authorities at Fort Henry were opposed by Supreme Court Chief Justice Roger Brooke Taney, then eighty years old, who had, only a couple of months before, administered the oath of office at Lincoln's inauguration. Taney and Lincoln were ancient enemies because of the Supreme Court decision in the famous Dred Scott case.

Taney ordered Merryman brought before him in Baltimore; the Army authorities refused. Taney then issued a writ to compel the appearance of General George Cadwalader. A U.S. Marshal was refused admittance to Fort Henry to serve this writ.

Citing the Constitution's provision that "no person shall be deprived of life, liberty, or property without due process of law," Taney said,

if the authority which the Constitution has confided to the judiciary department and judicial officers, may thus, upon any pretext or under any circumstances, be usurped by the military authority, at its discretion, the people of the United States are no longer living under a government of laws, but every citizen holds life, liberty, and property at the will and pleasure of the army officer in whose military district he may happen to be found.

Taney's opinion said that the President had no authority to suspend the writ of *habeas corpus* or to authorize a military officer to do so. Merryman was released not long afterward.[22]

The old Chief Justice's words were to have a familiar but hollow ring eighty-one years later.

III

At the end of January, seven weeks after Pearl Harbor, there had been no attempts at sabotage, no evidence of any fifth column activity on the West Coast. But by then there was no longer any doubt about Evacuation for the people of Japanese blood. It was only a question of how soon, to what degree, and under whose direction.

The wheels were turning, and there were wheels within wheels, with a great confused clashing of gears. A partial chronology of the major events of that period follows:

January 29: As a result of requests from General DeWitt, U.S.

Attorney General Francis Biddle issued the first of a series of orders establishing strategic areas along the Pacific Coast, and requiring removal of *all enemy aliens* from such areas.

February 2: The FBI staged a mass raid on Terminal Island. California Attorney General Earl Warren convened State peace officers, and warned them of the dangers of sabotage and fifth column activities.

February 13: A West Coast Congressional delegation wrote to President Roosevelt recommending "immediate evacuation of all persons of Japanese lineage, . . . aliens and citizens alike" from the "entire strategic area" of California, Oregon, and Washington.

February 14: General DeWitt sent a memorandum to the Secretary of War, recommending evacuation of "Japanese *and other subversive persons*" from the West Coast.

February 19: President Roosevelt signed Executive Order No. 9066, authorizing the Secretary of War, *or any military commander designated by the Secretary,* to establish military areas, and to exclude therefrom *"any or all persons."*

February 20: Secretary of War Henry L. Stimson wrote to General DeWitt, designating him as a military commander empowered to carry out an evacuation within his command under terms of Executive Order No. 9066.

February 21: The Tolan Congressional Committee convened in San Francisco to investigate the problems of evacuation of enemy aliens and others.

It can readily be seen that the cart had been put before the horse insofar as the Tolan Congressional Committee was concerned. It had a high and fancy title; it represented the Seventy-seventh Congress and was a Select Committee Investigating National Defense Migration, with a subtitle: "Problems of Evacuation of Enemy Aliens and Others From Prohibited Military Zones." But when it convened in San Francisco on February 21, General DeWitt had made his decision to evacuate the Japanese a whole week earlier, and on February 19 he had been given the authority to evacuate them.

Any testimony given before the Tolan Committee, therefore, could have been all sound and fury, signifying nothing. The Committee had no authority to cancel General DeWitt's orders, even had it been inclined to do so.

But the testimony the Committee heard was most revealing in that, as far as the West Coast Japanese were concerned, it at least divided friends and foes.

IV

There was an increasing public demand for the evacuation of the Japanese when the Tolan Committee met on February 21, 1942. The Committee had been set up by House Resolution 113 to "inquire further into the interstate migration of citizens . . . caused by the national defense program."

There was some unintended ironic humor in the description of the committee's function. There *were* migrations, to be sure: men from Arkansas loaded their families in cars and headed for San Francisco to get jobs in Hunter's Point shipyard. But "migration" connotes travel ordinarily instinctive, and, at the least, voluntary. The movement of Japanese from the West Coast was neither.

Representative John H. Tolan of California was the Committee chairman. The other congressmen serving with him were John J. Sparkman, Alabama; Laurence F. Arnold, Illinois; Carl T. Curtis, Nebraska; and George H. Bender, Ohio. The Staff Director was Dr. Robert K. Lamb. Congressman Curtis was not present when the Committee convened in the San Francisco Post Office building.

The group probably would have gone to the West Coast sooner or later, but the February visit was in response to an urgent request made by Carey McWilliams, chief of the Division of Immigration and Housing of the California Department of Industrial Relations. McWilliams had written to Dr. Lamb informing him that the situation was bad, that many Japanese had already lost their jobs, that discrimination was increasing. Committee hearings, he thought, would give the various pressure groups a chance to blow off steam, and would allow the Japanese to present their side of the question.[23]

McWilliams, enlightened and vocal, had already published a book called *Factories in the Field,* and a February issue of *New Republic*—on the newsstands when the Committee met—carried an article he had written expressing the belief that a Congressional investigation would result in opposition to any wholesale evacuation of the Japanese.

But 1942 was an election year. Politics colored the thinking of public officials and candidates for public office. The Committee was no sooner in San Francisco than Hearst's *San Francisco Examiner* quoted Congressman Tolan as saying the West Coast was certain to be bombed.[24]

Resident Japanese had little opportunity to tell their story, but the politicians turned out *en masse.* Carey McWilliams did not get a chance to testify until March 7, after the Committee had moved to Los Angeles. By then it was obvious that the hearings had backfired, insofar as McWilliams' constructive hopes were concerned; there was strong internal evidence to suggest that at least some members of the Committee had come to the Coast with their minds already made up.

In the San Francisco sessions, only nine persons of Japanese ancestry were heard, out of a total of forty-three witnesses. Out of a total of forty-seven written statements accepted by the Committee, only six were from Japanese. Twenty-five letters from district attorneys and sheriffs were introduced into the testimony by California's Attorney General Earl Warren.

When the Committee went on to Portland and Seattle, there were four Japanese witnesses out of fifty, and three written statements from Japanese out of fifty-four. In Los Angeles, six Japanese were heard out of forty-four witnesses, and Japanese submitted six statements out of forty-two.[25]

The Tolan Committee worked hard and covered a lot of ground, most of it already sowed with the seeds of suspicion and prejudice. Its first witness was San Francisco's mayor, Angelo J. Rossi, a dapper man sometimes accused of trying to be the Jimmie Walker of the West. Rossi, a florist, always had a fresh carnation in his lapel. He was of Italian extraction. He read a prepared statement recommending that the problems of German and Italian aliens "be considered separately from those of the Japanese."

The Japanese situation, Rossi said,

admits of no delay. The activities of the Japanese saboteurs and fifth columnists in Honolulu and on the battle fronts in the Pacific have forced me to the conclusion that every Japanese alien should be removed from this community. I am also strongly of the conviction that Japanese who are American citizens should be subjected to a more detailed and all-encompassing investigation. After investigation, if it is found that these citizens are not loyal to this country they, too, should be removed.

Rossi repeated his conviction that "evacuation of Axis aliens, other than Japanese, should be avoided unless deemed imperative" and stressed the "extreme hardship, mental distress, and suffering" which would be put upon German and Italian aliens by evacuation. He said nothing about hardships, mental distress, or suffering on the part of the Japanese.[26]

Mayor Rossi was not alone in this attitude. On the day before Rossi gave his testimony, Secretary of War Henry L. Stimson had written to General DeWitt:

I desire, so far as military requirements permit, that you do not disturb, for the time being at least, Italian aliens and persons of Italian lineage except where they are, in your judgment, undesirable or constitute a definite danger to the performance of your mission to defend the West Coast. . . . I consider such persons to be potentially less dangerous. . . . Because of the size of the Italian population . . . their inclusion in the general plan would greatly overtax our strength.[27]

In his own way, Mayor Rossi set the tone for the Tolan hearings; a study of the transcript suggests that Committee members were already persuaded that Axis aliens posed no threat. Chairman Tolan early expressed concern about one important thing: he wondered why no custodian had been named to protect the property of the evacuees. In the next breath, he admitted the Committee's impotency. "This Committee hasn't any idea of coming out here and dictating to the Army any more than you have."

An interesting exchange a little later showed that if one had to be an alien residing in San Francisco, it helped a great deal to have a son who was a *real* Yankee—*à la* Babe Ruth.

Chauncey Tramutolo, a former Assistant United States Attorney, testified as a representative of the Citizens' Committee to Aid Italians Loyal to the United States. Chairman Tolan informed the committee members that he had known Mr. Tramutolo for twenty-five years. Suddenly the witness was prompted:

THE CHAIRMAN. Tell us about the DiMaggios. Tell us about Di-Maggio's father.
MR. TRAMUTOLO. Neither of the DiMaggio seniors is a citizen. They have reared nine children, five boys and four girls, eight of whom were born in the United States, and the other one is a naturalized citizen. Three of the boys are outstanding persons in the sports world. Joe, who is with the Yanks, was leading hitter for both the American and National Leagues during the years 1939 and 1940. His younger brother, Dominic, is with the Boston Red Sox, and his older brother, Vincent, is with the Pittsburgh team of the National League. . . . To evacuate the senior DiMaggios would, in view of the splendid family they have reared and their unquestioned loyalty, present, I am sure you will agree with me, a serious situation.[28]

Mr. Tramutolo had just hit a home run, with the bases loaded, for the Italian alien team. Nobody had yet been to bat for the Japanese. Nobody would bat for them, very much.

A short time later, when the Evacuation went into gear, it included a Berkeley florist and nurseryman named Tatsu Ogawa, who was fifty years old. Ogawa had served with the 91st Division of the American Expeditionary Forces in France in World War I; he had been shot in the shoulder in the Meuse-Argonne campaign. Tatsu Ogawa was a Hawaiian

born American citizen. He had borne arms for his country and
had shed blood for it. One would assume that he was at least
entitled to his freedom.

The Army put Tatsu Ogawa in an Assembly Center and
later he went behind the barbed wire at Camp Topaz, Utah.
His family happened to be visiting in Hawaii at the time or
they would have been interned, too.[29]

V

A native Californian, Congressman Tolan also had known
other witnesses for a quarter century, and occasionally a nostalgic whiff of Old Home Week and hail-fellow-well-met spirit
permeated the proceedings. To Earl Warren, Tolan promised
"the widest latitude," and added:

We are not here to cross-examine any witnesses—not that you
could not take care of yourself. I found out twenty-five years ago
that in the trial of a lawsuit you could take very good care of yourself.[30]

California's Attorney General would be running for the
office of Governor that year, and would be elected. At the
time of the Tolan hearings, whether politics could be blamed
or not, his views and those of the incumbent Governor, Cul-
bert L. Olson, were quite divergent and occasionally vacillating where the Japanese were concerned. On February 2, Governor Olson discussed the problem with Army officers, and
later announced that a mass evacuation would not be required.

This was the same day on which Warren called a mass
meeting of sheriffs and district attorneys, which adopted a resolution urging that "all alien Japanese be forthwith evacuated . . . to some place in the interior . . . for the duration
of the war."

Governor Olson sanctioned action by the California Department of Agriculture to revoke the licenses of enemy aliens

handling farm produce. Attorney General Warren was immediately on the other side of the fence, asserting on February 17 that such revocation was illegal.[31]

More than a year later—in December, 1943—when Olson appointees to the State Board of Agriculture persuaded the Board to pass a resolution favoring return and fair treatment for the evacuees, Warren—by then Governor—made new appointments to the Board, and their votes caused the action to be reversed.[32] How much of this was politics? Earl Warren was very prominent in the American Legion. He was a member of the Native Sons of the Golden West. Both groups, in 1942, were all out against the Japanese.

At the time of his appearance before the Tolan Committee, Warren's stand easily could have been considered ambiguous. The Associated Press on January 30 quoted him as stating that the Japanese situation

may well be the Achilles heel of the entire civilian defense effort. Unless something is done it may bring about a repetition of Pearl Harbor.

By February 2, he was doing something about it by convening the sheriffs and district attorneys. He told them:

I have talked to General DeWitt, I have talked to subordinate officers, I have talked to the Army, I have talked to the Intelligence Unit of the Navy, I have talked to the FBI, I have talked to every federal agency that there is in this part of the country, trying to get some relief from this situation.

Now Governor Olson's State Personnel Board barred from State civil service jobs all citizens who were descendants of enemy aliens. In practice, the order was enforced only against American born Japanese. Attorney General Warren, who had been all out against the Japanese on February 2, swapped horses five days later.

On February 7, he declared that the civil-service ruling "discriminates against naturalized citizens and citizens by birth"; he pointed out that neither the Constitution nor any existing law allowed such discrimination. Naturalized citizens and their American born children, he added,

have in the past and do now represent the highest standards of American citizenship, . . . To question [their] loyalty or place them in a category different from other citizens is not only cruel in its effect upon them but is also disruptive of the national unity which is so essential in these times.

Next day, Warren said in a press statement,

If we start discriminating against people because of their fore-bears, it will bring about disunity in our war effort. Anybody can think of individuals who will be affected by such a ruling. Even Wendell L. Willkie could hardly hope to hold public office, as his parents were emigrants from Germany.

Having struck that blow against discrimination on February 7, having morally aided the cause of the Nisei, Earl Warren went to another meeting, to address members of the California Joint Immigration Committee, long the leading anti-Japanese group.

He reminded this audience that American born Japanese were citizens until Congress acted or the Constitution was changed. "These things," he said, "take time." He thought the military command could move "any or all Japanese out of the combat zone," and added that it "should be done. . . . The Army . . . has the right to do it."

A political approach to the problem, Warren said,

is just too cumbersome; it is involved with too much red tape for us to do anything to protect our situation now. We are likely to get it before this day ends; we don't know; we are fighting an invisible deadline. There is only one group in the last analysis that can pro-tect this State from the Japanese situation and that is the armed forces of this government. What we need now it seems to me, is action, and I think we ought to urge the military command in this area to do the things that are obviously essential to the security of this State.[33]

Earl Warren appeared before the Tolan Committee the day after President Roosevelt signed Executive Order No. 9066.

He said that the order was most wise and had obviated the necessity of saying many of the things he had intended to say.

VI

The Army, whether it asked for it or not, had been handed the can of worms by the President's Executive Order No. 9066. Now Earl Warren could speak freely, because it was out of his hands, and he told the Tolan Committee:

I want to say that the concencus of opinion among the law-enforcement officers of this State is that there is more potential danger among the group of Japanese who are born in this country than from the alien Japanese who were born in Japan.

At the meeting of law-enforcement officers on February 2, he had asked those present to prepare maps showing all lands owned, occupied or controlled by Japanese, both alien and American born. (It must be remembered that the 1913 Alien Land Law prevented Issei from buying land. What they had bought previously was poor and marginal.) Now Warren showed the maps to the Tolan Committee and said they indicated a "disturbing situation." Japanese farmers were close to defense plants, "within a grenade throw of coast defense guns," in the vicinity of leading beaches, air fields, railroads, power lines, gas and water mains, and so on.

Warren provided the Committee with a detailed list of locations of Japanese in thirty-three counties. The list did not distinguish between alien Japanese and American citizens, but simply said things like:

Butte County—Jap adjacent to Chico airport; two Japs along Cherokee Canal and Northern Canal; Japs in the vicinity of numerous highway and railroad bridges near Gridley, Biggs, Oroville and Chico; numerous Japs in the vicinity of Feather River levees between Gridley and Oroville.

Sacramento County—Many Japs along important Sacramento River levees and near important highway and railroad bridges across the river at Sacramento and other places; many Japs adja-

cent to Sacramento Municipal airport; Japs adjacent to Pacific Gas
and Electric substation; Japs close to Mather Field; Japs close to
McClellan Field; Japs close to American River bridges.

Shasta County—Jap in vicinity of Hat Creek powerhouse and
dam.

Warren also placed in evidence twenty-five letters he had
received from law enforcement officials in answer to an inquiry he made by all points bulletin teletype on February 17.
Some of these said that *all* enemy aliens, regardless of nationality, should be moved back not less than two hundred miles
from the Pacific Coast.

"In this group," wrote S. T. Primmer, Chief of Police in
Santa Paula, "I include all Japanese, whether enemy aliens or
citizens." Sacramento Chief of Police A. K. McAllister advocated moving all alien Japanese at least five hundred miles inland. The Fresno Chief of Police said, moderately, that "as
long as that [racial] feeling exists, we will continue to get exaggerated reports of suspected sabotage." But he, too, favored
evacuation of all enemy aliens.

District Attorney A. H. Brazil of San Luis Obispo County
said:

If it were possible, I believe the best way would be to take every
Japanese alien in the United States and in the possessions of the
United States and send them to Japan.[34]

The hysteria was no longer creeping. It was running, fasten-
ing its tentacles on the minds of the public. Things were in a
bad way when a community, a state of millions of souls, was
able to take alarm at a statement that there was a "Jap in vicinity of Hat Creek powerhouse and dam."

The war news was still bad. General MacArthur was about
to abandon the Philippines; General Jonathan Wainwright
was taking over for his magnificent but hopeless stand, and his
troops were singing:

> "We're the battling bastards of Bataan:
> No mama, no papa, no Uncle Sam;

> No aunts, no uncles, no cousins, no nieces—
> No pills, no planes, or artillery pieces!"

Meanwhile, on the night of 24–25 February, there was fought the "Battle of Los Angeles."

There had been a full month of agitation against the California Japanese, and the public nerves were like fiddlestrings. At two A.M., radar picked up a bogey coming in from the Pacific. A blackout was imposed. Anti-aircraft guns began to fire. They got off more than 1,400 rounds of 3-inch shells.

Next day, the Army claimed there had been from one to five unidentified planes over the area. The Navy said there had been none at all, and that a weather balloon probably had been responsible for the entire drill. Critics guffawed. Few people remembered the night of October 30, 1938, when Orson Welles in a fictional drama on the radio reported heat ray-spurting Martians landing from rocket ships in New Jersey . . . and touched off a panic of unprecedented proportions.

There was really no difference in this case, but the American people were ready to believe the worst.

Sadly enough, the American officials were scared.

Five

Oh who is that young sinner with
the handcuffs on his wrists?
And what has he been after that
they groan and shake their
fists?
And wherefore is he wearing such
a conscience-stricken air?
Oh they're taking him to prison
for the colour of his hair.

—A. E. Housman, Additional
Poems, XVIII

I

If the Tolan Committee had convened on the West Coast
some two months earlier, it might have been a decisive factor
in forestalling the entire Evacuation program. As it was, the
record suggests that the group had been preconditioned
toward acceptance of all the anti-Japanese testimony it heard.
Reading the transcript today, one finds little evidence of good,
honest skepticism; apparently nobody said, "Now, . . . wait
a minute. Let's look at the other side."

Chairman Tolan not only continued to prompt the witnesses, but consistently showed that he believed the rumors of
sabotage and fifth column activity in Hawaii. What were the
accusations and what was the evidence?

*Japanese were living along the railroads, handy for sabo-
tage.* No one had much of a chance to explain that the early
Issei immigrants had laid a great deal of the railroad tracks,
and that many of them were paid in land grants along the right
of way. This was land nobody else wanted. It was cheap, and
loud with the noise of passing freight trains. The Japanese
made it fruitful.

Japanese lived near the airports. Airports were fairly recent: the term itself was not in use until the 1920's. Airports had to be established out in the sagebrush—nobody wanted the noise, or planes falling on their houses. A lot of the Japanese had been living in such areas while the Wright Brothers were still flying kites.

Japanese lived close to Signal Hill and had truck farms adjacent to the huge Northrup and North American aircraft factories. At Terminal Island, they were near the naval shipyard. Californians conveniently forgot that the Issei had settled and farmed Signal Hill years before oil was discovered there; they forgot that the truck farms around Inglewood and Hawthorne antedated the aircraft plants or the Los Angeles Municipal Airport.

Japanese lived under the transmission lines bringing power down to the metropolitan areas from the High Sierras. If a man could afford better land, would he want to live under a power line?

General DeWitt came up with a fence-straddling explanation of the need for military control and for the Evacuation:

It could not be established, of course, that the location of thousands of Japanese adjacent to strategic points verified the existence of some vast conspiracy to which all of them were parties. Some of them doubtless resided there through mere coincidence. It seemed equally beyond doubt, however, that the presence of others was not mere coincidence.[1]

Doubt admittedly existed. But the Japanese Americans were not given the benefit of it.

II

Earl Warren told the Tolan Committee:

I believe that we are just being lulled into a false sense of security and that the only reason we haven't had a disaster in California is because it has been timed for a different date. . . . Our day of reckoning is bound to come in that regard. . . .

THE CHAIRMAN. On that point, when that came up in our committee hearings, there was not a single case of sabotage reported on the Pacific Coast, we heard the heads of the Navy and the Army, and they all tell us the Pacific Coast can be attacked. The sabotage would come coincident with that attack, would it not?

ATTORNEY GENERAL WARREN. Exactly.

THE CHAIRMAN. They would be fools to tip their hands now, wouldn't they?

ATTORNEY GENERAL WARREN. Exactly. If there were sporadic sabotage at this time or if there had been for the last 2 months, the people of California or the Federal authorities would be on the alert to such an extent that they could not possibly have any real fifth column activities when the M-day comes.[2]

Although Warren earlier had paid warm tribute to the FBI, he told the Tolan Committee: "We don't know in this State who the enemy aliens are, and it is not permitted for us to know." He explained that the President ("and I think wisely") had placed internal security in the hands of the FBI. California local and State officers had "played the game" and turned over all information to the FBI. But . . .

we are not permitted to have the names, even, of the alien enemies in our midst. And at the present time every police station in this State, every sheriff's office, every law-enforcement agency can be flanked by aliens with weapons that we know absolutely nothing about. Gentlemen, I say to you that if we expect local law enforcement officers to compete against a situation of that kind, it is just like putting a blindfold over a man's face and asking him to go out and fight someone that he cannot see.

THE CHAIRMAN. What is the objection to your not [sic] having that information?

ATTORNEY GENERAL WARREN. I am afraid you will have to get that from the Department of Justice. . . .[3]

The Tolan Committee did get it from the Department of Justice five days later when it opened hearings at Portland, Oregon. One of the first witnesses was N.J.L. (Nat) Pieper, West Coast chief of the FBI, who had hurried up from San Francisco.

Pieper launched immediately into his grievance.

An article appeared in the *San Francisco Examiner* on February 22, 1942, stating that Mr. Earl Warren, Attorney General for the State of California, had . . . revealed that local law-enforcement officers are fighting in the dark against fifth columnists because the FBI will not take them into its confidence. This statement is not true. . . . I have so advised Mr. Clarence R. Lindner, the publisher of the *Examiner*.

In a conversation with Congressman Tolan . . . I advised that this newspaper article was not based on fact, and that Attorney General Earl Warren on reading the article, called me and stated that he had made no such statement, that the facts were to the contrary, since the FBI had been cooperating fully with local law enforcement officers and himself.[4]

The matter rested there, unresolved.

III

The Tolan Committee hearings showed that West Coast officialdom was almost solidly arraigned against the Japanese. The few who championed their cause were mainly private citizens, and the Committee gave them short shrift.

Louis Goldblatt, secretary for the California State Industrial Union Council in San Francisco, was a forthright and eloquent witness. The group he represented was an affiliate of the Congress of Industrial Organizations. It was unlikely, in San Francisco, that Goldblatt would get a fair shake, because the CIO was still anathema to newspaper publishers and business men. (Harry Bridges, shrewd and militant and suspected Communist leader of the Longshoremen's Union, had generated considerable anti-union sentiment because of waterfront tie-ups, so much so that a wry joke of the latter 1930's ran: "Have you seen our bridges—Bay, Golden Gate, and Harry?")

Goldblatt told the Committee:

We feel that a great deal of this problem has gotten out of

hand . . . inasmuch as both the local and State authorities, instead of becoming bastions of defense, of democracy and justice, joined the wolf pack when the cry came out, "Let's get the yellow menace." As a matter of fact, we believe the present situation is a great victory for the yellow press and for the fifth column that is operating in this country, which is attempting to convert this war from a war against the Axis Powers into a war against the "yellow peril." . . .

I am referring here particularly to the attack against the native-born Japanese, an attack, which, as far as we can find out, was whipped up. There was a basis for it because there has always been a basis on the Pacific Coast for suspicion, racial suspicion, which has been well-fostered, well-bred, particularly by the Hearst newspapers over a period of 20 to 25 years.

Frankly, to date we haven't seen either civic or State leadership that is competent to handle the problem. . . . I think the only people who have shown a semblance of decency and honesty and forthrightness in this whole situation are the second generation Japanese, who, on their own accord, have made the statement . . . that in their opinion the thing they ought to do is get out of here. They are in accord with evacuation . . . not in principle, but . . . because they realize that, perhaps, the only thing they can do now to avoid vigilantism, mob rule and hysteria, beatings and riots, is to evacuate. Of course that doesn't speak well for either our State or local authorities. . . .

This was nearer oratory than anything the Committee had heard. Tolan wanted to know how Goldblatt would determine the loyalty and disloyalty of 120,000 Japanese?

In exactly the same way I would proceed to tell who was a loyal or disloyal Italian or German. I think the second generation of Japanese in this Nation should not be distinguished from the second generation of any other nationality. . . .

Where is this to end, Mr. Tolan? Italians will be the next to be evacuated, then the Germans. . . . The so-called American . . . came out of a crystal into which has been poured the peoples of all the world. We forget what was written on the Statue of Liberty. I have the words here. I would like to read them.

THE CHAIRMAN. I don't think you better. . . . I think you would make a very dangerous talker the way you are going here today. I think you are wonderful.[5]

Goldblatt's written statement was admitted as evidence. It said:

We assumed that the exclusion of aliens of enemy nationality from specified military areas was based upon information in the hands of the Government and performed as part of a general program against fifth column danger. Almost immediately . . . came a widespread campaign demanding the removal from coastal areas of all Japanese, whether alien or born in this country. The old flames of racial suspicion were fanned to full blaze. . . . Politicians saw a good chance to garner publicity. Soon the wolf pack was in full cry.

Let it be said that within this State there was heard but one voice of reason and understanding. It came from second-generation Japanese, some of them members of our unions. They proposed the evacuation of all Japanese, both alien and citizen. Their proposal did not come from agreement with those who were leading the pack. It rose out of a realization that the forces of hysteria and vigilantism had won out over decency and government. . . .

As some of these Japanese express it: "We want to leave. Perhaps that is the greatest contribution we can make right now to the war. Maybe people will settle down to fighting the enemy instead of us and go after the real fifth columnists." . . .

This entire episode of hysteria and mob chant against the native born Japanese will form a dark page of American history. It may well appear as one of the great victories won by the Axis Powers. . . .[6]

Governor Olson of California—who testified at the Los Angeles session—was not nearly as positive for evacuation as Attorney General Warren. He felt there were loyal Japanese, and pointed out that some five thousand of them were already serving in the armed forces. But he also feared that a considerable part of the Japanese population would help Tokyo if an opportunity were given

They all looked alike, Olson said, thus perpetuating an ancient untruth. He complimented the California Japanese for

being willing to coöperate "and voluntarily evacuate themselves," and felt the rest of the country should do its duty by
absorbing the West Coast Japanese. As for German and Italian aliens, he favored a "selective" evacuation, since in their
case the FBI could pick the loyal from the disloyal.[7]

Selective evacuation had not only been suggested to the Tolan Committee by a number of reputable witnesses, but actually was being currently practiced by the FBI. At the time
the Committee met, there were one thousand Italian and six
hundred and fifty Japanese aliens already in the internment
camp at Missoula, Montana.[8]

Galen M. Fisher, advisor to the Institute of Pacific Relations and secretary to the Committee on National Security and
Fair Play, told the Tolan group he was convinced that a
sweeping evacuation of Japanese, whether aliens or citizens,
would hinder, not help, the maintenance of national security
and victory in the war. Fisher said:

> Removal of persons of any race or nationality should be con-
> fined to such as special investigation shows to be dangerous or de-
> cidedly suspicious. Identification cards, fingerprinting and photo-
> graphs are all desirable. . . . Any organized and extensive fifth
> column activity by residents of Japanese stock would presumably
> have to be led by experienced alien Japanese. Most of the natural
> leaders have already been detained, and others can be, without
> evacuating the thousands of rank and file Japanese.[9]

Richard H. Neustadt, Regional Director of the Social Security Board in San Francisco, advocated eliminating certain
groups from evacuation, including those who satisfied Federal
investigators that they were loyal and those who had sons in
the armed forces. He said, "There are cases of Japanese families in which the one you are moving is the mother, and the
son is in the Army." [10]

Even the representative of the California Joint Immigration
Committee, an organization which had been the arch enemy
of the Japanese for years, favored a selective evacuation. This
was Robert H. Fouke, who testified:

I feel in the case where there is no doubt as to the loyalty of the individual, be he Japanese, or be he of any other social group or religion, citizen or alien . . . that that party should be permitted to remain. . . .[11]

But one must read the fine print. The Joint Immigration Committee submitted, at the Tolan hearings, its "Exhibit E," a copy of a report it had prepared for the Dies Committee, which did no one any honor. After a considerable discussion of the Japanese problems, the report says:

These conditions, while unfortunate, are the result of the determination of the Caucasians to keep their country and their blood white, and involves [sic] no claim of superiority. Our laws against which the Japanese protest were enacted to keep out immigrants who cannot be absorbed into the lifeblood of the country, and who form unassimilated racial blocs. *The Founding Fathers of the Republic stipulated that citizenship should be granted only to free white persons. But a grave mistake was made when citizenship was granted to all born here, regardless of fitness or desire for such citizenship. Another grave mistake was the granting of citizenship to the Negroes after the Civil War* [italics supplied].[12]

The report went on to say that a bill introduced in the California Legislature in 1939, "to curb espionage activities of Japanese fishermen in Southern California," had been beaten by a lobby headed by Walter Tsukamoto, former national president of the Japanese American Citizens League, Sacramento attorney, and a U.S. Army Reserve officer.

At the time "Exhibit E" was submitted, Captain Walter Tsukamoto had been filing repeated requests to be called to active duty with the Army. He finally made it. He served in World War II, and in the Korean conflict; he died as a full colonel in 1963.

The testimony given the Tolan Committee in favor of a selective evacuation fell on deaf ears everywhere. General DeWitt had already made up his mind and had been given sweeping authority for the Evacuation under Executive Order No. 9066.

California's Governor Olson perhaps had not made up *his* mind. At least he changed it a few times: he was liberal at first, then took a tougher attitude, and in May of 1942 wanted all the Japanese removed. But in July he was worried about the shortage of labor to deal with the California farm crops, and he wanted Japanese to be left in California to work as harvest hands. By then it was too late.

And what was the sentiment in the Northwest and in Los Angeles?

Oregon's Governor Charles Sprague had wired U.S. Attorney General Francis Biddle, on February 17, that steps taken so far were inadequate, that

people on this coast demand more thorough action for protection against possible alien activity, particularly by Japanese residing on coast. . . . We want no repetition of Honolulu experience here.

The record does not show that Sprague testified before the Tolan Committee.

Washington's Governor Arthur B. Langlie expressed more moderate views, but was ready to "go all the way on any program that is set up by the Army or by the Federal agencies." His State had had no serious difficulties, and he urged that every precaution be taken to "be humane and American, in the way we do this particular job." [13]

Smith Troy, Attorney General for the State of Washington, was greatly concerned for the protection of the Washington forests from incendiarism—and almost equally so over the possibilities of mob violence against the Japanese. He was for evacuation of both alien and citizen Japanese as quickly as possible, but added:

By that, I don't mean total internment of all citizen Japanese for the duration of the war, but at least moving them out of here for their own protection.

He, too, felt "that we know the Italian and German people better." He said:

You can't take people with blue eyes and say, "You have got to get out of here," and people with brown eyes can stay. But I do think that our first problem is the Japanese.[14]

Seattle's Mayor Earl Millikin felt that the sentiment of people in that city was overwhelmingly in favor of evacuation, and that it was "utterly impossible" to separate the loyal from the disloyal. He estimated the Japanese population of Seattle to be 8,000, and stated for the record:

There is no doubt . . . that 7,900 probably are above question but the other 100 would burn this town down and let the Japanese planes come in and bring on something that would dwarf Pearl Harbor.[15]

Portland's Mayor Earl Riley told the Committee that the business licenses of all Japanese nationals and other aliens of Axis governments had been revoked. He was asked if he expected trouble in finding out who were loyal and who disloyal among Italian and German aliens.

THE MAYOR. As far as I am concerned, I do not propose to have any trouble; because the only way I look at it at this time is that every Axis alien is under suspicion . . . and I do not want them in my locality.
MR. SPARKMAN. How about those who are not aliens, but are second generation?
THE MAYOR. That would apply only with the Japanese.
MR. SPARKMAN. That would not apply to German and Italians?
THE MAYOR. No.
MR. SPARKMAN. Would it apply to the Japanese?
THE MAYOR. Yes.
MR. SPARKMAN. You think that they ought to be evacuated, too?
THE MAYOR. I do.
MR. SPARKMAN. Even though they are American citizens?
THE MAYOR. Indeed.[16]

Los Angeles' Mayor Fletcher Bowron told the Committee he thought the problem had been solved by the United States Army. One fifth of all the Japanese in America were located

within the sprawling Los Angeles city limits. The Japanese
had been law-abiding, industrious, and coöperative . . . but,

I know of no rule, no way to separate those who say they are patriotic and, are, in fact, loyal at heart, and those who say they are
patriotic and, in fact, at heart are loyal to Japan. . . .

He had discovered that the city employed people of Japanese
ancestry

who could, if they had been so minded, entirely sabotage our electric light distribution system. . . . While it was voluntary, it was
suggested to them in such a way that all applied for [such leaves of
absence] and we have no Japanese employees at this time.[17]

Mayor Bowron had conferred with General DeWitt and
others; he was a strong advocate of evacuation. He was to
prove himself also an honest man, willing to acknowledge a
mistake. Twelve years later, on September 2, 1954, Bowron
appeared before a Congressional Committee which was looking into property claims resulting from the Evacuation. At this
time, he said:

I was mayor during all of the war period . . . and I know of
the hysteria, the wild rumors, the reports, that pervaded the atmosphere and worried a great many of us in responsible positions. We
were quite disorganized. . . . There were many rumors floating
around, as a result of which, this order of evacuation was
made. . . . I rather hold myself somewhat responsible, with
others. . . . I realize that great injustices were done. . . . I
thought it was the right thing to do at the time; in the light of after
events, I think it was wrong, now . . . I have been impressed
with the fortitude of the Japanese people, the way they took it, and
then how they came back and reëstablished themselves in this
community.[18]

Mayor Bowron may have been unique in admitting he was
wrong. An attempt was still being made, in 1965, to manufacture political hay out of the stand West Coast leaders took on
the evacuation question. The California Young Republicans,

in convention at Millbrae, attacked Chief Justice Earl Warren, charging that he,

having been swept along by the general hysteria, without any evidence before him, slandered these [Japanese American] citizens by saying they were more dangerous than aliens.

The outgoing CYR president, Attorney John Gromala of Fortuna, said, "This man who is now all-out for civil rights was something else at another time."

A supreme and very judicial silence followed.[19]

IV

Suspicions of disloyalty on the part of West Coast Japanese, as voiced before the Tolan Committee and elsewhere, were for the most part based on three factors:

1. The Japanese Language Schools. General DeWitt stated that "in California alone there were over 248 schools with an aggregate faculty of 454 and a student body of 17,800."

2. Dual Citizenship. From 1899 until 1924, Japan held to the European rule of *jus sanguinis*—law of blood—which meant that a child born anywhere was a Japanese citizen if the father was a Japanese citizen. In the United States, the rule was *jus soli*—law of the soil—which made any child born in this country an American citizen.

3. The *Kibei Shimin,* or "Returned to America Citizens," already mentioned: American born Japanese partly educated in Japan.

The plain truth concerning any or all of these factors might have refuted many of the arguments presented by the advocates of evacuation. There was nothing mysterious about the situation at all, yet people insisted in shrouding it in an Oriental mystery.

Japanese language schools were late coming under attack by such groups as the Japanese Exclusion League, probably because they operated under supervision of the California

State Board of Education. When wartime hysteria uncovered the "peril" they presented, the fact that the entire country had always had parochial schools—a counterpart—was conveniently overlooked. Nobody had any quarrels with parochial schools.

A large number of the language schools, especially in rural areas, were conducted for missionary purposes by Protestant churches, and some were Buddhist. In the bigger towns, they were principally sponsored by Japanese American organizations and often served as day nurseries—where English was taught. After 1927, when all foreign-language schools were removed from State control in California, it became a popular belief that Japanese children were being taught "Emperor worship" and other forms of Japanese nationalistic propaganda.

This was never proved in any way, and appears most unlikely. The language schools did try to inculcate a few ancient and central virtues into the hearts and minds of the young Nisei. Michio Kunitani of Berkeley, who had been a Federal employee and a member of the Young Democrats, Incorporated, of California, a product of one of these schools, explained it this way:

> Our parents thought that the fine parts of Japanese culture could be integrated into American life and that the second generation of Japanese, if they were able to read and write [Japanese], could thereby discover the better side of Japanese culture.
>
> We were discriminated against in private industry, and therefore the only other channel into which the Japanese people could gain an economic livelihood was in the Japanese group. It was essential for us to learn the Japanese language so that we could converse intelligently with our employers.

Kunitani pointed out that the time spent in the language schools was about an hour a day, two or three days a week. These periods followed a regular day of six to eight hours in the public schools, and were not popular with the young students who longed to be outdoors playing.

I went to a Japanese language school for about four years. I did not like to go at all. . . . I just went to the equivalent of about the third grade in the Japanese school. Even then I attended only haphazardly.[20]

The Young Democrats, Inc., to which Kunitani belonged, was in favor of evacuation if the military authorities deemed it necessary. They asked only assurances of food, shelter, and clothing, and a plan by which the evacuees could take a positive part in the defense effort; they wanted such people as doctors and lawyers to be allowed to practice their professions after being evacuated.

The accuracy of the testimony concerning the inefficiency of the language schools was borne out considerably later in the war, when the Army, needing men with Japanese language skill to act as interpreters in the Pacific, interviewed an initial group of 3,700 Nisei. Of these, 3 percent spoke the language fluently, 4 percent were fairly proficient, and another 3 percent could be useful after intensive training. Fifty-eight Nisei were selected for the first six months course at San Francisco's Presidio—and fifteen failed. But by the fall of 1944, the Army school had taught Japanese to 1,600 enlisted graduates, 142 officer candidates, and 53 officers. A large number of these went on to serve with distinction in the war.[21]

Dual citizenship seems never to have caused any official national concern in this country, but the phrase had a mysterious and ominous sound to the man in the street and was early seized upon by the Japanese Exclusion League and other West Coast racist groups. As early as 1921, California State Controller John S. Chambers said an objective of the Exclusion League would be to amend the Constitution of the United States so that children born in this country of parents ineligible to citizenship would themselves be ineligible to citizenship.

Mr. Chambers did not mention the fact that Congress, in an Act passed March 26, 1790, gave American citizenship to children born abroad to American citizens.

This was exactly what Japan was doing until the Exclusion Act of 1924. After America put that act into effect, Tokyo changed her law to require a baby's birth abroad to be registered, within fourteen days, at a Japanese consulate, to give the child status as a dual citizen. This was done at the insistence of the JACL and Nisei in Hawaii who wanted clarification on the dual nationality situation. From that time on, the number of dual citizens steadily declined. For example, three years before the war it was estimated that of 60,000 Nisei who had been born in Hawaii since 1924, only 10,000 had been registered with the consulate.

It also had become possible for any dual citizen to expatriate himself, legally, from Japan—simply by giving the address of his parents in America. In earlier decades, any dual citizen who went to Tokyo to study and reached the age of twenty while there was subject to service in the Japanese army. The expatriation amendment to Japanese law made a big difference. In Hawaii, where some 53,000 Nisei had been born *before* 1924, some 30,000 took advantage of the expatriation measure.

In other words, there were not as many dual citizens around, in 1942, as the anti-Japanese groups claimed. The term was not really very meaningful, but it was dusted off and used—against the Nisei, only. Nobody paid any attention to the fact that both Italy and Germany claimed dual citizenship for the children of their nationals, regardless of where they were born.

Thus, the DiMaggio boys, whose batting averages became a shining part of the Tolan Committee's transcript, could have been dual citizens. For that matter, Mayor Angelo Rossi, with the carnation in his buttonhole, could have been one.

The Dies Committee got into the act after Pearl Harbor and told Congress, "It has been conservatively estimated that about 75 percent of the Nisei, or American-born Japanese, have dual citizenship."

This estimate was neither conservative nor accurate. Figures from a survey made as far back as 1930 were available. They showed the same trend later found in Hawaii: only about a third of Nisei children had been registered at a Japanese consulate, 40 percent of older Nisei had legally renounced all ties with Japan.

On the mainland, thousands of Nisei scorned to take any advantage of the procedure to divest themselves of any so-called Japanese citizenship, lest they lend dignity to the situation. They stressed the fact that they were *not* Japanese citizens, that Japan had no jurisdiction over them, that dual loyalties were utterly false. They were determined to take no action that would hint, in the slightest way, that they were not a hundred percent American.

There are, of course, dual citizens among us today. In June of 1965, stage and film star Yul Brynner renounced his rights as a naturalized American citizen to become a Swiss citizen only. He explained that he wished to avoid being separated from the members of his family who lived in Europe and were not U.S. citizens.[22]

The Kibei, or returnees from Japan, will be dealt with later in this story. It is enough to say here that an exaggerated importance probably was attached to them. It is true that a few of them, who had stayed too long in the land of their ancestors, at an impressionable age, were neither fish nor fowl when they returned to this country. Some of these were potentially disloyal. The manner in which they were treated during the Evacuation was enough to tip the balance.

Six

Lysander said that the law
spoke too softly to be heard in
such a noise of war.

—Plutarch, *Life of Caius Marius.*

I

The Department of Justice had been in charge of the enemy
alien problem from December to February 19, when President
Roosevelt issued Executive Order No. 9066. General DeWitt
had been blowing hot and cold through most of that indecisive
period, but he was sure of one thing: the Attorney General's
staff was not being tough enough. Even if they had wanted to
bear down harder, they couldn't have; there were simply not
enough of them.

The FBI continued its efficient work, unaffected by the prev-
alent hysteria. After Earl Warren and Walter Lippmann and
a number of other liberals called for concentration camps for
even the American born, J. Edgar Hoover went on record
with a protest that the demand for evacuation was "based primarily upon public and political pressure rather than upon
factual data." [1]

The hot-line telephones were busy between San Francisco
and Washington; a series of conferences was held at General
DeWitt's Presidio headquarters. The Justice Department sent
Assistant Attorney General James Rowe, Jr., and the War De-
partment sent Major Karl R. Bendetsen, who was chief of the
Aliens Division in the Provost Marshal General's Office. [2]

Major Bendetsen was a young and brilliant graduate of the
Stanford Law School, Class of 1932; he had joined the National Guard while still in his teens and was well grounded
both in military and legal affairs. In 1941 he had been a spe-
cal representative of the Secretary of War to General MacAr-

92

thur. Although he was a field-grade officer, a rank that is rarely listened to in high ranking circles, his opinions already carried weight. He was shortly to be promoted, and before long he would be running the show.

At the conference table, Bendetsen advocated the establishment of strategic areas to be prescribed by the Army and declared off limits to all enemy aliens. Assistant Attorney General Rowe later recalled that General DeWitt was strongly opposed to any mass evacuation, but wanted the FBI to have blanket authority for search and seizure. The strategic areas were set up some two weeks later, but either DeWitt was not satisfied or had changed his mind.

He telephoned Bendetsen, who was back in Washington, and said the steps being taken by the Justice Department might control sabotage, but wouldn't stop it. He added:

The only positive answer to this question is evacuation of all enemy aliens from the West Coast and resettlement or internment under positive control, *military or otherwise* [italics supplied].

With the initial announcement of the first "strategic" areas, aliens living in such districts as the San Francisco waterfront had to get out. The order was well publicized.

General DeWitt, in his Final Report, said:

There was much conjecture that this was the forerunner of a general enemy alien evacuation. . . . Public excitement in certain areas reached a high pitch, and much confusion, the result of conflicting reports and rumors, characterized the picture. However, in essence, there was no substantial dislocation or disruption socially or economically of the affected groups.

Actually, there was a tremendous disruption, socially and economically, at this early stage. Even then, Japanese were approached by profiteers who wanted to buy their cars, refrigerators, and radios. Some of the dislocated people could double up with friends or relatives outside the restricted zone, but, even so, they had to abandon their shops and businesses. Everybody lost something. Many people lost everything.

II

No military or naval commander, in any Army Corps Area or Naval District, can escape or ignore civilian pressures. The Army and the Navy have always been subject to civil control. But this policy, while wise, also makes a military commander very conscious of what a Governor thinks, or a local Congressman, or the head of the Chamber of Commerce. A great deal of social activity is required of the military commander, and his thinking can also be influenced by what has been called "pillow politics"—when his wife, for example, says late at night, "Dear, So-and-so was asking me why you don't do thus-and-thus . . ."

Back in December, 1941, General DeWitt was unsure of a number of things, including his statistics. On December 26, in a telephone conversation with Major General Allen W. Gullion, Provost Marshal General in the War Department, DeWitt said:

If we go ahead and arrest the 93,000 Japanese, native born and foreign born, we are going to have an awful job on our hands and are very liable to alienate the loyal Japanese from disloyal [sic]. I'm very doubtful that it would be common-sense procedure to try and intern or to intern 117,000 Japanese in this theater . . . those people should be watched better if they were watched by the police and people of the community in which they live and have been living for years . . . and then inform the FBI or the military authorities of any suspicious action . . . rather than try to intern all those people, men, women, and children and hold them under military control and under guard. I don't think it's a sensible thing to do. . . . I'd rather go along the way we are now . . . rather than attempt any such wholesale internment. . . . An American citizen, after all, is an American citizen.[3]

Somewhere along the way, somebody sold General DeWitt a bill of goods. Just over a year later, well after the tide of battle had turned in the Pacific, he was saying, "A Jap's a Jap," and calling American citizenship "a piece of paper" insofar as it applied to men and women of Japanese ancestry.

The phone talk with General Gullion came about because a representative of the Los Angeles Chamber of Commerce had just visited DeWitt to urge a roundup of all Japanese in the Los Angeles area. DeWitt said no. Gullion agreed with De-Witt's stand and delayed submitting a plan to transfer the alien program from the Justice Department to the War Department.

But Gullion thought it would expedite matters if DeWitt could bypass the chain of command in the War Department and deal directly with the Provost Marshal General's Office. This was arranged. The official U. S. Army History says:

As a result . . . the responsible Army command headquarters in Washington had little to do during January and February 1942 with the plans and decision for Japanese evacuation [italics supplied].[4]

The question naturally arises, who *was* responsible? General DeWitt?

Perhaps. But as ten Broek points out in his *Prejudice, War, and the Constitution,* the program was

initiated by the generals, advised, ordered and supervised by the civilian heads of the War Department, authorized by the President, implemented by Congress, approved by the Supreme Court, and supported by the people.

In a telephone conversation with Bendetsen on February 4, 1942, DeWitt said:

I have never on my own initiative recommended a mass evacuation, or the removal of any man, any Jap, other than an alien. In other words, I have made no distinction between an alien as to whether he is Jap, Italian or German—that they must all get out of Area A, that is, the Category A area. The agitation to move all the Japanese away from the coast, and some suggestions, out of California entirely—is within the State, the population of the State, which has been espoused by the Governor.[5]

Three days later Assistant Secretary of War John J. Mc-Cloy decided to send Bendetsen to San Francisco to—in the words of the Provost Marshal General's daily Record of Operations—"confer with General DeWitt in connection with mass evacuation of all Japanese."

DeWitt made new and detailed recommendations as a result of this conference, and referred to them collectively as "the plan that Mr. McCloy wanted me to submit."

Some explanation is needed here. The official history published by the Department of the Army in 1964 calls Bendetsen the War Department's "most industrious advocate of mass evacuation." This was unfair. DeWitt and Bendetsen have both been maligned in connection with the Evacuation, and some of that was unfair, too.

The same official history of the Army reveals that an unsigned "Memo for Record" dated 8 February, 1942, was found in the War Department files. In part, it read:

Japanese Evacuation, West Coast

Prepare definite instructions for DeWitt on following basis:
Select key points where danger is great and size not too large.
Put them in order of importance.
Evacuate everybody, aliens and citizens.
Institute system of permits.
Whole matter to be handled by Army authorities.
Then, as matter progresses, we will soon find out how far we can
    go.[6]

What actually happened was this:

General DeWitt, charged with defense of the West Coast, was quite understandably alarmed at the success of the Japanese in the Pacific. He was subject to a vast amount of pressure from politicians and commercial groups who wanted the Japanese removed. He was further concerned with the possibility that unless the Japanese were sequestered, serious civil disorders would occur along the West Coast, with the Japanese as the victims.

There was some merit in this view, of course, when one

considers the times and the prevailing public mood. It would also seem that Secretary of War Stimson was caught up in the West Coast panic. No one of less political stature could have persuaded President Roosevelt to issue Executive Order No. 9066.

The mood of the people, and of the military officials, was both confused and confounded by certain intelligence reports. It was known that Japanese naval agents were active in almost all of their consulates; for six months before the attack on Pearl Harbor, it was known that reports of Navy ship movements were being sent to Tokyo. As early as August, 1941, Admiral Kimmel, Commander in Chief of the Pacific Fleet, was warned that a Japanese attack might come on a Sunday, and in November, 1941, Kimmel was instructed to take a defensive deployment so that there would be no ships in Pearl Harbor.[7] History attests that these warnings were not heeded.

Back on the West Coast, General DeWitt was on the spot. He had earlier recommended to the War Department that enemy aliens be removed to the Zone of the Interior.

The Army—and any other military organization—must have A Plan. Now the War Department asked DeWitt to submit a plan as to just how such evacuation would be handled. Major Bendetsen—he had not yet been promoted—was sent to confer with DeWitt. Bendetsen was only one of several General Staff officers who were asked to draw up a detailed plan on how the extremely complicated logistics and other problems of the Evacuation would be handled.

Karl Bendetsen's plan, which ran some nine pages of typewritten copy, was officially adopted. Through this, he later became known as the Army's most "industrious advocate of mass evacuation." Bendetsen may well have been the War Department's most expert officer in handling the problem, but he did *not* instigate the Evacuation. He merely set it up, under orders.

What happened here is quite plain. DeWitt asked for the

authority, McCloy came back at him with a request for a detailed plan, and Bendetsen wrote that plan.

Therefore, in a very large sense, no specific individual can be charged with having "authored" the Evacuation. General DeWitt, alarmed at what was happening in the Pacific, wanted it. The War Department approved it. Bendetsen, under orders, came up with a workable plan of operation. And the President issued Executive Order No. 9066.

Original plans called for exclusion of the Japanese from the coastal areas, and would have permitted their voluntary removal inland to any point they chose. This movement began in March, but the plan was neither fair nor workable. Some of the people had no money for travel, many did not speak English and did not know where to go. They heard daily reports of hostility on the part of inland communities; governors and other officials in the western states said bluntly that the Japanese were not wanted. Armed posses turned back migrants at the Nevada line. "No Japs Wanted" signs sprouted at the town limits of many inland municipalities. A number of Japanese were jailed overnight and then told to be on their way.

The voluntary evacuation plan lasted three weeks. On March 27, General DeWitt issued his fourth public proclamation, instructing the people to stay where they were until further orders.[8]

III

The spread of hysteria on the West Coast was nourished both by rumors and by what the people considered official reports. Some of the latter were not always "official." For example, Secretary of the Navy Frank Knox had flown to Pearl Harbor for a first-hand inspection of the damage there. He was not only smarting, officially, from the bludgeoning of the sneak attack, but he also suffered personally because the then current issue of *American Magazine* seemed to leap out from every newsstand with a cover blurb quoting him: WE CAN WIN IN BOTH OCEANS.

Knox's official report did not mention fifth column activity in connection with the Pearl Harbor attack. But, back in Washington on December 15, he held a press conference and was quoted as saying, "I think the most effective fifth column work of the entire war was done in Hawaii, with the possible exception of Norway."

Secretary Knox was known to newspapermen as Chicago's "Evening Colonel," because he published an afternoon newspaper in competition with one published by "Morning Colonel" McCormick. He handled press relations well, and newsmen liked him. What he said usually was regarded as official. But what he said on December 15 later turned out to be based purely on rumor.

Curtis B. Munson, a special State Department representative who made a less hurried investigation of Pearl Harbor, respectfully suggested that instead of using the term "fifth column," Knox should have employed that of "complete physical espionage."

[The latter] is supplied unwittingly by the gabble of Navy wives, by the gabble of loyal second generation Japanese, by the gabble of the postman and milkman, and [is] classified by definite agents of a foreign government.[9]

Munson might have added that members of ambassadorial and consular staffs were pretty active, too. These people enjoyed diplomatic immunity, just as our people did in diplomatic positions abroad. We should not forget that they were paid, as part of their jobs, to get as much military information as possible. The old cartoon gag of, "I'll trade you the dope on our new artillery for the plans on your new heavy cruiser," is funny, but not at all far-fetched. It was all in the day's work.

Vice Admiral John Wills Greenslade, Commander Western Sea Frontier (a billet junior to DeWitt's Western Defense Command), was an old sea dog who had kept his feet on many a heaving deck and did his best to keep them on solid ground now that he was ashore.

Back in 1934, when he was a Rear Admiral and Commander Submarine Forces Pacific, Greenslade had advocated measures to eliminate racial prejudice, by finding means" to establish an immigration quota for the Japanese."

When war came, he was alert, but still broad-minded. In an appeal to striking welders to return to their shipyard jobs, Admiral Greenslade revealed, on December 20, that Japanese submarines were attacking West Coast shipping.

And, indeed, they were. That same day, the tanker *Agwiworld* was fired upon near Monterey but returned to port under her own steam, and the tanker *Emidio* was sunk off Eureka with the loss of five crewmen. On December 22, the freighter *H. M. Storey* was fired upon, but not hit, off Point Arguello. Next day the tanker *Montabello* took a torpedo "somewhere off the coast." The *Larry Doheny* was shelled but got away.[10]

On Christmas Eve, an Army B-24 reported sinking a submarine off the mouth of the Columbia River. The Army's official history now discredits this claim, saying, "the Japanese submarine then assigned to this station, (the I-25), was the one that returned eight months later to wind up enemy submarine operations off the Pacific coast." [11]

There were no other submarine attacks worthy of mention. But just as President Roosevelt was beginning a "fireside chat" on February 23, the I-17 surfaced 2,500 yards off the coast at Goleta (California) and lobbed thirteen rounds of 5½ inch shells at an oil-tank complex.

No significant damage was done, but the Japanese might have been amused to learn about one casualty of the bombardment. San Simeon, the baronial castle of their ancient enemy, William Randolph Hearst, was not far away, and offered a vulnerable target. Fearing personal retaliation from Japan, Hearst closed San Simeon and fled with Marion Davies to Wyntoon, his other palatial hideaway on the McCloud River, two hundred and fifty miles north of San Francisco. Miss Davies was not amused. She hated this place, and always called it "Spittoon." [12]

Admiral Greenslade's public announcement of the submarine attacks was both wise and necessary, since returning crewmen do talk, and rumors in wartime are bound to spread. In this case, a jittery populace was in a mood to add two and two and come up with eight. The rumors spread despite official announcements, and many West Coast citizens believed they were blockaded by a whole fleet of Japanese submarines.

At that time, the Atlantic was having so many actual sinkings by Nazi U-boats that coastal pilots reportedly used the masts of downed vessels for navigational purposes, but there appears to be no similar record of hysteria along the Eastern seaboard. General DeWitt's official story of the Evacuation, the Final Report, *made fifteen months later,* still declared that *"for a period of several weeks following December 7, substantially every ship leaving a West Coast port was attacked by an enemy submarine* [italics supplied]." [13]

We come back, now, to a certain unfortunate lack of liaison between the Army and the Navy. DeWitt's statement was absurd, and had been disproved, on the record, a long time before it was made. But the General had made the same claim by telephone to the Secretary of War on January 24, when he added, "We know there are radios along the coast; and we know they are communicating at sea."

The Navy did not know this. And the official Army history now says:

Actually there had been no Japanese submarine or surface vessels anywhere near the west coast during the preceding month, and careful investigation subsequently indicated that all claims of hostile shore-to-ship and ship-to-shore communications lacked any foundation whatsoever.[14]

February was the month of decision.

The Roberts Commission report had been published on January 25. It said there had been widespread espionage in

Hawaii, both by Tokyo's consular agents and by Japanese residents of Oahu. After the war, the latter charge proved false, but at the time the report inflamed West Coast officials and citizens alike. General DeWitt met with Nat Pieper, the FBI chief, and Attorney General Earl Warren on January 29. He reported later that "Warren was in thorough agreement with Governor Olson that the Japanese population should be removed from the State of California," and expressed his own concurrence in the proposal. By telephone, he told Major Bendetsen in Washington that he was willing to accept responsibility for the program if it were given to him.

By February 1, DeWitt had agreed to submit a written recommendation for a mass evacuation.

Apparently there were second thoughts in the War Department. General Gullion informed DeWitt that both Secretary of War Henry L. Stimson and the Assistant Secretary of War John J. McCloy were against any mass evacuation of the Japanese. This was on February 4, the same day Major Karl Bendetsen was promoted to Lieutenant Colonel.[15]

Just two days before, on February 2, both Admiral Harold R. Stark, Chief of Naval Operations, and Brigadier General Mark W. Clark of GHQ had told Congress that there might be air raids on the West Coast but that the chances of any sustained attack or invasion were—in Clark's words—nil.

On 4 February, Colonel Bendetsen wrote General Gullion a lengthy memorandum saying that an alien enemy evacuation would not do much for safety, because the Issei were elderly persons who could do little harm and that evacuating them would antagonize the Nisei. Bendetsen went back to the designation of military areas and a system of passes for those who could enter or remain in such areas.

It went on that way until General DeWitt made up his mind on February 14 and presented the West Coast Japanese with a bitter Valentine's Day greeting.

Bendetsen was promoted again, to full Colonel, and was sent to San Francisco to be Assistant Chief of Staff for Civil

Affairs, General Staff, and Director of the Wartime Civil Control Administration. This military organization was established to evacuate the Japanese into temporary "reception"
and "assembly" centers. After the more permanent Relocation
Centers had been prepared, the Army would step aside and
the civilian War Relocation Authority would take over.

The Japanese Americans, meanwhile, were not without
champions who at least fought for fairer play. Lieutenant
Commander Kenneth D. Ringle of the Eleventh Naval District
(Los Angeles) office of Naval Intelligence was vocal in their
behalf. He submitted a report to the Chief of Naval Operations, charging that the problem had been "magnified out of
its true proportion" on racial grounds. The Army's proposal
of mass exclusion, Ringle thought, was both unwarranted and
unwise. He advocated review of cases on an individual basis,
by boards made up of Army and Navy Intelligence officers
and members of the Department of Justice.[16]

Such hearing boards were repeatedly urged in the spring of
1942 by educators, attorneys, and church leaders. It was suggested that the already existing Selective Service appeal boards
could handle the job and finish it in six weeks time.[17]

General DeWitt's headquarters turned a deaf ear. Such procedure, it said, would "cause delay when speed was urgent,"
and, besides, "it would be practically impossible to establish
the loyalty of any one of Japanese race.[18]

General DeWitt did not explain why the problem had suddenly become so urgent after it had lain dormant for nearly
three months, during which time neither sabotage nor fifth column activity had been reported.

IV

Several months before the West Coast Japanese were ordered
to line up to board buses for the Assembly Centers—taking
with them only such possessions as could be carried by
hand—a small group of people of Japanese ancestry had al-

ready been dealt with, but in a very different way.

When war came, the State Department was immediately
confronted with the problem of interning members of the enemy diplomatic corps, with their families.

This had to be done, of course, in the best gray glove and
striped pants diplomatic manner. It had to be carried out with
the thought that the Japanese, Germans, and Italians were
holding our own diplomatic people, and if provoked, might re-
taliate against them. International law and usage are very
stuffy about "diplomatic immunity."

In addition to the enemy diplomatic and consular staffs in
our own country, the State Department had to take care of
those from South America and Mexico. The fact that Americans were not going much of anywhere on rationed tires and
gasoline helped. State settled on three famous resorts: The
Homestead at Hot Springs, Virginia; Grove Park Inn at Asheville, N.C., and The Greenbrier at White Sulphur Springs,
West Virginia.

This was one of the ironies of war. Anybody ought to love
being incarcerated in such luxurious surroundings. The aliens
attached to ambassadorial and consular staffs were not necessarily "spies," of course, . . . but certainly a number of them
escaped being spies by that "diplomatic immunity" status, and
all of them were out to get and transmit to their homelands
every scrap of military information they could obtain by diplomatic means.

In August, 1941, a Japanese arrived in Honolulu under the
name of Vice-Consul Morimura. His real name was Takeo
Yoshikawa; he was a police officer's son who had been an en-
sign in the Imperial Japanese Navy but had resigned due to ill
health in 1936. He was young and brilliant: he had studied
English for four years after being shifted to Tokyo's Naval Intelligence upon his retirement. He became a junior official in
the Foreign Office, and when he went to Hawaii he was ordered to play the role of diplomat—but to send a coded report
through Consul Kita on the daily disposition of the U.S.

Fleet.[19]

To be completely fair, we must admit that Intelligence officers of the U.S. Navy were, at the same time, doing the same thing in Japan and elsewhere—or trying to. In the middle thirties, the author of this book, as a San Francisco newspaperman and a Reserve Intelligence officer, spent a great deal of time checking on the activities of one Lieutenant Commander Ohmae, who had entered the University of Pennsylvania as a language student, only to drop out a few weeks later and drive to the West Coast, where he acted as a Japanese agent.

Ohmae got nothing. He was very busy living it up with a pretty little Nisei girl from Hawaii who apparently went with the job: she was passed along to Ohmae's successor. Naval Intelligence bugged Ohmae's California Street apartment and listened in on all that went on, . . . and most of the events were of a very intimate nature. When Ohmae finally booked steamship passage for return to Japan, Naval Intelligence was looking over his shoulder. That evening, they stole everything he had, just to be sure there was nothing in the lining of his suitcases. There wasn't, and Ohmae was allowed to recover his luggage through the police pawnshop detail, by an arrangement with the police that probably didn't fool him at all. This bit of business scared hell out of Admiral (then Commander) Arthur H. McCollum, back in the Washington office of Naval Intelligence. "There were times," he told the author, "when I thought you guys in San Francisco were going a little too far."

Ohmae was allowed to sail, and one wonders just what he reported, orally, when he reached Tokyo. Letting him sail made it much easier to keep tabs on the officer who relieved him—and took over the cute Hawaiian Nisei girl.

Later, there was the Tachibana spy case. The details are shrouded in mystery and tucked into official files not readily accessible. At first glance, the name *Tachibana* might appear to be an alias, since it means "mandarin orange," and because *tachi-ban* means "guard," or "sentinel." But Admiral McCollum, an expert Japanese linguist, has pointed out that Tachibana is actually an old and honored surname in Japan. At any rate, a lieutenant commander of the Japanese Navy, Itaru Tachibana, thirty-nine, enrolled at the University of Southern California as a language student. He had an assistant, Toraichi Kono, who had been Charlie Chaplin's valet and personal secretary, but by June of 1941 was operating a small business.

The case was bizarre enough to satisfy any lover of spy stories. Kono approached a man named Al Blake, known in Hollywood as "Keeno, the King of the Robots." Blake, fifty, had been a yeoman in the Navy in World War I. He made his living by standing in a department store window alongside a wax dummy exactly like him, even to a tiny waxed mustache. Window shoppers and sidewalk crowds were invited to try to make him laugh or flicker an eyelid and to attempt to tell which was the dummy and which was Al Blake.

Kono asked Blake if he would get in touch with yeomen aboard the battleship Pennsylvania, then flagship of the Pacific Fleet, and obtain information from them. Blake agreed, but went at once to Naval Intelligence with the story. Naval Intelligence told him to go on with the deal.

Tachibana then came into the picture and paid Blake several thousand dollars—all of which Blake turned over to Naval Intelligence. Blake came out of his department store window and made a couple of trips to Hawaii. The Navy gave him a few old and outdated code books, as well as some harmless gunnery statistics from the cruiser U.S.S. *Phoenix*. Blake turned this material over to the Japanese agents.

Then, when Naval Intelligence was sure it had a case, the FBI was tipped off, and, early in June 1941, both Kono and Tachibana were arrested. A whole truckload of Navy information was found in Tachibana's apartment. He was charged with conspiracy to obtain national defense information for a foreign power. Japanese Consul Kenji Nakauchi promptly posted $50,000 bail for Lieutenant Commander Tachibana, but allowed Kono, whose bail was $25,000, to languish in jail.[20]

Disposition of the two cases is not known here. But Al Blake came out a hero for having been able to keep a straight face. And the papers that had been seized provided an almost complete list of Japanese agents in this country, so that the people named were speedily arrested on December 7.

"Diplomatic espionage" was old in 1941 and is still practiced today. *The Reader's Digest* for December, 1965, carried an article by Frederic Sondern, Jr., entitled "The Many Faces of the FBI." Among other things, Mr. Sondern said:

The greatest, and ever-present challenges to the disguise division are the tortuous intrigues of foreign espionage agents. They ordinarily have much higher IQ than that of most criminals. The number of these snoopers is growing continually as more and more governments—not only communist bloc, but Latin American, African, Middle and Far Eastern—become increasingly interested in American military and diplomatic moves.

These spies are based mainly at the official establishments in New York and Washington, D.C., cozily protected by diplomatic immunity. FBI agents have to be very careful: the State Department likes to avoid embarrassment. A case must be copper-riveted before it declares a foreign emissary *persona non grata*. Nevertheless, the FBI has accomplished just that in more than 30 important instances over the last ten years.[21]

In 1942, the diplomats lived it up while the aliens and citizens went off to live in stables and in desert concentration camps. The Homestead at Hot Springs, Virginia, had a tradition of seventy-five years. It was a playground of the rich, a 17,000-acre vacation paradise with golf courses, tennis and badminton courts, bowling alleys and ballrooms. It had luxurious suites, luxurious single rooms, and a superb cuisine. The Homestead also offered, through its natural hot springs, the *o-furo* so dear to Japanese hearts.

Being interned at the Homestead was one of the anomalies

of war. It was surely more reward than punishment.

The Homestead management got word two days before Christmas, 1941, that it had been selected as repository for the Japanese diplomats. Gordon Shoemaker, then and now prominent in the managerial staff, remembers that they had to move out all other guests by Christmas Eve.

The first contingent of what would be 334 Japanese arrived by train a few hours later.

"The FBI was in charge," Shoemaker says. "Roy Morgan was the head FBI man. The people came in bringing everything they had, including sacks of potatoes and other food supplies, which we stored in the basement of the Tower.

"They brought 150 cases of Old Paar Scotch."

Up from Texas came some sixty members of the tough U.S. Border Patrol to serve as guards at The Homestead, with a Captain Hudson in command. The Border Patrolmen entranced everybody by telling how many Mexicans they had shot along the Rio Grande. They never bothered about recovering bodies, they said, but they knew the Mexicans were dead, because "they didn't move again . . ."

The Homestead gave the Texans no trigger practice. But neither did the interned Japanese enjoy the famed hotel to the full, or live in the luxury their less fortunate West Coast kinsmen have supposed. In those days, the resort was virtually closed down for winter, not yet having a ski lift and other snow season attractions. The internees were so strictly confined to the hotel itself that temporary partitions had to be erected to keep them in particular areas.

"In general," Shoemaker recalls, "they had full run of the public rooms. But they could not go into the Club."

The Club was a place, in dry Virginia, where anybody who had suddenly become a member could buy a drink.

A baby was born that winter, making the total of internees 335. The baby was cradled in a dresser drawer, and thrived.

People interned at the Homestead came not only from Washington, but from the staffs in Mexico City and from embassies in Salvador and Cuba. Internment being a family affair, there were some seventy-five or eighty children. Besides the Border Patrolmen, three FBI men were on duty at all times.

"There was a big meeting every morning in the ballroom," Shoemaker says. "They had lectures on Chinese culture. But the meetings were a good thing, and not just to pass the time. When they first came, they were told that our waiters and the other help were largely dependent upon tips. You see, the hotel had started off under an arrangement by which Uncle Sam paid a family rate of $10 per head per day. After we had more than two hundred and fifty people in residence, this rate was cut to $9 per day."

It was winter. The Homestead would have been operating at a loss, under such rates, in summer time. And the $9 per day did not take care of the help.

But the Japanese got the word about the tipping system, and said, "Ah, so? How much?" Thereafter, they tipped $1400 a week, to be distributed among the employees. At first they turned in $500 bills, then got down to greenbacks of $100, later to $50 denominations, and finally—as if time and money were running out together—down to twenties, tens, and fives.

Every bill was terribly crinkled, as if it might have been tightly rolled and sewed into the seams of clothing.[22]

Did the internees enjoy the traditional services, the famed hospitality, and the internationally known cuisine of the well-known resorts?

At Grove Park Inn, Asheville, where 63 Japanese and 155 Germans were interned—all of them from embassies and consulates in South America—the usual menus were maintained, and the guests enjoyed shuffleboard, lawn bowling, badminton, and bridge, under guard of twenty-eight FBI men and forty-eight special guards hired in Asheville.

"At the Homestead," Shoemaker says, "the Japanese had

our regular menus for about two weeks. Then Admiral (Ambassador) Nomura and others had a meeting in the ballroom. They decided that when they had been exchanged they would not have food like that in Japan, and that it wasn't fair to other Japanese to eat it now; they thought they had better tighten their belts. So they went, voluntarily, on a fish and rice diet, and made their own menus. It certainly helped the hotel, which had not been operating at a profit under the old arrangement."

The guests were disciplined. At the Grove Park Inn, there were no incidents at all. Among the people interned at the Homestead were newsmen of the official Japanese Domei News Agency, who twice burned some papers—perhaps copies of exclusive stories. In each case, the burning set off the automatic sprinkler system, and the Domei news men were drenched, but fought their way out of the charred and sodden wreckage—and paid for the damage.

There were fifty small children at the Grove Park Inn, and an even larger number of small fry at the Homestead, where the Japanese kids found themselves in a fairyland. One little girl was asked if she believed in Santa Claus. She said yes, Santa had brought her a doll last Christmas. But she added, sadly, that she had heard that the FBI might not let Santa come this year.

Gordon Shoemaker heard a conversation between two boys of about nine. One said, "Stop talking that damned Japanese, and tell me in *English* what's troubling you!"

And a small boy ran under the American Flag that was and still is displayed on a staff projected from the balcony in the main lobby. His mother, the wife of a Japanese diplomat, called, "Georgie! Take off your hat! You're under the American Flag!" [23]

The Greenbrier at White Sulphur Springs, West Virginia, was in its one hundred and sixty-fourth year as a hostelry. Approximately two thousand Japanese, German, and Hungarian diplomats were interned there for six months; they, too, were guarded by the FBI and the Texas Border Patrol. But at The Greenbrier the internees had the run of the estate when spring came and enjoyed the traditional menus and other services insofar as they were not affected by wartime shortages. The hotel saw to it that Sears and Roebuck and Montgomery-Ward catalogue services were provided so that mail-order shopping could be done. Six babies were born, and three weddings took place during the six month period.

And every time the Germans entered the dining room, the orchestra struck up "The White Cliffs of Dover." [24]

On May 7, 1942, a total of 948 enemy nationals sailed for Lisbon on the Swedish liner *Drottningholm,* out of Jersey City; others would be leaving on the famous *Gripsholm.* Those aboard the *Drottningholm* included the people who had been interned at the Grove Park Inn, 426 Germans from the Greenbrier, and 215 Germans and Italians who had been held at Cincinnati.

They went aboard ship, newspaper dispatches said, in a somber mood . . . but many had dogs on leashes, and one small German boy was gaily singing a song the Border Patrol had taught him—"Deep in the Heart of Texas."

The comparatively small group leaving Grove Park Inn had 3,000 pieces of luggage, including 2,500 trunks.[25] The real ordeal for the West Coast Japanese was just beginning at that time. Out there, they could take no pets. They had to leave behind anything that could not be carried by hand when they boarded the buses.

Seven

"'Why, you fellows needn't
  bother,'
Said General Doug MacArthur,
As he called out his Navy and
  Marines;
'We'll just batten down the
  hatches
While I write a few dispatches,
And we'll have the Philippines!'"

—South Pacific Navy Song.

I

Everybody was putting pen to paper. On March 2, General
DeWitt's Public Proclamation Number One designated the
western half of the West Coast and the southern half of Arizona as Military Area No. 1 and set up prohibited and restricted zones from which residents of Japanese ancestry
would be required to move.

Some ten thousand did move, voluntarily, some to stay with
friends or relatives, many to discover that they were not welcome in Colorado or Utah. Those who had gone just outside
the restricted zones were dismayed shortly afterward when
creation of Military Area Number 2 forced them to move
again.

General DeWitt ordered cessation of voluntary evacuation
on March 29 and resumed writing Civilian Exclusion Orders.
Between February and April 30, there had been twenty-seven
such orders; the paper war went on until there was a total of
108 Civilian Exclusion Orders.

Number 27, on April 30, said in part:

1. Pursuant to the provisions of Public Proclamations Nos. 1
and 2, this Headquarters, dated March 2 and March 16, 1942, re-

spectively, it is hereby ordered that from and after 12 o'clock noon, P.W.T., of Thursday, May 7, 1942, all persons of Japanese ancestry, both alien and non-alien, be excluded from that portion of Military Area No. 1 . . . [description follows]

2. A responsible member of each family, and each individual living alone . . . will report between the hours of 8:00 A.M. and 5:00 P.M., Friday, May 1, 1942, or during the same hours on Saturday, May 2, 1942, to the Civil Control Station. . . .

[Instructions given the people included the following:]

Evacuees must carry with them on departure for the Assembly Center, the following property:

(a) Bedding and linens (no mattress) for each member of the family;

(b) Toilet articles for each member of the family;

(c) Extra clothing for each member of the family;

(d) Sufficient knives, forks, spoons, plates, bowls and cups for each member of the family;

(e) Essential personal effects for each member of the family. . . . No pets of any kind will be permitted. . . .

—J. L. DEWITT
Lieutenant General, U.S. Army
Commanding [1]

Commander Arthur H. McCollum had been at Pearl Harbor helping Admiral Chester W. Nimitz set up a Fleet Intelligence Center. He returned to San Francisco in May and found a telegram awaiting him from the Washington office of Naval Intelligence.

This was the first word McCollum had received concerning DeWitt's exclusion order. The Washington office urged him to do something to alleviate the situation and particularly to try to save the Navy's Japanese language school which was then located at the University of California at Berkeley.

McCollum recalls:

I went to see Admiral Greenslade, the Twelfth Naval District Commandant. Greenslade said he had not been informed of the Navy Department's interest in the matter, and expressed the view

that by now DeWitt was more or less publicly committed to the
Evacuation, and it would be difficult to get him to back down. I
went to see DeWitt, and he told me in effect that he had his orders
from the War Department, he was going to carry them out, and if
the Navy didn't like it, it was just too bad.

McCollum talked to an old friend, Lieutenant Colonel John
Weckerling, who was the head of DeWitt's Intelligence section,
and was given a new and somewhat more logical reason for
the Evacuation order. The General, Weckerling said, was convinced that unless people of Japanese ancestry were sequestered, serious civil disorders would occur all along the West
Coast, and the Japanese would be the victims.

Admiral McCollum believes today that there was some
merit in this view, considering the temper of the times. Perhaps there was. But DeWitt's Final Report, published a year
later, failed to stress any protective nature of the Evacuation
and emphasized, instead, that it was a "military necessity" to
avert sabotage and other aid to the enemy.

Eugene V. Rostow, Dean of the Yale University Law
School, in his book *The Sovereign Prerogative,* asserts that we
succumbed to an institutionalized sense of panic in California,
Oregon, and Washington, and describes the Evacuation as
"preventive custody"—a term much more true. Rostow also
says:

Studies . . . about conditions within the camps . . . make it
plain that [they] were in fact concentration camps, where the hu-
miliation of evacuation was compounded by a regime which ignored citizens' rights and the amenities which might have made the
relocation process more palatable.

On May 20, Colonel Bendetsen made a speech before the
Commonwealth Club of San Francisco.

By design, or by accident, substantial numbers of the Japanese
coastal frontier communities were deployed through very sensitive
and very vital areas.

Now, if you and I had settled in Japan, raised our families there and if our children and grandchildren were raised there, it is most improbable that during a period of war between Japan and the United States, if we were not interned, that we would commit any overt acts of sabotage acting individually. Doubtless, in the main, and irrespective of our inner emotions, you and I would be law abiding.

But when the final test of loyalty came, if United States forces were engaged in launching an attack on Japan, I believe it is extremely doubtful whether we could withstand the ties of race and the affinity for the land of our forebears and stand with the Japanese against United States forces.

Colonel Bendetsen added that it was doubtless true that many persons

of Japanese ancestry are loyal to the United States. It is also true that many are not loyal. . . . Contrary to other national or racial groups, the behavior of Japanese has been such that in not one single instance has any Japanese reported disloyalty on the part of another specific individual of the same race.[2]

This echoed the testimony of Earl Warren before the Tolan Committee. Both Warren and Colonel Bendetsen were uninformed. Naval Intelligence could have set the record straight, but it was being very close mouthed. Actually, a considerable number of Nisei had been giving all the suspicious data they could find to the FBI and Naval Intelligence, for several years. These Nisei were unpaid volunteers. At one time, with only three days' notice, they obtained and turned over all the records of the Black Dragon Society for the West Coast.

Colonel Bendetsen's "final test of loyalty" was predicated upon actual invasion. Two weeks after his talk, the Battle of Midway so badly crushed the Japanese Fleet that invasion of the West Coast was no longer possible. Captured documents proved that it had never even been planned.

But when General DeWitt wrote his Final Report, he was still asserting that no Japanese had ever informed on another . . . that there *had* been radio transmissions with the enemy—the latter in spite of the analysis of the Federal Communication Commission's Radio Intelligence Division, which proved just the opposite.

Another, and older, man was doing some writing in Los Angeles, and in the Santa Anita Assembly Center, and later in the Relocation Center at Gila, Arizona, where his wife died. He was an Issei who had learned English; he kept a journal in both languages because, "I may die before I can hear the ringing of a bell of Peace; if I do not write the detail of this distress to relatives in the old country nobody will because my two daughters could not write in Japanese very well." (One daughter was in her third year at the University of California; the other had entered Los Angeles Junior College.)

We will call the writer of this journal "Mr. H." [3]

This action is against American Constitution, a black spot for Democracy, but Army paid no attention. I educated my daughters to be best citizens of U.S.A., and America is my resting place after I am deceased. I will purchase war bonds and stamps if my financial resources will permit, but Alas, the daughters—typical American citizens—must face same music as Issei. I am Awfully disgusted. My sister, who was arrested by F.I.B. [sic] was released March 11 under police servilliance. . . .

We are now facing most disturbing and catastrophic situation, and we have not any solution. The West Coast Defence Commander General DeWitt issued the order of most merciless and ruthless one in all my life. The place we are going for temporary is famous race track, about twelve miles from Los Angeles. . . . Moving day was the most lamentable and sorrowful day in all our life on the Pacific Coast—our foundation, built by fifty years of hard toil and planning, was swept away by Army's Order. It was Awful Nightmare! . . .

I have had my chronic neuralgia coming back in this very unfortunate hour of evacuation. [My wife's] stomach troubles are getting worse for over-anxiety. If she eats, she vomits instantly. It may be symptom of Cancer, but I will not going to tell her what I am thinking. We have not time to go consult with Doctor.

We—everybody—ride the Buses. Fifty Buses altogether were

guided by M.P. Soldiers to Santa Anita Race track. We reached there in forty minutes. The place was very strictly guarded; they have barbed wire fence, the soldiers with machine guns watch the gate with alertness. We have no chance to step out to outside world. We are prisoners of WAR!!

Newly appointed police officers are very busy to examine our belongings, suitcases and boxes; everybody pretty near crazy to get their goods examined ahead of everybody. NO MANNERS AT ALL—I am Awfully disgusted. [My wife] complains her stomach is so painful. My Waist Line is still not so good yet. I worried how we could carry our belongings to our apartment or rooms. Just in time, Mr. W.K.'s son came and carried all our baggages to our temporary room—the stable. Then we went to the dining room, 3,000 capacity and were served Pork and Beans. We went back to our room and finally four of us lay on the bed for the night. It was eleven P.M.[4]

Mr. H. was a man of sensitivity. It is possible that he and some of the other older Issei, upon going into their quarters, Stable No.—, Stall No.—, and all unlighted, may have recalled a classical *haiku* written in the seventeenth century by the famous poet Matsuo Basho:

Nomi shirami	Plagued by fleas and lice
Uma no shito suru	I hear the horses staling—
Makura moto	What a place to sleep!

There were sixteen Assembly Centers, or "reception centers," to which the evacuated people were first taken—carrying by hand all that was permitted in the way of personal effects. The centers were set up at race tracks, fairgrounds, livestock exposition facilities, an abandoned CCC camp, a former mill site, and so on. They were located at:

Fresno, Manzanar, and Marysville, California; Mayer, Arizona; Merced, Pinedale, and Pomona, California; Portland, Oregon; Puyallup, Washington; Sacramento, Salinas, Santa Anita, Stockton, Tanforan, Tulare, and Turlock, California.

The length of operation of the Assembly Centers, until tarpaper barracks could be constructed at the desert War Relocation Camps, ranged from 27 days at Mayer, Arizona, to 215 days at Santa Anita. The maximum population figures tell a similar story: 245 at Mayer, 18,719 at Santa Anita.

Eighteen thousand people are a lot to have at a race track, even when the ponies are running.

II

The Army's roundup was thorough. George Enosaki, nineteen, and just graduated from high school in Montana, drove his car out to California intending to go to work—and arrived just in time to be picked up with the rest. Nobody gave him a chance to return to the Montana home of his parents. He was able to sell the car, which had new tires, for a good price.[5]

Sam Yoshimura, ten, from Florin, was all excited about going to the Assembly Center at Tanforan Race Track with his family—it would be, he thought, like camping out. Miné Okubo, the artist from Berkeley, was a little older and somewhat more sensitive to the fact of regimentation: she was given a number and was soon to be known as 13660. She had three days to prepare for the move to Tanforan. Her brother, in his last year at the University of California, had the same three days to make arrangements to protect his college record. It was now the first of May, and he would have gotten his B.A. degree in June. Nevertheless, he had to move.[6]

Miné Okubo and her brother went by bus to Tanforan and were searched for such things as knives and straight-edged razors and examined to see whether or not they had been vaccinated. They were assigned to Stable 16, Stall 50. The floor was covered with manure.

After an hour of standing in the mess line, they finally got boiled potatoes and two slices of bread—the canned Vienna sausages had just run out.

Fortunately, Miné Okubo's characteristically American sense of humor never did. She kept up her art work, despite difficulties, and in 1946 was able to bring out a book of sketches called *Citizen 13660*. She remembers, now, that after she and her brother had their skimpy supper, they were issued bed ticking bags and told to stuff them with straw. For a long time they sat on these, listening to the gradually subsiding murmur of hundreds of bewildered people.

"Then," says Miné Okubo, "we decided we might as well hit the hay." [7]

Accommodations at the Assembly Centers included milk stations, community showers, toilets, and laundries; each Center had a hospital and a post exchange.

Some of the people were flat broke by the time they were moved. They were given "nominal allowances" for incidentals in the form of coupon books. Any single adult was entitled to $2.50 per month, a married couple got $4, and children under sixteen received $1. The maximum for any family, even if it had seven or eight members, was $7.50.

If the people could get jobs helping run the Assembly Center, as some did, they were paid. A doctor assigned to the Center hospital, for instance, earned $16 a month, which was top pay. Unskilled workers got $8; skilled workers received $12.

All of them had to put in forty-four hours a week to draw these salaries.

Down at Santa Anita, Mr. H. was writing in his journal:

I took cook's job, pays only $12; my daughters, one at musical Department, the other at Paying Department. We thought the U.S. supplies everything at the camp and we don't need any money at all, but in due time we find this idea is absolutely wrong. The small salary we get from the jobs is not sufficient for my cigarettes or my daughters' necessities; the ready cash we carried from Los Angeles is getting low every day. If Peace will be restored in some future, I won't have any money left in my possession: this Problem worries me days and nights, but I don't have any idea for solution. [8]

The Army had no solution for the problem, either, but it was about to get off the hook. On March 18, the War Relocation Authority had been created by executive order, a civilian

agency with Milton Eisenhower in charge. It was working
with the Army toward establishment of a long-range program;
it was charged with operating Relocation Centers where the
Japanese would live for the duration of the war. Once the
evacuees had been moved to these Centers, under military es-
cort, the Army would be through with them—except that it
would maintain "protective military guards" outside the Centers.

The Army constructed and equipped the dreary tar-paper
barracks in the desert locations. By mid-June, 1942, eleven
Relocation Centers capable of handling 130,000 persons had
been approved by the Army. Ten were put into use. They
were:

Manzanar	California	Capacity	10,000
Tule Lake	California	"	16,000
Poston	Arizona	"	20,000
Gila River	Arizona	"	15,000
Minidoka	Idaho	"	10,000
Heart Mountain	Wyoming	"	10,000
Granada	Colorado	"	8,000
Topaz	Utah	"	10,000
Rohwer	Arkansas	"	10,000
Jerome	Arkansas	"	10,000
		Total	119,000

Eight

"The Army is not worried
about the Japanese in Hawaii.
Among them there may be a
small hostile alien group, but we
can handle the situation. It seems
people who know least about
Hawaii and live farthest away are
most disturbed over this matter.
People who know the Islands are
not worried about possible sabotage. I say this sincerely after my
years of service here. I am sold
on the patriotism and Americanization of the Hawaiian people as
a whole."

—Lt. Gen. Charles D. Herron, Commander Hawaiian
Department, in *Collier's*, Oct. 19, 1940.

I

In strange and marked contrast to the West Coast, the Hawaiian Islanders did not consider that mass evacuation of people
of Japanese ancestry was a matter of "military necessity."

Hawaii had suffered the major Japanese attack. It was
2,400 miles nearer the enemy, and in those first few months
after the crippling of the Pacific Fleet it could have been very
vulnerable, indeed. It had more than 157,000 residents of
Japanese blood who made up about 37 percent of the total
population. These, in 1941, included 37,000 Issei.

At noon on December 7, Hawaii's Governor Joseph B.
Poindexter declared martial law after telephoning President
Roosevelt. Habeas corpus was suspended, and the next day the
military authorities applied travel restrictions to all alien Jap-

anese fourteen years of age and older. The FBI began round-
ing up suspected individuals on a basis of selective internment
immediately after the attack, with Army and Navy Intelligence officers and the Honolulu police lending a hand. Thirteen squads fanned out to make the arrests of Japanese consular representatives and their families, alien language school-
teachers, Buddhist and Shinto priests, and commercial fishermen. Robert C. Shivers, wartime FBI chief in Hawaii, later
told a Congressional committee that the total number of Japanese held on suspicion during all the war was 1,440, and the
number actually interned and sent to mainland camps was
981, or about one percent of the adult Japanese population.

It is true that the Islands saw the only recorded instance in
which a Nisei turned violently and actively against the United
States and thus supplied rumor-mongers with material for
widespread stories of treachery.

On December 7, a Japanese pilot crash-landed on the small
and isolated island of Niihau—some four hundred miles short
of his target at Pearl Harbor. The residents of the island dis-
armed him and waited for a supply boat to make its regular
call. The boat was delayed. Five days after he crashed, the pilot recovered his weapons and went on a rampage.

Four Hawaiians rowed for sixteen hours to take the news to
Kauai. They said there were only two people of Japanese ancestry on Niihau, Ishimatsu Shintani, an Issei, and Yoshio
Harada, a Hawaiian-born Nisei. Both were called to serve as
interpreters after the pilot was captured.

What happened then could make an excellent suspense
movie. The pilot had no way of knowing how successful the
Pearl Harbor attack had been, and he must have realized that
his chances of rescue were zero. It can be said for him that he
still tried to carry out his orders, and was glib enough to make
Harada turn traitor. On December 12, he sent Shintani to a
ranch worker who had seized his pilot's papers, and offered a
bribe to have the papers burned.

Shintani was told that he could get into trouble for running that kind of errand. Shintani answered that the Japanese pilot would kill him if he refused—and then Shintani hid out somewhere on the island.

When the people on Kauai got the news, an Army lieutenant stationed at Burns Airfield volunteered to head up a rescue party to Niihau. Appropriately enough, this officer was a Nisei, Lieutenant Jack Mizuha, of Company M, 299th Infantry. (Mizuha later was wounded in Italy.) Mizuha took with him thirteen enlisted men, four ranch hands, Aylmer Robinson (whose family owned Niihau), and two other civilians. The lighthouse tender *Kukui* put the expedition ashore at Niihau on December 14, and the party made a seven-mile hike to the ranch village only to find, anti-climactically, that the Japanese pilot was dead. So was Yoshio Harada, who had joined forces with the pilot. It took a little time to get the details from the excited villagers.

On the preceding day, a Hawaiian named Benhakaka Kanahele—who must have been quite a man—had run afoul of the rampaging pair. The pilot shot Kanahele three times—in the stomach, the groin, and the leg. Kanahele was understandably enraged but obviously not incapacitated: he picked up the Japanese invader by the ankles and swung his head against a stone wall, dashing out his brains just as he might have broken a ripe coconut.

Seeing this, Yoshio Harada promptly shot himself to death.[1]

Nisei belonged to the Territorial Guard and the island militia, and soon after Pearl Harbor the public took alarm at the fact that they were helping to guard vital installations. The Guard commander diplomatically discussed the situation with them, and the Nisei reluctantly agreed that they should be inactivated. But 155 of them wrote a petition to Lieutenant General Delos C. Emmons, U. S. Army, who had succeeded General Walter C. Short as military governor ten days after the sneak attack:

Hawaii is our home; the United States our country. We know but one loyalty and that is to the Stars and Stripes. We wish to do our part as loyal Americans in every way possible and we hereby offer ourselves for whatever service you may see fit to use us.

General Emmons saw to it that the Nisei were organized into a labor corps to work with the engineers. They were known as the Varsity Victory Volunteers, and they did so well that Gregg Sinclair, president of the University of Hawaii, called VVV "the most honored initials in Hawaii."

On the West Coast, at least 45,000 working adults were being withdrawn from productive labor, and Galen M. Fisher, writing in *The Christian Century,* estimated that the resultant loss to the economy for the first year was $70,000,000. It took another $70,000,000 from the Federal Treasury to establish and maintain the Relocation Centers for that first year.

In Hawaii, people of Japanese blood supplied the principal labor corps for the plantations, and it was estimated that these people produced 90 percent of the food grown in the islands.

Therefore, some attempts to explain the difference in the two policies have held that the economic situation in the islands was the reverse of that on the mainland, where the Japanese were held to be in competition with other agriculturists. It also has been said that it would have been impossible, in 1942, to provide enough ships to transport 157,000 people to the mainland for internment.

The latter argument does not hold up. Relocation Centers could have been set up in Hawaii, at the cost, of course, of using fighting men to guard them. In the final analysis, it comes back to another theory: that the military command in Hawaii was "more intelligent" than General DeWitt's military command on the West Coast.

DeWitt was not listening to the Navy. Commander Kenneth D. Ringle, an Intelligence officer in Los Angeles, despaired of getting the official ear and wrote an article for *Harper's Magazine* in which he said the actual agents had been known, and that at least fifteen Nisei had been doing Intelligence work—

thus refuting Earl Warren's testimony before the Tolan Committee, and the Final Report a year later. Lieutenant Commander Coggins, of Hawaii, wrote in the June, 1943 issue of *Harper's* that,

By their actions an overwhelming majority of Japanese Americans have shown hatred of the enemy and have made brilliant records in all of the war effort in which they have been allowed to participate.

In Hawaii, military and civil authorities set up a "morale section" to forestall interracial disunity and mob violence and to check hysteria. It worked well. The plan could have worked equally well on the mainland. Instead, the Evacuation began to roll, under direction of Colonel Karl Bendetsen, who had been named head of the Wartime Civil Control Administration. This agency functioned with laudable, if impersonal, efficiency.

Why did the Evacuation have to go on, inexorably, without modification? When the U.S. Navy so decisively smashed the Japanese at Midway, on June 3–6, any danger of invasion was past, and the plan could have been tempered. By August 7, 1942, when the Western Defense Command announced completion of the first phase of the Evacuation—removal of 110,000 people from their homes to the Assembly Centers—it was high time for a second look, for modification or even cancellation of the program. But nothing was done. On that same August day, U.S. Marines went ashore on Guadalcanal to dispossess the real Japanese enemy. It took a little while, but after that there was no doubt about the outcome of the war.

II

"Military necessity" is a fine phrase, but it needs more to support it than the Army offered. There were spot raids by the FBI on the West Coast, and the newspapers played up the seizure of a large number of shotguns, rifles, and a supply of am-

munition—without adding an explanatory clause that would
have spoiled a good story. The raid was on a Nisei-owned
sporting goods store that had been carrying such merchandise
for years.

There was an interesting exchange of letters in *The Nation,*
in the summer of 1942, having to do with the problem of the
Japanese in Hawaii—where they were having no problem at
all. Albert Horlings wrote on July 25:

> The United States . . . is gambling the internal stability of its
> greatest base in the Pacific—the anchor of the whole Pacific battle
> line—on the loyalty of 150,000 Japanese and Japanese Ameri-
> cans, 40,000 of whom are aliens, the majority of whom cannot
> read or speak English, and few of whom have ever seen America
> or have a clear understanding of what America stands for.

Perhaps unintentionally, Horlings was very sharply con-
trasting the Hawaiian situation and method with that of the
West Coast.

He went on to say that a Japanese fifth column in Hawaii
could do great damage during an attempted invasion . . .
that sabotage would be easy . . . that "the Japanese population is forty percent of the total, and its members hold hundreds of strategic positions."

He suspected that we were making the gamble for the
wrong reasons . . .

> not because the military authorities in Hawaii really trust the Jap-
> anese, but because (1) pressure has been brought on them, and
> (2) they have been told that the economic life of the Islands will
> collapse without the Japanese . . . and in the background hovers
> the case for Hawaiian statehood.

The Japanese in Hawaii, Horlings said, had long been held
up to the mainland as first-class citizens by the people who advocated the Islands' admission to the Union, and it was feared
that any doubt cast upon Japanese loyalty would ruin the
chances of that admission.

I never found anyone in Honolulu, [Horlings went on] not even
the most enthusiastic member of the Japanese Chamber of Com-

merce, who would say that Hawaii's Japanese were overwhelmingly loyal to the United States. Why should they be, and why
should they want us to win the war? . . . The majority have
nothing to gain by the defeat of Japan.

Horlings presented scholarly and solid argument. The prestige of the expatriates, he pointed out, largely depended upon
the prestige of the Japanese empire; the economic fortunes of
the Issei were often tied more closely to Japan than to America. He favored evacuation for all, versus a large scale internment, because "there is no doubt that the vast majority of Hawaii's Japanese will work with alacrity with the Emperor's
forces if Japan ever takes the Islands."

"If Japan ever takes the Islands" was a defeatist phrase;
both the Army and the Navy were determined it would never
happen. The Issei of Hawaii may have been more truly American than Horlings knew. It would have been an impossible
task to determine their degree of Americanism, evaluating
such things as their condition in Japan and the improvements
gained by emigration.

But the Horlings article brought a prompt response in the
form of a letter to *The Nation* from Thomas W. Ige, a Nisei
living in Madison, Wisconsin:

I will not deny for one minute that some agents of Tokyo and
their dupes are still running loose, but the overwhelming majority
of us here proved that we will stand by America when the zero
hour strikes.

Ige insisted that evacuation of the Japanese on the West
Coast did not justify the same treatment in Hawaii:

In reading through the Tolan Committee hearings and reports, I
am far from convinced such drastic steps were necessary, especially since they were instigated not by the military, but by hysteri-
cal civilians and interested groups. I suggest further that we young
men of fighting age be given the same opportunities in the armed
forces as other American boys, and, secondly, some assurance of
equality in the post-war world.

Horlings replied to this letter in the issue of *The Nation* for August 15, and said he still favored evacuation. In defense of his stand, however, he fell back upon a claim that had been well disproved, and even he cited it only as a rumor: the report that automobiles of civilian Japanese had clogged the road to Pearl Harbor on the morning of December 7. He still believed that there were at least a few Japanese sympathizers in Hawaii . . . "and if we can't find out *who* they are, only blanket measures will suffice."

The debate rested there. I have not been able to find out whether or not Thomas W. Ige, of Madison, Wisconsin, fought for his country. But a perusal of the roster of the 442nd Regimental Combat Team shows that seven men named Ige were on the job, winning their share of Purple Hearts and other awards.

III

On the West Coast, meanwhile, the people who had been hastily crowded into racetrack and fairground Assembly Centers were fortunate in having the leadership of the Japanese American Citizens League.

The JACL was still a very young organization, and its officials were young, too. But they spoke English. They had been born Americans, and these young men believed whole-heartedly in America. Men like Saburo Kido, Dr. Thomas T. Yatabe, Mike Masaoka, Masao Satow, and William Hosokawa early began to assume a sometimes unpopular and often dangerous responsibility. Once evacuation became inevitable, they urged the older Issei and their own contemporaries to comply with the Evacuation orders as the only way they could demonstrate their faith in the ultimate workings of American democracy.

There were others, lesser known. John Yoshino, from Alameda, and Joseph D. Sasaki, head of the Fresno chapter of the JACL, were active. Sasaki kept up a running correspondence with Congressman Bertrand W. Gearhart and higher officials, using a broken-down typewriter in the Fresno Assembly Center, and writing "not as an authority, but as a helper for our complete victory." [2]

All of these JACL people were asking a lot when they could actually promise very little, and some of them were physically beaten, later. But all the Americans of Japanese ancestry were well disciplined, and none had ever been on the juvenile delinquency lists. For the most part, they listened to the JACL spokesman, and heeded. Their parents, the Issei, needing some sort of interpretation of the strange and frightening thing that had happened to them, listened, too.

Life in the Assembly Centers began as a temporary stay but stretched out for as much as five or six months. The time was passed in schooling and adult study programs: dramatics classes, needlecraft, Junior Forum groups studying "American Living and the Nisei," and many other subjects. Boy Scout programs flourished, church services were headlined in the weekly mimeographed newspapers, and social welfare workers were busy. Blood Bank donations were high.

One of the most noteworthy achievements of the JACL was in the arrangement to have all the evacuees vaccinated before they left for the Assembly Centers. The Army had recommended this but did not provide it.

A hundred humble, every-day problems intruded in each of the Assembly Centers. There were matters of plumbing in a race track that now housed thousands of people. There were matters of keeping the records, of filling straw tick mattresses, of messing and housing and garbage and sanitation. Schools had to go on, as did religious services—both Christian and Buddhist. There was still spare time, and it hung heavily.

Sam Yoshimura had thought it would be like camping out. In a way, it was, except that when camping out an average family tries to find seclusion. There was no privacy here, not even in the showers or toilets. There was no personal or individual initiative. Everybody had been reduced to a faceless number.

The Assembly Centers were hard to get used to. They were filled with rumors and speculation, and the people were bewildered.

Then the time came to move on to a Relocation Center. The very name had an even more impermanent sound.

Nine

Thrown unceremoniously together through a matter of necessity, we have experienced our primary trials and tribulations of readjusting ourselves to shape a living community out of bare nothing. We have found the importance of coöperation and mutual understanding. . . . It is to this spirit of coöperation manifested in each individual that the editors of the *Vignette* dedicate this souvenir yearbook. May it serve not only as a glamorized review of our brief Fresno Center life, but an inspiration to achieve far nobler heights for the duration wherein we must all unite to share in the American War Effort.

—Dedication of the *Vignette,* a yearbook made up of material from "The Grapevine," a mimeographed newspaper published in the Fresno Assembly Center.

I

The *Vignette,* quoted above, was as purely American—and as corny—as any college annual. It got in the names of everybody from the teaching staff to those in charge of garbage disposal, from the administrative officers and their Nisei secretaries to the security guards. The old college cheer is in its pages—but between the words one can sense the pathos. The people were bewildered and hurt; they were whistling in the dark.

Dr. Sasaki was still writing to his Congressman, to the Department of State, and others. He urged President Roosevelt to establish a Scientific Board to develop electronic gear for the successful prosecution of the war. Some of the letters were acknowledged by George Atcheson, Jr. Assistant Chief, Division of Far Eastern Affairs; some brought replies from M. H. McIntyre, Roosevelt's secretary. Another was answered by Paul V. McNutt.

Dr. Sasaki signed all of his letters, "Respectfully yours for Victory through Unity." He never lost faith.[1]

The Assembly Center days were perhaps the darkest days of the Evacuation. The Japanese Americans were fortunate in having a few staunch friends who did not desert them. Typical were Judge and Mrs. K. E. Morrison of Santa Ana, California.

Judge Morrison had been a friend a long way back: in the early 1900's, he helped a number of Japanese to study English; around 1920, he was seeing that Japanese farmers got loans so they could raise sugar beets. During the war, he wisely counseled the Japanese Americans to accept evacuation, and at the same time arranged to get many of the Nisei youngsters into Eastern and Midwest universities. "I feel happy about this program," he says today, "because we have an outstanding surgeon in Orange County as a result." [2]

The last day in Fresno Assembly Center was a sad one for Dr. Sasaki. Many of the people had already gone to the Relocation Center, and the dark, flimsy, dusty rows of empty barracks and their shadows left him with a chilly and lonesome feeling. Here, for several months, he had been a part of the crowded population: he remembered the cries of children at play, "the troubles of the aged and poor, the angers of the rich and the selfish, and the whispers of the rumors and gossips." As night came on, he could see the Fresno skyline through the leaves of the oleanders and palms and eucalyptus trees.

He loved Fresno. It was his birthplace, and he had lived there for more than thirty years. He had prospered in Fresno and had built a pretty white stucco home on a hill that overlooked the whole city. On October 24, 1942, he and his wife would have given anything to see their home again, but this was not permitted. October 24 was the day when all the people in his block had to leave for the Relocation Center at Jerome, Arkansas.

Both his wife and his son had come down with the measles at the time of the Evacuation. Dr. Sasaki had to handle all the details of packing and storing, as well as taking care of the two patients. His wife's eyesight was poor, and in the Assembly Center she was forced to limit her activities; she could never understand what they had done to be evacuated. Again and again they had pledged allegiance to the United States.

Dr. Sasaki was appointed Pullman monitor in charge of all Pullman cars for the special train leaving Fresno with the evacuees. His young son was very excited, because he had never before ridden on a train.

There were thirty-nine people in Pullman Number One, twenty-seven on Pullman Number Two, and nine on Pullman Number Three. Another Pullman car was to be dropped off at the Gila River Relocation Center in Arizona. There were ten persons in this car.

Mrs. Sasaki wanted to know why the Arizona project was included.

"Most of the ten are TB cases," Dr. Sasaki told her. "It hasn't been good for TB patients living here for five months or so—poor diet and poor living conditions didn't help."

Dr. Sasaki kept a meticulous record. At 12:30 P.M. on Saturday, October 24, 1942, the Santa Fe train pulled out to the southward. Captain E. T. Martin of Reno was in charge; the conductor was E. L. Bogg, of St. Louis; there were two registered nurses aboard and two nurse's aides. There was a doctor, but Sasaki did not get his name.

Near Bakersfield, California, two people became patients—

one suffering from high blood pressure that caused nosebleed, the other having fainting spells.

As the train went over the Tehachapi Mountains, a young Nisei cried for water. The nurses gave him water, but he was a tubercular case, and water was not sufficient. Dr. Sasaki recalls:

The train stopped, but it was too late. His heart stopped beating. He should not have been forced to travel, due to his condition, according to the physician on the train. But this was war hysteria, with the order to ship all Japanese to the War Relocation Centers. I saw him die. Nothing could be done due to the high altitude, oxygen insufficiency and the high humidity and heat in the Pullman.

Life ran its common course. Saturday night, Dr. Sasaki recalls, saw a battle of love affairs in the third Pullman—one girl, and three men. The situation was eased somewhat when one of the men had to get off at Gila.

Sasaki had to get off the train to buy Coca-Cola and candy; there were problems with paper diapers and formulas for the babies. It was a long haul. He noted that in Fort Worth they heard a Texas accent for the first time when they spoke to some girls. Sunday evening, they were in Arkansas, but it was Monday morning before the train pulled into Jerome.[3]

II

Mr. H. was writing in his journal:

It is a very well-known fact that Santa Anita is our temporary home, but when we must move to another place everybody has some kind of funny feeling or sentiment. . . .

The nasty smelling stables, the dust piling barracks . . . yet, we have lived here more than five months, and feel a little affection for the place. . . . October 18 at 4 P.M. we departed to our new camp at Gila, Arizona, bade *sayonara* to our friends. As we passed the city of Los Angeles by nightfall, windows on the train were closed tight, and we could not even peep outside. The train passed Indio, Yuma, at two o'clock next afternoon and we reached Gila

Bend, but there was some kind of trouble . . . we finally reached Gila Relocation Center, at 10 P.M. . . .

Gila Center is an Indian Reservation of more than 15,000 acres. It is a genuine desert, no grasses grow. Nearby little streams by irrigation ditch grows the cotton [wood] trees. On the height huge Cactus standing just like a Ghost, 20 or 30 feet high, having no leaves or branches. The whole place was so Lonely and hideous looking as I ever saw. . . . The scene in this desert looks like a picture I saw on the wall of some church a few years back—Moses Leads the Jewish Multitudes to Palestine. They wandered many years in a desert. . . .[4]

So, the people were being moved for the second time. There was confusion in California, in those summer months of 1942. The farmers were especially bewildered: government agencies were exhorting them to raise bumper crops to feed American troops and America's allies. On the other hand, the government was putting Japanese farmers into internment camps while their crops were still in the ground and taking away the farm hands before harvest time.

One of the earliest and loudest howls went up from poultry producers all over the United States; it had to do with a very mysterious practice called "chick sexing."

The science of chick sexing—i.e., determining whether a day-old chicken is a rooster or pullet—was discovered by a Japanese. In 1942 people of Japanese descent made up about 90 percent of the professional chick sexers in America, and now most of them were in Assembly Centers.

Poultry producers could not profitably operate without these experts. The egg industry depends upon their skill in the swift segregation of male and female, since it does not pay to raise too many nonlaying chickens. Chick sexers are paid according to the number of baby chicks they handle, and here is a curious thing: most so-called Caucasians are not able to process more than four hundred chicks an hour, while Nisei turn out as many as twelve hundred per hour, and make very good money. Twelve hundred chicks in sixty minutes means examining twenty fluffy little babies every minute—and not injuring them.

Was the virtual Japanese monopoly in this field due to the smaller and more graceful hands of the Japanese and their quickness of movement? This seems logical, but today Sam Yoshimura is a chick sexer, and Sam is more than six feet tall and has hands that would make him formidable in football as a passing back.

"How does one become a chick sexer?" I asked Sam.

"Well, I went to school for six months. But it takes a couple of years of actual work before you have really been graduated."

There are chick sexing schools in Hattiesburg, Miss., in Tucker, Georgia, and in Pennsylvania. I asked the Pennsylvania proprietor, "Just how do chick sexers determine sex, anyway?"

He grinned. "They look at the chick's rear end." [5]

The scream that went up from poultrymen in the summer of 1942 was so loud that the Government released all the qualified chick sexers from the Assembly Centers so they could practice their profession. None was allowed to work in the West Coast restricted zone, however. This was reported in *Newsweek* and other publications, and many a slightly confused reader probably thought the chickens in California's famed Petaluma had to do without sex for the duration.

As soon as the evacuees were out from under Army administrative control, the WRA encouraged church groups who were active in sending young Nisei to colleges east of the restricted zone, and also began allowing them to leave the Centers for seasonal farm work. Once again an ancient foe—the American Legion—had visions of potential sabotage. The Legion, in convention at Kansas City in September, 1942, protested both the educational and the harvest programs and wanted all the evacuees kept confined.

But in October—again during the peak period of the following year—more than eight thousand Japanese Americans were helping save such things as the sugar beet crop. They went on leave to such places as Townsend, Montana. George

Enosaki, who had come from Montana originally, just in time to be picked up, returned to top sugar beets, along with a number of other Nisei.

Things had changed with the war. As a boy, George had known no discrimination at all in Montana. Now the restaurants in Townsend refused to serve the Nisei. The local movie palace would not admit them. But the movie show proprietor either had an understanding heart or was out to garner a few extra bucks. He would run, he said, a special matinee for the boys of Japanese extraction who were working in the sugar beet fields. But this was pure segregation, and the Nisei audience was not fooled. Promptly, and with ironic humor, they dubbed the show the "Joe Jap Matinee." [6]

A sense of humor like that was heart-lifting and soul-saving. It found expression in such wry things as renaming the Santa Anita Assembly Center "Japanita." When the people went on to such dreary desert places as the Relocation Center at Topaz, Utah, they called it "Camp Topaz—the Jewel of the Desert." When in every Relocation Center the camps were divided into "blocks," with "block leaders," the irreverent Nisei promptly came up with the title of "Blockheads."

The Nisei were Americans and could laugh at their own predicament. The older Issei shrugged their shoulders and said in Japanese that all this was *shikata ga nai*—a "can't be helped thing."

Seen in hindsight, the tragedy is multiplied. It *could* have been helped, of course, any number of times after the inception of the program, and if it had not been for the initial hysteria on the West Coast, the program need not have been started at all.

Now the Nisei, the young American citizens, were getting angry. James Y. Sakamoto, Seattle editor of the *Japanese-American Courier* and General Chairman of the JACL's Emergency Defense Council, had told the Tolan Committee:

The suggestion of evacuation is repugnant to us from this viewpoint: You wish to send us to a place of safety. What we want to do is to remain here and shed our blood, together with other Americans, to save our country and our homes. We don't want to be sent to a safe place and let other Americans save our homes and possibly die in the effort. We don't like that idea.[7]

The Evacuation went on through its Assembly Center stage; and just when these places had been made liveable to a degree, they were abandoned for the Wartime Relocation Centers and the work had to be done all over again.

Christian agencies helped a great deal during both moves. So did individual Caucasian citizens who had known the Issei and Nisei as good neighbors. Marge Shimomoto, who now lives in San Diego, was sent with her family to the Poston Center. She kept a diary there, and the entry for October 25, 1942, reveals that an Imperial, California, rancher named Roy Westmoreland came to the camp,

bringing with him such lifesavers as washing machines, a baby buggy, a baby bathinette and other necessities. The washing machines were *truly* life savers. I had been washing, rinsing and wringing the heavy sheets and bedspreads by hand. In the heat, it was very hard.

Mrs. Shimomoto's baby was born in camp, and her mother died while there. At Poston, dust storms came suddenly and without warning, and residents caught even a block or two from their own barracks had to take shelter wherever they could find it. The barracks had second roofs about eighteen inches above the main roofs, to provide a little coolness from the circulation of air. The dust storms were so strong that many of the extra roofs were ripped off and went sailing away to the peril of life and limb.

The first meals in camp were really terrible, although the cooks worked hard and did the best they could with what they had [Mrs. Shimomoto recalls]. Somehow, families became separated at the tables, with the oldsters grouping together and the young people merging with other young ones and eagerly getting acquainted.

This did not meet with the approval of many parents, and so mess in the "family style" was established. . . .[8]

Life went on at Poston, with births, deaths, and marriages. One of the saddest things to the Japanese was the pitiful lack of flowers for the funerals. But a number of florists were in the camp, as well as many gardeners. They got together. The gardeners made the desert blossom, and the florists fashioned elaborate wreaths for both funerals and weddings.

How does Marge Shimomoto feel now about the Evacuation?

We don't dwell on the past. We feel sometimes that some good must have come from this experience, and we do not feel bitter— sometimes bitterness is another word for "self-pity."

Last year her daughter Gwen was graduated from high school after winning three scholarships and being chosen to accept the Freedom Foundation's Award for her school in Washington, D.C. Only forty-five schools in the nation were so honored.[9]

Mr. and Mrs. Roy Westmoreland were honored, too. The Japanese American Citizens League put them on its honor roll for the good neighbor work they did during the Evacuation years.[10]

III

The pure mechanics of the Evacuation, *i.e.*, the actual displacement of 110,000 people, were admittedly a marvel of military efficiency. The schedules clicked, the buses and trains were on time, and all logistics (the science of supply) had been provided, including even diapers for the babies.

In October, 1942, a *Harper's* article entitled "The Japanese in America, the Problem and the Solution," presented a very clear and unbiased analysis of the situation. Unfortunately it had been written in May and was therefore overtaken by events.

The article, done anonymously by "An Intelligence Officer," was the work of Lt. Commander (later Admiral) Kenneth D. Ringle, of the 11th Naval District Intelligence Office.
Carey McWilliams, in his *Prejudice: Japanese Americans,
Symbol of Racial Intolerance,* was the first to attribute the article to Ringle.

Ringle's idea was that individual examinations of Japanese
in this country could well determine loyalty. He pointed out
that the people of Japanese blood felt that to deny them individual hearings only proved that the Evacuation was being
handled solely on a racial basis.

Ringle believed that 75 percent of the American born Japanese were utterly loyal. He was being very conservative,
here; he did not trust too many of the Kibei. He brought out
the fact that Japanese consular staffs did not trust the Nisei
and that Nisei going to Japan after they had become of age or
had reached their late teens were ridiculed as being Americans. He pointed out that about five thousand Nisei had already gone into the U.S. Army as a result of the Selective Service Act. He reminded his readers that Japanese Americans
paid taxes, performed jury duties, and were supposed to enjoy
the full protection of the Constitution and the Bill of Rights.

On the favorable side, Ringle noted only one thing: Nisei
children could attend public schools. Aside from that concession, no effort had been made to cement their loyalty to the
United States. Much in the form of anti-Japanese agitation in
the press, on the radio, and so on, had been done against it.

Ringle was strongly opposed to any general evacuation
which would put loyal and disloyal Japanese Americans into
the same camp. He felt that some of the Kibei were dangerous—if they had gone to Japan too early and stayed too
long—but he thought one of the surest ways to make an
American was to send a Nisei to Tokyo after he was seventeen
or older. At that age, he said, they

couldn't live on the Japanese standard of living or the Japanese
diet; they couldn't accustom themselves to Japanese ways of life.

The majority of them returned after a short time, more thoroughly disillusioned with Japan and more than ever loyal to the United States.

Ringle insisted that the identity of the Kibei could well be ascertained from Government records. He reversed the usual thinking here and thought Kibei should be presumed guilty until proven innocent beyond a reasonable doubt. Above all, he did not think Kibei and Nisei should be put together.

Ringle's plan made considerable sense. But either he was of too junior a rank, or the Army wasn't listening to the Navy, or events had moved too far. At any rate, his plan was not adopted. It would have:

Permitted any person of Japanese blood to announce himself as a loyal citizen of Japan, without prejudice, irrespective of whether or not he held American citizenship;

Determined the identity of any Nisei who had spent three years or more in Japan since the age of thirteen and after 1930 (parents, spouses, and dependents would be included in this list);

Set up boards in each relocation or assembly center to determine whether or not individual cases were dangerous.

Commander Ringle's plan would have taken into consideration the dominant role of the male in Japanese society, and in the Japanese household. If a Kibei male were married to a Nisei female who had never been to Japan, Ringle would have put the entire family in the Kibei category and listed them as potentially dangerous. He would have classified Issei on the basis of how many trips they had made to Japan since coming to America. And so on.

Viewed in the light of history today, the plan appears to be both sensible and more just than the way things were handled. But in 1942, its publication hardly caused a ripple. Too many people in high places were against the Japanese Americans; too many pressure groups opposed them. And sometimes the opposition combined the prestige of high office with the mass influence of organization.

Only a few weeks before Ringle's article was published, Attorney General Earl Warren, campaigning for Governor, told the California State Convention of the American Legion, at Los Angeles:

I say to you now that they must not come back to our State—we must keep them away from California so long as the flag of Nippon is flying over the Philippines.[11]

One is tempted to say that the qualifying time limit in that utterance was shrewdly fortuitous.

Ten

Some Americans need hyphens in their names, because only part of them has come over; but when the whole man has come over, heart and thought and all, the hyphen drops of its own weight out of his name.

—Woodrow Wilson.

There is no hyphen in "Japanese American." We explain that by saying that "Japanese" is only an adjective describing the wonderful noun, "American." We may be short, but we are *not* hyphenated.

—Mike Masaoka.

I

Manzanar became the first War Relocation Center due to the fact that it had been activated, originally, as an Assembly Center. It was unique in the sense that the people who went there did not have to move again until they returned to life "outside."

Manzanar in Spanish means "apple orchard." The place was a few miles south of the town of Independence, in California's Owens Valley. This is east of the Sierra Nevada range and somewhat isolated. It was an area of violent natural contrasts.

The days were hot, and the nights were cold. When the wind blew, as it did often, dust devils and full-grown sandstorms swirled across the land—and yet there were green tracts, irrigated by the Owens River, that produced flavorful cantaloupes and other truck-garden specialties. Nearby to the westward was Mt. Whitney, stabbing the sky at 14,495 feet, the highest mountain in the continental United States. Not far to the southeast was Death Valley, and the lowest point in the nation—282 feet below sea level.

Before the evacuees left their homes, mainly in the Los Angeles area, they were subjected to rumors which ran to the same sort of extremes: Manzanar was crawling with snakes. It was populated by thieves. Worst of all, as it affected morale, was the story that if the Japanese invaded California Manzanar would be bombed by U.S. planes.

The rumors about snakes and thieves caused many of the evacuees to spend what little money they had left in buying boots and padlocks. They arrived at Manzanar to find only one real enemy—the dust.

Owens Valley residents were a hardy and conservative lot, given to minding their own business. They were inclined to be a bit suspicious of outsiders, and yet they were usually quick to offer traditional western hospitality to any stranger in need. Not many years before, charging that the State Water Authority had infringed upon their riparian rights, some of them had dynamited the aqueduct that carried Owens River water to the city of Los Angeles.

Now, in March 1942, they learned that with the establishment of the Manzanar Reception Center, they would shortly have new neighbors. A large number of the Valley residents wanted no Japanese in their "front yard."

Tom Clark, chief of the civilian staff of the Western Defense Command, asked the Owens Valley people to set up a Citizens Committee to work toward an amicable solution of the anticipated problems. One of the most prominent men in the area, Ralph P. Merritt, became chairman of this group— and later was Project Director of the Relocation Center. George W. Savage, editor of the influential Owens Valley

Progress Citizen, did much to reassure the worried and belligerent Valleyites. Robert L. Brown, a prominent Valley resident, lent the Committee his prestige and assistance, and later became Public Relations and Reports Officer for Manzanar.[1]

How much of the hostile attitude toward the evacuees was based on idle talk will never be known. At any rate, the Citizens Committee did a good job, and the first contingent of displaced people—sixty-one men and twenty women—arrived on March 21, 1942. It was the first day of a Spring that promised no blossoming for them. But at least there were no incidents.

Manzanar was not really ready. The first arrivals were put to work immediately, mainly in the mess hall. People were coming in fast—much too fast for the carpenters, the plumbers, and even the administrative officials. By the first week of May, Manzanar had a population of 7,200; two weeks later the count was well past 9,000—and this made it California's biggest community east of the Sierra Nevadas.

If living conditions in the Centers were always a little rugged, they were especially so in the early days. Like most other WRA Camps, Manzanar began with fourteen barracks each partitioned into one room apartments, twenty by twenty-five feet, and each apartment was to be shared by two families numbering eight to ten souls. All too often, the families were total strangers.

There was no furniture. The administration supplied Army cots and bed ticking for the straw-filled mattresses. During the first two weeks, only two of the barracks had showers and flush toilets; the other twelve were supplied with cold water and Chic Sale outhouses with chemical receptacles.

Hospital facilities, of sorts, were set up immediately, but it was some time before they were anywhere near adequate. Dr. James Goto and a nurse named Fumiko Gohata happened to arrive with the first contingent of evacuees, so they were pressed into service. They pioneered, with one room, five beds, an operating table, and some instruments and drugs.

They did not have sterilization equipment or toilet facilities. However, the hospital was expanded with reasonable speed, and by July it had two hundred and fifty beds, seven wards, six doctors, six dentists, and a fair number of nurses and technicians.[2]

These professional people, of course, were all Japanese. The doctors and dentists were paid $16 a month. But even this wage was hardly what it seemed.

There were some ambitious plans for war work at Manzanar, including the manufacture of camouflage netting. The first evacuees were subjected to a flood of rumors. Many were under the impression that if they did war work, they would be paid prevailing wage scales. They were due for a rude awakening. They went to work, but the Wartime Civil Control Administration made no announcement about salaries: there was only the scale of "nominal allowances," with a maximum of $7.50 per month for any family. For two months after Manzanar opened, the WCCA said only that wage policies were being "formulated."

The wage scale was announced on May 14. Eight dollars a month for unskilled labor, $12 for skilled labor, $16 and up to $19 a month for professional work.

This meant that a Nisei who held a medical degree or was qualified as a high-school or college teacher could work in the Centers at such wages—alongside often inexperienced and unqualified Caucasian personnel who did the same work at salaries based on regular U.S. Government scales.

Even then, no payment was made until after the War Relocation Authority had taken over control of Manzanar from the WCCA. In the last week of June, payment was started for work done in March. The early arrivals had worked for three months before they were paid at all.

The delay, and the difference between Center wages and those paid war workers on "the outside," quite understandably provoked an angry reaction. There were charges of "broken promises," and the theme of broken promises later keynoted no end of troubles.

II

Practically every adult worked in Manzanar. More than five hundred people were employed in the administration of the community. A hundred and twenty acres of land was cleared for farming, and a year later this enterprise yielded a profit. A garment factory was established and did well. But it was the camouflage net factory that caused all the headaches.

In June, two large buildings were set aside for the making of camouflage netting for the Army. The Army needed a vast amount of camouflage netting, and the internees were eager to make it. The whole thing was a splendid idea, except that—like many great ideas—it went off half-cocked.

Under the provisions of the Geneva Conferences, aliens could not do war work.

Government officials suddenly ruled that the manufacture of camouflage netting was "war work." This provided one of the earliest and most unfortunate splits between Issei and Nisei and fed fuel to the flames of a political fight that was already brewing to decide who would control the War Relocation Centers.

Insofar as the Issei were concerned, not only were many of them alien in name only and not only did they want to help the war effort, but those evacuated from Terminal Island had had a great deal of experience in making fishing nets and could manufacture them with ease.

Now these people were told they could not work at the camouflage net factory; only citizens could perform this task. Early in August some 650 Nisei were busy at it. There was a new dispute over the fact that people were supposed to work an eight-hour day, but the Army had said it expected a quota of five camouflage nets per day per crew. Some of the crews did their quota in half a day and then went back to their barracks. Other evacuees—who couldn't work as quickly—objected. The net factory was temporarily shut down.[3]

Bonuses were paid, later, and everything was done to smooth over the discontent. At long last, the net factory was abolished.

In all probability, [Richard Brewer Rice wrote later] this end was not a sad one, as the net factory had more and more served to pit two classes, the Issei and the Nisei, against one another, creating bad feelings.

What happened at Manzanar could never have happened in Tokyo, where all citizens bowed to the will of the Emperor. In Manzanar, a knockdown and drag-out political fight was developing. It was in the best tradition of Democracy in action.

Money was not involved, since the top pay had risen to only $19 a month. This was, instead, a clash of ideologies. The outlook of the Issei—without being at all un-American—was Japanese. That of the Nisei was purely American, and a rebellion against all the old Japanese reverence for the elders.

A whole slew of organizations began to blossom at Manzanar. Self-government had admirably been encouraged. The Center soon had a Manzanar Work Corps and Fair Practices Committee. The Work Corps set up a Representative Assembly. Elections were held. Employees of the Mess Division distrusted the Work Corps and decided to organize their own Kitchen Workers Union.

And the Nisei, active both in political and labor circles, had established the Manzanar Citizens Federation. Everybody belonged to something.

War Relocation Authority administrators, perhaps innocently, compounded the situation: they formed the Consumers Coöperative and turned it over to the internees as an incorporated company. Various coöperative stores were opened under a board of directors—all Japanese—but many people felt that this was a trick of the Center administration to take

the last of their savings. Too many former business competi-
tors were executives of the coöperative. Their old rivalry continued in the Center, and there was more competition than
coöperation. By November, promised dividends were far over-
due—and somebody tried to set fire to the general store located in Block 21.[4]

The store had to be moved before calm prevailed.

III

Manzanar saw an unfortunate number of changes in management, and these contributed nothing to the internal stability.
The first Camp Manager was C. E. Triggs, who was so bom-
barded with queries that he opened an information office. This
establishment grew and fed upon itself. Under the Wartime
Civil Control Administration the Information Service was attached to the Service Division, headed by J. M. Kidwell.

Kidwell planned to have one Information Office for every
fifteen hundred evacuees . . . six offices for the entire Center
when its population reached ten thousand. By the time the
War Relocation Authority took over Manzanar, the Information Service alone had a formidable staff of fifty-seven people.
In addition, the Information Service had organized a Voluntary Service Corps to help newly-arrived persons find their
quarters, and to carry their baggage. There were four hundred
and fifty Japanese attached to this Voluntary Service Corps,
and for awhile the Information Service was wagging the dog
as far as the selection of Block Leaders was concerned.[5]

Politics now really began to boil in Manzanar, just as it
would later boil at Poston, Tule Lake, and other Centers.

It may well have been that proper development of a system
of self-government was hampered by too many organizations,
some of them overlapping. And there were "empire builders."
As soon as new blocks were filled by incoming evacuees,
Block Leaders were chosen. Kidwell's Information Service
and his Voluntary Service Corps had been controlling selec-

tion of these leaders. Older men were usually chosen, and while this conformed to the traditional Japanese reverence for age, it also meant that most of the Block Leaders were Issei.

Nisei made up two thirds of the Manzanar population, but only 14 percent of them were twenty-five or older, so that they did not swing a proportionate legislative weight. But they were extremely active.

In early 1942, the Japanese American Citizens League had some fifty chapters in the United States, most of them on the West Coast. The JACL was well aware of Caucasian hostility toward the Issei and in essence had turned completely against the Japanese heritage in striving to protect Nisei citizenship rights. It was known among the Japanese that the JACL had coöperated in the national defense effort by turning over information to Naval Intelligence, and this did not sit well with many of the Issei and even some of the older Nisei. The Japanese have a word for "informers," *inu*—it also means "dog."

There were charges that the JACL was much too reactionary, and was guilty of attempting to "oversell" relations with Chambers of Commerce, American Legion Posts, and other groups. In turn, the JACL lashed back volubly and vigorously and accused some of its critics of being radicals, if not Communists.

The Kibei constituted a third party at Manzanar and elsewhere. Some Kibei had enjoyed living in Japan and shared, or at least understood, their parents' nostalgic feeling toward the old country. Others were very bitter about having been sent to Japan, where they were not always accepted, and where they lost ground in really mastering English and becoming fully Americanized. In many instances, the Kibei came close to being citizens without a country.

Therefore, Manzanar had three divided camps.

Mature Nisei were in the minority, but they spoke English, and many of the Issei did not. Meanwhile, a Block Leader was not really popular with the rank and file: being appointed

Block Leader made him suspect as a stooge of the administration. Later, when the Block Leaders were elected, not appointed, their prestige rose.

But in the summer of 1942 another plan of self-government was announced and with it such things as a Temporary Community Council, an Executive Committee, and a Judicial Committee. The Temporary Community Council would be made up only of citizens of the United States, who were to be elected only by citizens of the United States. In other words, the new directive issued by the Director of the War Relocation Authority left the Issei without vote or voice in this particular field.

The Project Director at Manzanar ignored it. Older Issei remained in council but were crippled by another order. The use of the Japanese language was forbidden, both in public meetings and in the Center newspapers.

It was a period of bewilderment and frustration and even physical hardship for the evacuees, so there was little surprise when they turned upon each other. People who did not belong to the JACL forgot that the members of that organization had done a great deal of laudatory work in nonpolitical fields: they had helped Japanese Americans facing eviction because they could not pay their rent. They arranged the vaccination program; they had aided bankrupt travelers; they helped families of Issei who had been interned, and translated the Army's ever-changing Exclusion Orders for those who could not read English.

One small mob "incident" had taken place at the Santa Anita Assembly Center on August 4, during a search for articles of contraband, and one evacuee suspected of being an informant, or *inu,* was severely beaten. The Military Police were called, and restored order.[6]

This was seemingly insignificant. But it pointed the way toward more serious incidents which would occur at Manzanar, at Poston, and later at Tule Lake.

IV

"Intake" (or arrival of new groups of evacuees), was a focus of interest and solicitude on the part of the administrative staff. The Project Director said it was one of the things he would remember longest out of the whole experience at Poston. He thought the people looked lost, not knowing what to do or what to think. He once found a woman standing, holding her four-day-old baby, and sent her to rest in his room. The Associate Project Director said that one of the pictures that would always stay in his mind was one he saw in an "apartment" where people had just arrived. An elderly mother who had been in a hospital some years sat propped on her baggage gasping and being fanned by two daughters, while her son went around trying to get a bed set up for her. The old lady later died.

Alexander H. Leighton, *The Governing of Men* (Princeton University Press, 1945).

To be sure, a number of births and deaths and marriages were bound to crop up as vital statistics concerning 110,000 people.

Over in the Gila Center, Mr. H. was keeping his Journal:

Chiyo [his wife] working very hard every day to arrange room, and wash Linen at Laundry room. The hard work and big changes on the food have her stomach pains every day . . . her face became paler day by day.

Three weeks after we came to Gila, I took her to hospital for examination. Doctor examined her very carefully and says a hard spot on the breast may be cancer, so she better be in-patient.

Next day she went to hospital for stay, two weeks to take care of her resisting strength, and took her X-ray pictures. Doctor's verdict was breast cancer; Doctor's opinion was we must operate as quickest we can, if not, pain will increase every day and she cannot live more than two years.

I told her about Doctor's Verdict. In answer Chiyo said "I leave everything to God Almighty." Chiyo is a very good Christian; she educated her daughters in a Christian way, and believes.

Mr. H's wife underwent her operation, but lived only two weeks after going to the hospital. The hospital staff was short-handed, and she was forever getting up out of her bed to assist more helpless patients.[7]

The personal tragedies such as that suffered by Mr. H. and his daughters might well have occurred outside the Relocation Centers, but they were more sharply felt under detention, and added fuel to the flames. Some of the Nisei were angry, now—and certainly with good and sufficient reason. They no longer listened to the JACL's voice of moderation.

The leaders of the JACL had been scattered throughout most of the Relocation Centers by the Evacuation. Mike Masaoka was allowed to travel around the country to conduct JACL activities and do liaison work with the WRA and other government agencies, but his family was in Manzanar. Saburo Kido, the organization's wartime president, was at Poston. Dr. Thomas T. Yatabe, the first constitutionally elected national president, was at Jerome. Masao Satow was behind the barbed wire at Granada. William Hosokawa, already a good newspaperman, was editing the weekly paper for the Center at Heart Mountain, Wyoming. (He is, today, Associate Managing Editor of the *Denver Post*.)

These and others pleaded with the evacuees to keep their faith in the ultimate good of American democracy, but there were hotheads, and the JACL came under spirited attack.

What happened to Joseph Kurihara also happened to a number of other Nisei . . .

Kurihara had been born in Hawaii in 1895, and therefore was considerably older than the average Nisei. In 1942 he was still single, stout, and getting bald; he was a devout Catholic and had an exemplary record for honesty and integrity. A graduate of a Catholic high school, he had originally planned to study medicine and become a doctor. In 1915 he moved to California and attended St. Ignatius College in San Francisco. He had never known any racial discrimination in Hawaii, but he found it now on the West Coast and was so discouraged that he dropped out of college and went to the Midwest.

He remembered that he and a Nisei companion had been stoned by boys in Sacramento, and this worried him. While in Michigan in 1917, he enlisted in the Army.

I had purchased $500 worth of Liberty Bonds, but I felt ashamed of myself in civilian attire. . . . I solemnly vowed to fight and die for the U.S. . . . In California my animosities against the Californians were growing with ever-increasing intensity, but in Michigan my liking for the American people was getting the best of me.

In the summer of 1918 I was sent to France. . . . After the armistice, I was assigned to Coblenz, Germany. At every meal time the little German boys and girls would line the walk to the garbage can for whatever scraps the boys were throwing away. I could not bear to see these little ones suffer, so I always made it my duty to ask for as much as my plate would hold and give it to them. O Lord my God, so this is the price of war. Why should these innocent children be made to suffer the hardships of war? [8]

Kurihara was far above the average man in intelligence, a man who was perhaps too sensitive. He made a mistake, after World War I, in going back to California. He became a navigator on a fishing boat cruising from Terminal Island. Not long after Pearl Harbor, his boat returned to San Diego Bay, and Kurihara was picked up and somewhat roughly treated. He reminded one interrogator: "Say, officer, I wore that uniform when you were still unborn. I served in the U.S. Army and fought for Democracy. I may be a Jap in feature, but I am an American. Understand?"

This did him no good. He tried in vain to get a job in a shipyard. Then, like Tatsu Ogawa and some other World War I veterans, he was caught in the dragnet of the Evacuation, and his resentment really began. Being older, and having been around, he decided that the JACL leaders who were urging compliance with the Evacuation orders were "a bunch of spineless Americans."

The government [he said], could easily have declared martial law to protect us. It was not the question of protection. It was because we were Japs! Yes, Japs!

After corralling us like a bunch of sheep in a hellish country, did the government treat us like citizens? No! We were treated like aliens regardless of our rights. . . . This matter of proving one's loyalty to enjoy the rights of an American citizen was nothing but a hocus-pocus.[9]

Kurihara had not urged noncompliance or noncoöperation prior to the Evacuation; he became embittered after the fact. His charge that the JACL leaders were "spineless Americans" was made in unreasoning anger and was ridiculous. It obviously required a very great deal of backbone and courage, indeed, to maintain the stand of the Japanese American Citizens League under such trying conditions. The League opposed the Evacuation, but once the government issued its evacuation orders the JACL's official belief was that compliance with the Evacuation orders could be a positive demonstration of loyalty to the United States under the most difficult of circumstances. It also felt that only through compliance and coöperation could the threat of bloodshed and violence be averted. The JACL believed, too, that such a course would help secure a better life for the people in the camps and an "early" return to their normal lives.

Both Saburo Kido, at Poston, and Dr. Thomas T. Yatabe, at Jerome, were beaten up because of their counsel of moderation. Neither swerved from his beliefs, however, nor did any of the other JACL leaders.

All the Nisei owe them a great debt today.

Eleven

It is sobering to recall that though the Japanese relocation program, carried through at such incalculable cost in misery and tragedy, was justified to us on the ground that the Japanese were potentially disloyal, the record does not disclose a single case of Japanese disloyalty or sabotage during the whole war. . . .

It is easier to say what loyalty is not than to say what it is. It is not conformity. It is not passive acquiescence in the *status quo*. It is not preference for everything American over everything foreign. It is not an ostrich-like ignorance of other countries and other institutions. It is not the indulgence in ceremony—a flag salute, an oath of allegiance, a fervid verbal declaration. It is not a particular creed, a particular version of history, a particular body of economic practices, a particular philosophy.

It is a tradition, an ideal, and a principle. It is a willingness to subordinate every private advantage for the larger good. It is an appreciation of the rich and di-

verse contributions that can come
from the most varied sources. It
is allegiance to the traditions that
have guided our greatest states-
men and inspired our most eloquent poets—the traditions of
freedom, equality, democracy,
tolerance, the tradition of the
higher law, of experimentation,
co-operation, and pluralism. It is
a realization that America was
born of revolt, flourished on dis-
sent, became great through experimentation.

—Henry Steele Commager, "Who Is Loyal to America?"
Harper's Magazine, September, 1947.

I

The Evacuation fell far short of applying any of Dr. Commager's tests of loyalty, since it had already violated freedom,
equality, democracy, tolerance, and the tradition of the higher
law—*i.e.,* the constitutional rights of the American citizen.
Before long, the War Relocation Authority would be conducting loyalty tests of its own . . . and bungling them terribly.

Meanwhile, August, 1942, was a troubled month at Manzanar and other Centers, and things were building up to a
crisis.

The Issei, Nisei, and Kibei were still divided, each group
striving desperately for power. The Manzanar Citizens Federation was formed on July 24. Its membership showed too
many former JACL leaders to suit some of the other people
concerned. Its stated aims were: Improve conditions in camp;
educate citizens for leadership; participate in the war effort;
prepare a post-war program for evacuees . . .[1]

These were laudable purposes, but in some way they failed of achievement.

In Washington, Dillon S. Myer, Director of the War Relocation Authority, was doing all he could to formulate a policy for handling the evacuees. Myer has been described by a Nisei leader as "respected and responsible." He was held in high regard. But some of his own people, down the line, could not quite agree on the best program.

The problem was indeed a tough one. The more the WRA stepped in to improve such things as welfare, education, health, employment, compensation, housing, religion—and many others—in the Centers, the more the earlier objectives of self-contained, self-supporting and self-governed communities receded into the distance. The Centers were in danger of becoming nothing but havens where the people could live until they were allowed to return to their West Coast homes. The WRA wanted them to move out, to relocate elsewhere, but the people feared discrimination. The WRA was caught between a desire to treat the internees well and the need to avoid making life in the Centers so attractive as to deter the voluntary outward movement.

Joe Kurihara, the World War I veteran who should never have been evacuated, was growing more and more rebellious. He led a group that attacked the Citizens Federation as an attempt to establish the JACL all over again . . . and the cleavages among Issei, Nisei, and Kibei were widened.

On August 3, the Manzanar people were informed that relocation was open to Nisei who had never lived in Japan, or attended school there. This was a blow at the Kibei, and they resented it.

Kurihara made a talk against the Citizens Federation. Somebody reported it to the Center authorities. On the evening of Saturday, December 5, 1942, a Nisei named Fred Tayama was severely beaten for this on grounds that he was an informer, an *inu*.[2]

Tayama, a former restaurant owner in Los Angeles, and

chairman of the Southern District of the JACL, was badly injured. Next morning several persons suspected of being members of the gang that had attacked Tayama were arrested.

These included Harry Ueno, a Kibei, one of the cooks who had been trying to organize a union of mess-hall workers. Ueno also had publicly accused the Assistant Project Director and the Caucasian Chief Steward of stealing sugar and meat from the Center's warehouses. Such accusations made him a marked man, while the other suspects were placed in the Center's jail, Ueno was taken to the county jail at Independence.

There was an immediate popular reaction. Crowds formed at Manzanar. A public address system was set up. Kurihara and others demanded Ueno's immediate and unconditional release. Speakers wanted an investigation of conditions at Manzanar by the Spanish Consul, Spain being neutral in the war. They demanded further action against Tayama and other "informers." They read off blacklists naming men like Tokutaro Slocum, a World War I veteran who had openly boasted of his work with the FBI and Naval Intelligence. They were out to get Joe Grant Masaoka, one of Mike Masaoka's brothers, a documentary historian in the WRA Reports Office.

And so the mob spirit was incited and set afire. There were more assemblies that afternoon, and by evening a number of people were ready to invade the hospital with the intention of killing Fred Tayama.[3]

Tayama was no "informer" in the derogatory sense of the word; he was a hundred per cent American who believed in speaking out for Americanism. He had already been quoted in the October issue of *Harper's Magazine:*

My parents came over here many years ago. They desired quite earnestly to adapt themselves to the ways and customs and life in this country. They were poor and had to work very hard. They were anxious that we attend American schools, that we children who were born here and were citizens should have every opportunity to make our own place in this country. Nevertheless, we suffered somewhat in that our parents could not fully bridge the gap, largely because of language, and were not able to take effective part in American activities like the Parent-Teacher Association and so on. We Nisei feel that we have bridged that gap. My little girl is ten years old. She plays the violin in the school orchestra and works in the school library. We are members of the Parent-Teacher Association and freely and frequently consult with our daughter's teacher. As far as we are able to tell, she mingles with her Caucasian schoolmates on terms of absolute equality. She can understand a very little bit of Japanese which she has picked up from her grandmother, but cannot and will not speak the language at all. We value her association with her teacher and playmates above everything else, *and those are the things which we are being asked to give up by this evacuation program* [italics supplied].

But now there were threats against Fred Tayama's life . . .

The Project Director, Ralph P. Merritt, conferred with the commanding officer of the military police, Captain Hall, and with Chief of Police Gilkey. Then Merritt told Joe Kurihara that if the mob would disperse, hold no more mass meetings, and not attempt a jail delivery, and if the Manzanar Judicial Committee would help round up Tayama's assailants, Harry Ueno would be brought back to the Center's jail.

Kurihara agreed. But in the talk he made to the crowd, to inform them of the settlement, he spoke in a Hawaiian dialect that few could understand—except when he told the people there would be a meeting at six o'clock in Kitchen 22. In doing this, Kurihara violated the agreement he had just made.[4]

II

Merritt upheld his end of the bargain, but things got out of hand at Kitchen 22. A list of suspected informers was read; small groups of evacuees went looking for them. The crowd split in two divisions: half to get Tayama at the hospital, half to free Ueno at the jail.

Merritt called upon the military police to enforce martial law.

More than 200 Japanese aliens were taken into the custody of the FBI during a surprise raid in the Santa Maria-Guadalupe area on February 18, 1942. Here, some of them are unloaded from an army truck at the Court House at Santa Barbara, Cal., where they were brought for examination.

A policeman frisks one of the Japanese arrested in a roundup that followed Japan's Declaration of War on the U.S. on December 7, 1941. Norfolk, Va., police and sailors stand guard in the police lecture room.

The Nisei proprietor of this grocery store in California proudly proclaimed his American heritage, but it did no good. The sign at the top shows what happened: the grocer was evacuated and his store had to be sold.

Mute testimony, on the door of a Japanese American businessman, that the business was closed by evacuation.

Civilian Exclusion Orders posted on the West Coast, early in 1942, to instruct persons of Japanese ancestry.

The imminent evacuation of the Japanese Americans was played up by all the California newspapers. William Randolph Hearst, owner of the *Examiner,* was a long-time foe of all Oriental immigration to the West Coast.

Tokie Slocum (left), a Japanese granted American Citizenship by Congress for his services in World War I, tells a House Investigating Committee in Los Angeles, on March 7, 1942, that Japanese living there would go all-out with America to help win the war. He said he and other patriotic Americans of Japanese ancestry were gladly evacuating their homes as their sacrifice in the war effort.

Issei and Nisei line up at the California Wartime Civil Control Station to register for evacuation under the eye of an Army sentry.

Evacuees waiting in San Francisco, with their luggage, for buses to take them to the Assembly Center at Tanforan. They were not permitted to take anything along that they could not carry by hand.

◁
Under the Army's Exclusion Order, this group of orphans from a San Francisco orphanage was sent off to Assembly and Relocation Centers.

This young Nisei soldier was among the thousands of Japanese Americans already in the U.S. Army before Pearl Harbor. He was given leave so he could help his mother harvest her crop of strawberries. Then he went back to the Army, and his mother was sent to a Relocation Center, behind barbed wire.

◁
Trim in a Sam Browne belt and U.S. Army buttons, this young man, named Takeuchi (Number 21393), was one of a group of evacuees at Centerville, California.

Horse stables and flimsy temporary structures housed the first Japanese American evacuees at the Tanforan Race Track Assembly Center. Furniture consisted of army cots and sacks stuffed with straw for mattresses.

An elderly Issei sits in his Assembly Center barracks room. It has a bed and a small light bulb. A new partition has been added. There is no other furniture.

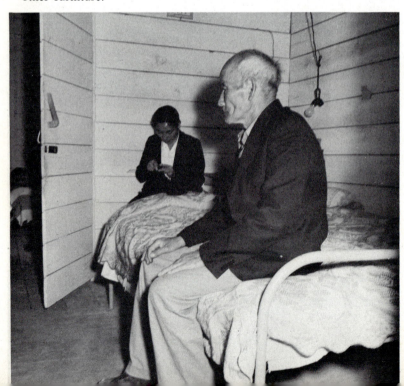

Evacuees line up for a meal in one of the temporary tar-paper structures housing a mess hall at Tanforan Assembly Center.

This group, at a California Wartime Relocation Center, was simply discussing the matter of laying a water pipeline when this photograph was taken. Nothing in the picture violated military security, or gave aid or comfort to the enemy, but the photograph was censored by the Office of War Information because an Army sentry with fixed bayonet walked into the scene. It was not policy, in the war years, to admit that our country was guarding more than 70,000 of its own citizens in concentration camps behind barbed wire and bayonets.

At the Manzanar Relocation Center, this internee created beauty in his small back yard by fashioning a miniature pool with a rock and cactus garden.

One of the frequent and sudden dust storms at the Manzanar Relocation Center sends residents scurrying for shelter.

Nisei girls making camouflage netting at the Manzanar War Relocation Center. Issei were doing this important task, too, until it was discovered that under the Geneva Convention, aliens could not perform war work. In the long run, the whole enterprise failed.

Italians of the Livorno area welcome troops of the 100th Japanese American Infantry Battalion, 34th Infantry Division, in July, 1944.

camouflage netting that for
hile was manufactured in the
rtime Relocation Centers
d these Nisei fighting men in
d stead in Italy. They are
ner Corporal Edward
amura and Cannoneer Pfc.
rge Tanma, both from
olulu, firing a 105-millimeter
itzer in the battle for Livorno.

quad leader of the 442nd
imental Combat Team watches
Germans from his front-line
ole in the St. Die area, France.
men of the all-Nisei
ments, mostly from California
Honolulu, found the snow,
, and mud hard to take.

e St. Die area, France, in
ember, 1944, men of Company
nd Battalion, 442nd Regimental
bat team, move out of
old command post in the
lines.

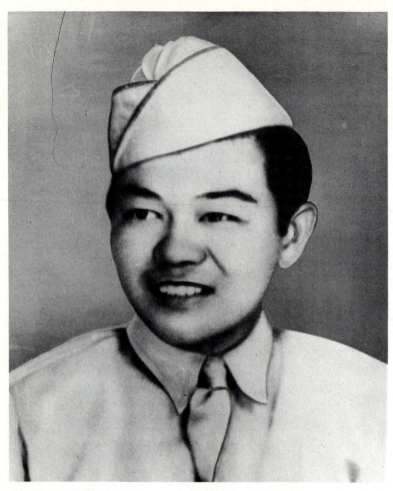

Pfc. Sadao S. Munemori, a young Nisei from California, won America's highest award for bravery — the Congressional Medal of Honor — in the Italian campaign. Near Seravezza, Italy, on April 5, 1945, Munemori singlehandedly wiped out two Nazi machine gun nests, killed three and wounded two of the gunners, and then gave his own life by throwing himself upon an exploding grenade to save the lives of two comrades from the 442nd Regimental Combat Team.

This scene was enacted hundreds of times on the West Coast, in Hawaii, and in the Relocation Centers where parents of Nisei heroes were still behind barbed wire. Here, Mrs. Risaku Kanaya is presented the Silver Star medal, posthumously awarded her son, Pvt. Walter E. Kanaya, for gallantry in action near Bruyeres, France, October 17, 1944. Chaplain (Colonel) Corwin H. Olds makes the presentation to Kanaya's parents on August 25, 1945.

Nisei troops of the famed 442nd Infantry Regimental Combat Team marched up Washington's Constitution Avenue on July 15, 1946, to pass in review before President Harry S. Truman and other notables. The 442nd suffered the greatest percentage of casualties of any unit in U.S. Army history.

President Harry S. Truman and Secretary of War Robert P. Patterson honor the 442nd Infantry Regimental Combat Team as it passes in review near the White House on July 15, 1946.

Then it happened. Soldiers pushed the crowd away from the police station, and lined up there with submachine guns, rifles, and shotguns. The crowd jeered. The soldiers put on gas masks and threw tear gas bombs. At first the evacuees fled, but they came back.

A teen-ager supposedly started the engine of a parked automobile, headed the car toward a machine gun mount, and then jumped out. The troops opened fire, reportedly without orders to do so.

One young Nisei—who had a brother serving in the U.S. Army—was instantly killed. A Nisei, nineteen, was so badly wounded that he died a few days later. Ten evacuees, all told, were treated for gunshot injuries.[5]

The mob quickly dispersed after the shooting, but small crowds kept gathering, soldiers patrolled the camp all night, and bells tolled endlessly. Next day, most of the people wore mourning bands.

Within a fortnight, sixteen troublemakers were transferred to a camp at Moab, Utah, and about sixty suspected informers were removed, for their own safety, to an abandoned CCC camp in Death Valley. This became an object of scorn to Manzanar residents, and canned goods sent to it were labeled "Dog and Cat Food for the Spy Camp." [6]

Richard Brewer Rice, who was there, has correctly observed that the Manzanar riot was not actually a clash between JACL and anti-JACL factions, although the presence of these groups enabled the incident to take place. The smaller third group, mainly Kibei, was anti-administration, and it exploited the rift between the other two. It also capitalized on the broken promises—the difficulties of the camouflage net factory, the failure of the administration to make a clothing allowance to the evacuees when such an allowance reportedly was being distributed in other Centers, and other things fancied or real.

The Center police force was composed of evacuees, with two Caucasian officers. It evaporated before the mob. The

Center administration could do very little, because the entire project depended upon Japanese personnel for water, heat, light, fire protection, and office maintenance. Mob action paralyzed the whole camp.

Rice observed that from 90 to 95 percent of the evacuees took no part in the outbreak of violence. "The vast majority," he says, "seems to have played the role of spectator."

On Christmas Day, Manzanar returned to normal. On December 27, the Manzanar Peace Committee was formed and soon a stabilized system of community self-government was functioning admirably.[7]

III

Manzanar was not the only Center having troubles. There were some difficulties even in Topaz, the Central Utah camp, which was isolated from everything.

Camp Topaz—"the Jewel of the Desert"—was fortunate in many ways. Its first director was Charles F. Ernst, a Harvard graduate who had handled unemployment relief in Washington state and remembered that people of Japanese descent had not been on the relief rolls at all. A number of Utah citizens who later became prominent in state affairs were helping manage Topaz, and the camp had a group of evacuees who had already attained prominence.

There was Chiura Obata, who had been Professor of Fine Arts at the University of California and was famous to a whole pre-war generation for his landscape paintings. The artist Miné Okubo went to Topaz and continued her graphic sketches of camp life. Other notables included Toshio Asaeda, a photographer, botanist, icthyologist, ornithologist, and all-around adventurer; Frank Takeuchi, a *judo* star in vaudeville; Joseph Ito, head concessionaire of the Barnum and Bailey Circus; Kantaishi Nishimura, remembered as leader of Utah mine unions in World War I; the gardener who had been landscape architect for the estates of Shirley Temple and Charles

Boyer, and the chief surgeon of the Los Angeles County Hospital.[8]

These and other leaders were determined to emulate the early Mormon pioneers in Utah by building Topaz into a community America could be proud of. At least they made the desert blossom.

"We will survive," Professor Obata said, "if we forget the sands at our feet and look to the mountains for inspiration." [9]

Topaz had its own tragedy on April 11, 1943. For about six months the Army had enforced a ruling that no alien Japanese would be permitted within a mile of the outside fence around the Center. On April 11, James Hatsuki Wakasa, an elderly Issei, was shot to death by an Army sentry who said Wakasa was crossing the inner boundary fence and ignored the command to halt.[10]

Residents understandably felt that the infraction of the rule might have been handled in a less drastic manner; the morale of Camp Topaz suffered for a whole year as result of the shooting.

As the first WRA Director, Milton Eisenhower had envisioned detaining the evacuees in ideally planned communities until the war was over, and tolerance and understanding had tempered the bitterness against the Japanese. But the program was costing the United States millions and millions of dollars both in its operation and in the withdrawal of a large segment of able-bodied people from agriculture, factories and defense plants.

Eisenhower's successor, Dillon S. Myer, believed that a program of resettlement could be worked out, based on formal investigations of loyalty. In effect, Myer was advocating "selective internment," which was working well in Hawaii.

The chief difficulty in implementing this policy was the fact that every FBI agent's dossier was terribly overloaded. Loyalty clearance of an individual took at least three months, and outside jobs that had been promised the evacuees would not wait that long.

Now the WRA hit upon the idea of an all-inclusive examination, a blanket test of loyalty to determine whether or not an evacuee was eligible for indefinite leave from the Centers to resettle or to take a job outside the West Coast's restricted areas. It may have been an unfortunate coincidence that at the same time, early in 1943, the War Department decided to have all male Nisei of military age fill out a "loyalty questionnaire." This was a piece of exploratory planning looking toward the formation of a Japanese American fighting unit.

The JACL had been actively working both for a resettlement program and the right to fight for America. As far back as the Thanksgiving weekend in 1942, a special emergency meeting of the JACL National Council was held in Salt Lake City, and the WRA allowed two representatives from each Center to attend. This conference voted approval of the resettlement plan and adopted a formal resolution insisting on the privilege of bearing arms.

The wheels of Government, however, turned slowly. Early in January, 1943, three young Nisei wangled leave from the Centers and went to the White House, to try to convince President Roosevelt that they belonged in uniform.

These were Larry Tajiri, then editor of the *Pacific Citizen,* the JACL's weekly newspaper; Mike Masaoka, national secretary of the organization, and George Inagaki, the assistant secretary.[11] A story got around to the effect that they had luncheon with the First Lady, and that she was sympathetic to their cause. (Mike Masaoka says, now: "I do not recall ever having luncheon with Mrs. Roosevelt in 1943.")

So much for a good story. How much the meeting had to do with subsequent events can hardly be evaluated, but on January 28, 1943, Secretary of War Stimson announced plans to organize a Japanese American combat team of Nisei volunteers from the mainland and from Hawaii.

Stimson said, "It is the inherent right of every faithful citizen, regardless of ancestry, to bear arms in the Nation's battle."

President Roosevelt said, "No loyal citizen of the United

States should be denied the democratic right to exercise the responsibilities of his citizenship, regardless of his ancestry." Dillon S. Myer said that the announcement made January 28 was "the most significant date of the last ten months for persons of Japanese ancestry."

Mike Masaoka was the first of all the Nisei to volunteer. In an ironic fashion, fighting and dying for America had become more of a privilege to be sought than a duty to be performed. Nevertheless, the Nisei were largely ready to "exercise the responsibilities" of their citizenship.

But after all those bugle-clear and patriotic words, the Nisei program in the continental United States got bogged down in a mire of misunderstanding and a swamp of semantics.

Although the Nisei were not reluctant to fight, some of them objected to being segregated in an all-Japanese Army unit and wanted to be dispersed throughout the entire Army. Mike Masaoka and some others, however, argued that such dispersal would mean complete loss of identity, while the segregated outfit offered the best chance in the world of proving what the Japanese Americans could do.

Meanwhile, the Army's plan of processing volunteers got tied in—on the mainland—with the WRA program to process the entire adult evacuee population for resettlement. Registration forms sent from Washington were of two kinds: one for Nisei males aged seventeen and older, the other for Nisei females and Issei of both sexes. The first was for military service; the second was for "War Relocation Authority Leave Clearance."

There were forty-two questions. For Nisei males:

Question 27: Are you willing to serve in the armed forces of the United States, in combat duty, wherever ordered?

Question 28: Will you swear unqualified allegiance to the United States of America and faithfully defend the United States from any and all attack by foreign or domestic forces, and forswear any form of allegiance or obedience to the Japanese emperor, or any other foreign government, power, or organization? [12]

These questions would have been a breeze for most Nisei boys, but there were pressures upon many of them that were not understood until later.

The questionnaire for females, and for Issei of both sexes, read:

Question 27: If the opportunity presents itself and you are found qualified, would you be willing to volunteer for the Army Nurse Corps or the WAAC?

Question 28: Will you swear unqualified allegiance to the United States of America and forswear any form of allegiance or obedience to the Japanese emperor, or any other foreign government, power, or organization? [13]

This last question should never have been asked in that form. Someone should have remembered that the Issei, by law, could *not* become citizens of the United States. Fully 90 percent of them had never planned to return, voluntarily, to Japan. A few, owning property and having relatives there, had intended to make a stake in America and then return to their homeland for their sunset years.

But now, after the way they had been herded into concentration camps, a great many Issei feared that in the long run they would be deported to Japan. They did not want to be stateless, people without a country. They felt that renunciation of the only citizenship they had certainly would bring reprisals if they were sent back to Tokyo after the war.

They wrote "No" to Question 28.

This set off a chain reaction. Many of the Issei were aging and ill, dependent upon their Nisei children. If the Issei answered "No," and the children answered "Yes," they could be separated. Japanese family ties were traditionally strong; few other people took so much to heart the commandment to "Honor thy father and thy mother." Nisei of fighting age wrestled with their consciences and were torn between blood bonds and love of America; many who were neither traitors nor slackers finally wrote "No . . . No" to the key questions.

There were other factors. Issei were afraid to accept relocation in some strange part of the Midwest or East, especially if their sons were going into the Army. How did they know what kind of treatment they would get? Who would interpret for them? Next, the old people in all the Centers outside California heard a rumor that a "No . . . No" answer meant they would be sent to Tule Lake. This was one way, at least, of getting back to California.

The "No . . . No" answers piled up. Out of some 20,000 men of military age in all the Centers, about 5,000 either said "No," gave qualified answers, or refused to respond at all. Thirteen percent of the young women did the same. Out of a total of 75,000 adults who were supposed to register, about 8,500 also answered "No."

The WRA, after sorting the questionnaires, had a bit of time in which to wonder why the Minidoka and Granada Centers had only 3 percent, or less, of young men saying "No . . . No," while Manzanar had 50 percent. How much local administration and management affected the answers in different Centers could hardly be ascertained. But in interviewing the Nisei who had answered negatively, the WRA

learned to distinguish between the 'No' of protest against discrimination, the 'No' of protest against a father interned apart from his family, the 'No' of bitter antagonism to subordinations in the relocation center, the 'No' of a gang sticking together, the 'No' of thoughtless defiance, the 'No' of family duty, the 'No' of hopeless confusion, the 'No' of fear of military service, and the 'No' of felt loyalty to Japan. . . . They knew that registration had indeed sorted people, but not in terms of loyalty to the United States and to Japan. In terms of feeling about the United States Government, *it had sorted people chiefly into the disillusioned and the defiant as against the compliant and the hopeful. As with any cross-section of humanity, even while deep in a trough of bitter experience, the vast majority continued to be hopeful* [italics supplied].

It developed that some of the younger and more impetuous Nisei boys had written "No" to Question 27 because they thought they should not be restricted to Army service, but should be allowed to go into the Army Air Corps, the Navy, and the Marines. Similarly, many were antagonized by the idea that they had to "forswear any form of allegiance or obedience to the Japanese emperor"—this, to them, was insulting, because they had never admitted any such allegiance or obligation in the first place.

As one WRA official said, "It was a time of testing, but less a testing of national loyalties than of nerves and family ties."

Doctor Commager has observed that loyalty is not really proved by an oath of allegiance or a "fervid verbal declaration." In retrospect, the entire registration program appears to have been a sophomoric and half-baked idea, if not, indeed, a stupid and costly blunder. In the long run, nothing could have been more certain or more simple than this: If there had been any actual Japanese agents or spies in the Relocation Centers, in February, 1943, they would have been the very first to profess their loyalty on paper, so that they could carry on their work.

Twelve

The Stranger within my gate,
    He may be true or kind,
But he does not talk my talk—
    I cannot feel his mind.
I see the face and the eyes and the
    mouth,
    But not the soul behind.

—Rudyard Kipling.

I

The Army teams that went into the Centers at the time of registration to seek recruits for the 442nd Regimental Combat Team had been carefully drilled, and each carried copies of a speech that had been written in the War Department.

The recruiting effort, the speech said,

is not a campaign or a drive. . . . Its fundamental purpose is to put your situation on a plane which is consistent with the dignity of American citizenship. You may object that this—your life here—is not freedom. The circumstances were not of your own choosing. . . . The only answer which needs to be made to such an objection is that if there were not millions of Americans who agree with your point of view we would not be here. . . . Your government would not take these steps unless it intended to go further in restoring you to a normal place in the life of the country, with the privileges and obligations of other American citizens.[1]

This eloquent statement may have helped a great deal. But in Topaz, a Committee of Nine wired the Secretary of War to ask for promise of restoration of citizenship rights before they registered. At Heart Mountain, a group sent telegrams to all the other Centers urging Nisei to stand together on "conditional" registration. At Granada, the WRA put a Nisei spokesman in touch with the War Department.

The War department answered the Topaz telegram, saying, "The present program is not complete rehabilitation, but it is the first step in that direction."

This satisfied the Committee of Nine, and registration proceeded at Topaz. But people in all the Centers had doubts.

In Minidoka:

"Will we be treated fairly in the Army? How much discrimination are we going to meet after the war? Will my family be secure? What will be the consequences if I do not volunteer?"

In Poston:

"My two brothers in Camp Savage and Camp Hare have been denied permission to visit our sick father in the Los Angeles County Hospital. Why can't they, who are in the uniform of the U.S. Army, visit their dying father whan Caucasians in Army uniforms may do so?"

"Why are Nisei not accepted in the Navy?"

"Why were veterans of the last war put in camps when they proved their loyalty then?"

"Why were Italian aliens in internment camps released while we were not released?"

In Gila:

Questions most persistently raised in this Center touched on democratic principles, and the fear of separating families. It was pointed out to the recruiting officer that the average age of the Issei was fifty-six, while that of the Nisei was twenty-one. In many cases, the Nisei was both family breadwinner and interpreter: if he went in the Army, the family could not really hope to resettle.

In Manzanar:

Most of the Issei felt they were about to be "liquidated" in America. Question 28 caused a stampede of requests for repatriation to Japan, and there was a campaign to urge the Nisei to answer "No . . . No" so that families would not be separated.[2]

The net results of the Army's recruiting campaign were

rather disappointing. It had been expected that at least 3,500 volunteers would come from the Relocation Centers. In Hawaii, where there was no evacuation, the muster rolls for the 442nd Regimental Combat Team were oversubscribed several times. On the mainland less than 1,300 signed up.

General DeWitt, who had put all of the people where they were, was not on the recruiting team at all. Secretary Stimson had announced the plan to form a Nisei fighting unit on January 28. The 442nd was activated on February 1, and its people began to converge on Camp Shelby, Mississippi, very soon afterward.

Two and a half months later, on April 13, 1943, General DeWitt was telling the House Naval Affairs Subcommittee, in San Francisco:

There is developing a sentiment on the part of certain individuals to get the Japanese back to the Coast. I am opposing it with every means at my disposal. . . . A Jap's a Jap. They are a dangerous element, whether loyal or not. There is no way to determine their loyalty. . . . It makes no difference whether he is an American; theoretically he is still a Japanese, and you can't change him. . . . You can't change him by giving him a piece of paper.[3]

On the very same day that General DeWitt said "A Jap's a Jap," 2,686 newly enlisted men, all Nisei, arrived at Camp Shelby from Hawaii. Their subsequent performance should have made the General eat his words.

II

The registration troubles had been continuing, meanwhile, and now they were centered principally at Tule Lake. The Tule Lake Relocation Center housed nearly 16,000 evacuees. Unlike some of the other Centers, where the interned people had come mainly from a common locality and therefore were with friends and neighbors, the Tule Lake population came from the entire Pacific Coast and consisted principally of farm families whose educational level was not as high as was found, say, in Topaz. It had what the WRA later described as

a strong-minded and resourceful minority, composed mainly of middle-aged Issei and adolescent Kibei, who were determined to prevent the successful operation of the [registration] program at almost any cost.

Tule Lake undoubtedly had more than its share of recalcitrants. It was isolated, it had its own irrigated farmlands more than capable of making the Center self-supporting—and it was about to be chosen as the official "Segregation Center," where all the Issei who had requested repatriation to Japan and all the Nisei who had renounced their American citizenship would be sent. These factors were enough to make it evident that the administration of Tule Lake was never a very desirable job. At the same time, the record indicates that the administration officials made a few blunders, too.

Registration at Tule Lake began with a vast amount of confusion. The Center administration (then under Harvey Coverley) did not clarify the issues but said that matters pertaining to military service would be explained by the Army recruiting team when it arrived on February 6. The team did not get there until February 9, and registration was to begin the following day. Evacuees had spent twelve days of uncertainty and had formulated a great many incorrect opinions of their own.

Block meetings were held as registration slowly began, and hundreds of questions were drawn up for submission to the Project Director. On February 15, Tule Lake officials met with evacuee representatives and told them that any interference with registration was punishable, under the Espionage Act, by fines up to $10,000, or twenty years imprisonment, or both.[4]

This was not true.

The trouble began in Block 42, which contained only males. Two-thirds of the residents of Block 42 did not report for registration. On February 18 and 19 the names of those failing to show were read in the mess halls. Trucks were dispatched to bring them to the registrar's office, but nobody boarded the trucks.

On February 21, WRA officials, accompanied by MP's with machine guns and bayonets, went to Block 42. Thirty-five young Nisei and Kibei already had their suitcases packed. They were taken to jail.

A general strike was proposed but was called off. Fire sirens wailed, mess-hall bells called the evacuees to block meetings, and the Community Council resigned in a body. Kibei, meeting in Block 4, demanded that they be treated as Japanese nationals; anybody who registered at all was suspected of being an *inu* and even children barked at them on the street. They barked because *inu* means "dog." A Christian minister and the Kibei translator for the camp newspaper were beaten, and a JACL leader was hurriedly taken out of the Center for his own safety.[5]

Then, embarrassingly, it was discovered that the officials had been hasty in locking up the young men from Block 42. FBI agents told the Center attorney that refusal to answer the registration questionnaire was *not* a violation of the Selective Service Act. The Project Director queried National Director Dillon S. Myer, who checked with the War Department and answered that the War Department did not consider answers to the registration form compulsory.

For some reason, however, the evacuees were not given this information, and the false threat of a $10,000 fine or twenty years imprisonment was still held over them.[6] Further arrests were made, although an Army document posted in the mess halls stated that Nisei and Kibei who answered "No" to Questions 27 and 28 "cannot anticipate that the Army of the United States will ever ask for their services or that they will be inducted into the armed forces by Selective Service." The announcement went on to say that a "Yes" answer to both questions would mean liability to induction.

On one hand, men of military age met with dire threats if they did not register; on the other they were assured that if they answered "No" the Army would not take them. It was bewildering.

Tule Lake's registration fell far short of that in the other Centers. About a third of the people, including 3,000 Nisei, did not register at all, 1,238 said "No" to Question 28, and only fifty-nine volunteered for the Army.

Minidoka, Idaho, with more than 6,000 fewer evacuees, provided 308 volunteers.

III

Registration was supposed to end on March 2, but because results had been so disappointing at Tule Lake the Project Director announced an extension to March 10. Also, he ordered all single Kibei males of registration age to fill out the forms.

Many of the Kibei were in such a rebellious mood that they would have refused almost any order. Those who ignored this one—about a hundred young men—were isolated in an adjacent and deserted CCC camp. Project Director Coverley issued a new bulletin which said that nonregistrants "will be considered as having violated the orders of the War Department and the War Relocation Authority and subject to such penalties as may be imposed."

Actually, it had been known since February 26 that the War Department planned no penalties, and that any authority of the WRA to impose punishment was dubious and limited. National Director Dillon Myer had ruled on February 27 that registration of all aliens and of Nisei females was not compulsory, but no announcement of this was made at Tule Lake.[7]

"This is a great chess game," said one of the young Nisei there. "The Government makes all the moves."

In Minidoka, where things went more smoothly, another Nisei saw the registration more clearly. He said, "What we face is the acid test. If we flunk it, we damn ourselves and our posterity."

At Heart Mountain, a newly organized Citizens Congress made up of Nisei felt that registration should be accompanied by some reservations, purely on American principles.

[The Government] has permitted damaging propaganda to continue against us. Also she has failed to reinstate us in the eyes of the American public. . . . Our firm conviction is that we would be useless Americans if we did not assert our constitutional rights now; for, unless our status as citizens is cleared and we are really fighting for the high ideals upon which our nation is based, how can we say to the white American buddies in the armed forces that we are fighting for the perpetuation of democracy—especially when our fathers, mothers and families are in concentration camps even though they are not charged with any crime.

We believe that our Nation's good faith is to be found in whether or not it moves to restore full privileges at the earliest opportunity.

Belatedly, Question 28 was changed to read, simply, "Will you swear to abide by the laws of the United States and to take no action which would in any way interfere with the war effort of the United States?"

That avoided the issue of Japanese citizenship and thus did not require Issei to renounce the only citizenship they had. After the question was changed, the majority of the Issei answered "Yes." But registration was still an "Application for Leave Clearance," and the elder residents of the Centers— having for the most part already lost their little farms, their shops or jobs, and their possessions—had a growing fear of being sent to some strange part of the country.

The best bet was to stay in the Centers for the duration. And if you answered "No-No," you could at least be assured of a stay in Tule Lake.

WRA began interviewing the dissidents, and in some cases a fuller explanation brought a retraction of the "No-No" answers:

A Nisei woman, married to an Issei, was asked if she was disloyal. She said yes.

Q. Why?

A. Well, no reason. If I say "loyal," will they take me or leave me here?

Q. We don't split families. If one member is on the segregation list the others in the family are given their choice of leaving or remaining. We don't want you to answer a certain way just because your husband does. This hearing is just to determine your loyalty.

A. Then it doesn't have anything to do with staying?

Q. No, you'll just be given the choice of following your husband or not.

A. Then I'm loyal.

Two high school graduates from Venice, California, were interviewed together:

Q. Have you thought over what you want to do about this question?

A. We want to keep it as it is.

Q. Do you realize that means we'll have to send you to Tule Lake?

A. Our parents wish to go; to be segregated.

Q. We are more interested in how you feel on this citizenship status than how you feel on the family status.

A. We'd like to sit in Tule Lake for awhile. We don't want to relocate. The discrimination is too bad. I see letters from the people on the outside. There are fellows in Chicago who want to come back [to camp] but who are not allowed to.

When a twenty-one-year-old Nisei from Sacramento was asked about his loyalty, he quickly brought up the issue of race prejudice:

Q. Do you feel that you'd fit in well in Japan? Where do you think you'd best fit in, here or in Japan?

A. I can't say because of racial prejudices in this country.

Q. We're fighting against racial prejudices and persecution.

A. I don't know, the colored people have faced it ever since they came here.

Q. You mean the Negroes?

A. Yes.

At Manzanar, an angry Nisei was asked if he was a dual citizen.

A. No. . . . But in the first place, if we are citizens, how come we are in these camps? The FBI had a record of all the bad ones. How come they took the rest? How come they took the citizens? How come they didn't intern Willkie, LaGuardia, and Mayor Rossi?

Q. This is wartime and things were done because of military necessity that would not be done in normal times.

A. I'd rather leave the answer the same as it is. . . . I answered "no" because of resentment and because of how they treated us. When they asked us to come here, they told us that they would pay us union wages. They even used the Catholic church for such lies. How can I have faith in this country? I lost all my ideals about this country. In school I was even an Ephebian [member of a California high school honor society]. Do you know what that means? What will it be when the soldiers come back? I don't speak much Japanese, but at least I'll be among Japanese . . .[8]

IV

The Registration aroused fears and tore at family ties and was as fully an emotional strain upon the Japanese Americans as the Evacuation itself had been. And then—just as had happened in the period between the Pearl Harbor attack and the first Evacuation order—the pressures began again.

Press and radio branded the "No-No's" as politically disloyal and dangerous. Demands were made in Congress for their segregation. California State Senator Clarence C. Ward of Santa Barbara stumped the state urging that they be interned and eventually deported to Japan. Opportunists among the California pressure groups were advocating that Issei and citizens alike be included in that deportation.

The WRA itself came under investigation, first by a subcommittee of the Senate Committee on Military Affairs early in 1943, and then under a direct and unfair attack in the House of Representatives Special Committee to Investigate Un-American Activities, which came to be known as the Dies Committee. Its claims were wild and unsubstantiated, but these were seized upon and perpetuated by anti-Japanese organizations in California.

Director Dillon Myer was a long time in being asked to testify. He stood up to the Dies Committee, and said the investigation had been conducted "in such a manner as to achieve maximum publicity of sensational statements based on half-truths, exaggerations and falsehoods; statements of witnesses have been released to the public without verification of their accuracy, thus giving a nationwide currency to many distortions and downright untruths." [9]

Mr. Myer put into well-chosen words what many thinking Americans already felt about the Dies Committee. The attack on the WRA may not have been a purely politically inspired onslaught on the Roosevelt administration—there were glory-grabbers in Congress who avidly sought newspaper publicity. But 1944 was an election year, and by summer of 1943 the politicians were beginning to saddle and ride.

The evacuees had long known that Tule Lake was going to be the Segregation Center. In early July, 1943, this was made official when a Senate Resolution asked the WRA "to take such steps as may be necessary for the purpose of segregating persons of Japanese ancestry in relocation centers whose loyalty to the United States is questionable or who are known to be disloyal. . . . (The wording of this resolution, as the reader may judge, barely escaped being gobbledygook.)

On July 15th, WRA's hundredth Administrative Instruction named Tule Lake as the Segregation Center. On August 16, Raymond R. Best relieved Coverley as the Project Director.

It should be mentioned that a Project Director, appointed by the WRA, had very considerable authority. The Project Directors were responsible for the administration of justice in the Centers; they could act as lawmakers, prosecutors, and judges; they could decide what acts by evacuees were offenses and rule where the cases would be tried—by evacuee-composed judicial boards, by Relocation Center courts, or by state or Federal court. They could impose fines up to $300 or hand down a maximum sentence of three months in the Center jail. They were authorized to remove troublemakers from their Centers and send them to an "isolation center," or—in cases of aliens—could recommend internment in an alien detention camp to the Department of Justice.

Isolation Centers had been set up at Moab, Utah, and at Leupp, Arizona. The latter camp was disestablished in December, 1943, after one troubled year of existence.[10]

The WRA was taking no chances with inexperience when Tule Lake became the Segregation Center. Raymond R. Best, named as the new Project Director, had opened and headed both the Moab and Leupp camps.

Although Mr. Best's new job at Tule Lake was hardly calculated to make him universally popular with the people who had to live there, still he had many friends among them. His background was varied. A native of Michigan, he was educated in Los Angeles, served with the Marine Corps in World War I, then participated in oil, banking, and general merchandising enterprises in Idaho. He was appointed to the Federal Land Bank at Spokane, and then put in eight years as a soil conservationist with the Department of Agriculture. He was with the War Relocation Authority from its inception in 1942.[11]

It is obvious that the WRA regarded Mr. Best as a "trouble shooter," and gave him the most difficult jobs. The young Nisei who said that the Government made all the moves in the chess game gave a description more apt than he knew. Now the chess game began in earnest: moving the "disloyal" from all the other Centers to Tule Lake, and moving the "loyal" at Tule Lake to the other Centers.

Here was another bit of questionable expense for the American taxpayer. Would it not have been better to leave the small percentage of trouble-makers, the "bad apples," scattered throughout *all* the Centers, where they actually stood very little chance of corrupting the loyal and patriotic Nisei . . . and might have been converted to the cause of Americanism themselves? Or was it best to put all the bad apples in one box, and thus make spoilage certain and quick?

Fast spoilage was what happened at Tule Lake.

The big switch began in mid-September, 1943: the chess game with human beings for pawns. It took more than a month; it required thirty-three troop trains to swap more than 20,000 evacuees. Every incoming train dumped more problems into Raymond Best's lap. To be sure, many of the defiant dissenters elected to go to Tule Lake. But thousands of the older Issei chose to go there simply because it offered a haven in California, as against being resettled in some strange and perhaps unfriendly section of the Midwest or East.

Over 6,000 "loyal" evacuees left Tule Lake, and the chess game went on until the spring of 1944, when about 1,800 people from Manzanar were finally transferred after more Tule Lake barracks had been built.

A train bringing the "No-No's" into Tule Lake from the other Centers passed a train taking the loyal out. "Yes-Yes'es" thrust their heads out of the windows and yelled: "Okay! Go back to Tokyo, you Jap bastards!" [12]

Thirteen

But through the shift of mood and
mood,
　Mine ancient humour saves
　him whole—
The cynic devil in his blood
　That bids him mock his hurry-
　ing soul;
That bids him flout the Law he
makes,
That bids him make the Law he
flouts,
Till, dazed by many doubts he
wakes
　The drumming guns that—
　have no doubts . . .

—Rudyard Kipling, *An American.*

I

Any fair-minded and patriotic American who looks back upon
the events of 1942 and 1943 could hardly escape the feeling
that the incredible and the impossible happened. It was emi-
nently fitting, in those days, that we hated the Japanese nation
with a hot and patriotic hate, enough to wake "the drumming
guns that—have no doubts . . ." It was unfortunate that we
did not know what some other Americans, of Japanese ancestry, were doing.

The war was progressing. The Navy and the Marines had
taken bloody Guadalcanal in January, 1943, and were beginning their island-hopping campaign up through the South Pacific. Less publicized was the fact that the 442nd Regimental
Combat Team—the all-Nisei fighting outfit—had been acti-

181

vated on February 1, 1943, and its cadres were converging on Camp Shelby, Mississippi, to begin what seemed an interminable and hopeless battle with mud, leaky barracks, cold snaps, and the rigors of basic training.

The men from Hawaii arrived, and the 442nd was in business.

Nisei troops of the 100th Infantry Battalion had already pioneered Stateside. They had sailed from Hawaii on June 4, 1942, while the Battle of Midway was being fought and the fate of Hawaii hung in the balance. A transport, the *Maui,* carried 1,432 men of the Hawaiian Provisional Infantry Battalion. They still did not know whether or not their families would be interned or evacuated, but at least after they had reports on the Battle of Midway, they felt their loved ones would be safe.

The *Maui* carried Army and Navy families being sent home; it made a fifteen degree change of course every twenty minutes, blacked out at night, had regular boat drill, and otherwise impressed everybody that there was a war on.[1] The Nisei men were young and eager and flexible. They had money, they had cards and dice and ukuleles . . . and always a song. Only one thing worried them. They were being sent to the mainland for combat training. Didn't it make more sense for Hawaiian born soldiers to be trained for combat in the Pacific in Hawaii?

Navy blimps looking like fat sausages escorted the convoy into the Golden Gate; the *Maui* docked at Oakland. The men went aboard three troop trains, and each train took a different route toward its destination.[2] At train stops, people asked whether the uniformed men were Chinese soldiers or Japanese prisoners? At a Colorado station, Red Cross girls dispensing coffee and doughnuts expressed surprise that "these Chinese soldiers" could speak English.

The troop movement was conducted with what was called commendable secrecy. Unless the 100th Infantry Battalion was considered a secret weapon, there was no reason why its movement should not have been publicized. Such publicity would have been of inestimable value to the morale of the people in the Relocation Centers.

The boys from Hawaii wound up in Camp McCoy, Wisconsin. McCoy had been a maneuvering area for the Wisconsin National Guard; it consisted of 14,000 acres of woods, fields, low hills, and gullies. Not enough barracks were available, and the men of the 100th Infantry Battalion suffered at night but were kept busy and warm in the daytime.

Training was long and arduous but an *esprit* was developing. All at once no officer would stand for any derogatory comment from an outsider—from a mainlander. The Army manual said that sixteen seconds was a satisfactory time for setting up a heavy machine gun; Fort Benning considered eleven seconds very fast, indeed. An officer of the 100th Infantry Battalion was boasting that his boys were ready to open fire in five seconds.

Sixty-seven of the men were fluent enough in Japanese to go to the Military Intelligence Language Training School at Camp Savage, Minnesota; most of them later served in the Southwest Pacific.

The soldiers at McCoy spilled out to Chicago (four hours away by car) on leave, and some got as far as Washington. They fought the winter and successfully passed a three-months course of outdoor sleeping. They made many friends in Wisconsin, and on December 31, 1942, when they were ordered to Mississippi's Camp Shelby, they threw a huge *luau* for the people who had been kind to them and served more than a hundred pounds of steak, Hawaiian style.

The 442nd Regimental Combat Team not only had to battle Mississippi mud, but it had to fight snakes as warm weather came on. A Texan in one of the other outfits gave the Nisei a piece of Texas philosophy: "Every man," he said, "has to kill his own snakes." Other units of the 442nd included the 522nd Field Artillery and the 232nd Engineers; they, too, were composed of Nisei enlisted men. All of them were determined not to be outdone by regular U.S. Army outfits; they drilled and soldiered hard.

Before long, they were passing the hat and raising money to have Nisei girls come over on weekend passes from the Relocation Centers at Rohwer and Jerome, Arkansas, which were not too far away.[3] Some delightful dances, some pleasurable dates, and a number of permanent romances and marriages resulted from this practice.

On July 7, a new unit was added, the company that had been studying Japanese at Camp Savage; it was ready, now, as interpreters and translators, to learn how to relate Japanese to combat terms and military equipment.

II

While the Japanese Americans were earnestly training at Camp Shelby, on the West Coast, a bitter and very well organized campaign had begun rolling. It was aimed at keeping the Japanese from ever coming back.

General DeWitt's "A Jap's a Jap" pronouncement either set off or closely paralleled an extensive California sentiment. Around the same time, it was announced that General Delos Emmons, who had been Commander of the Hawaiian Department, would relieve DeWitt as Commander Western Sea Frontier.

General Emmons was well known for his liberal policy toward the Japanese in Hawaii. When it became known that he would be taking over the West Coast command, a near panic resulted. Several California Congressmen fought DeWitt's replacement and went on record against permitting Nisei servicemen even to visit the West Coast.

Almost all of the old racist groups—and some hastily formed new ones—were suddenly activated.

We don't want to see the time return when we have to compete with the Japanese again in this valley, [said C. L. Preisker, who had been chairman of the Board of Supervisors in Santa Barbara

County for thirty years]. We should strike now, while the sentiment over the country is right. The feeling of the East will grow
more bitter before the war is over, and if we begin now to try to
shut out the Japanese . . . we have a chance of accomplishing
something. . . . Congress could easily pass an act ordering all
nationals of Japan to return after the peace and forbidding the immigration of others after the war. . . .[4]

Immigration, of course, was already forbidden. The sentiment "we don't want to see the time return again when we
have to compete with the Japanese in this valley" was a stark
admission of motive, intelligence, and competency. There
would be a great deal more of this sort of thing during the next
year and afterwards, even after all rumors of sabotage and
fifth column activities both in Hawaii and on the mainland
had been officially scotched, even after the Nisei soldiers of the
442nd Regimental Combat Team and their brothers in the
Southwest Pacific had made their shining records. In fact, the
anti-Japanese groups on the West Coast were now more active
and better organized than ever before.

Early in 1943, a subcommittee of the Senate Committee on
Military Affairs began what was purported to be an investigation of the WRA. Kentucky's Senator Albert B. Chandler
whizzed through the Centers, asked a few questions, and took
off. His recommendations were mild.

Then the Dies Committee got into the act. Dies Committee
investigators had been out on the West Coast in 1941, when
they distinguished themselves by firing off "informational"
telegrams to Washington, including such classical absurdities
as the one that said:

JAPANESE PREFECTURAL SOCIETIES ARE CALLED KENS X SIXTEEN
SHINTO TEMPLES IN LOS ANGELES X THIS IS NOT A RELIGION BUT
WORSHIP OF THE JAPANESE RACE PERSONIFIED IN THE EMPEROR
X [5]

Even at night-press-rates, such alleged information was costly
to the taxpayer. All of it, and more, was available in any ency-

clopedia, in accounts that would have diminished a great deal of the menace that was implied.

The Dies Committee on Un-American Activities indulged in some of the most un-American activities that had ever been seen. A member of the Committee, Congressman J. Parnell Thomas of New Jersey, arrived in Los Angeles and began putting out press releases before he was within a hundred miles of any WRA Center. Newspaper headlines shouted "Stop Freeing Interned Japs!"; "Dies Prober Charges Whole Relocation Plan Is Farce," and "Rep. J. P. Thomas Reveals Jap Army in L.A." [6]

Newspapers must bear their share of the guilt, here. At the time Thomas charged that a Japanese army was in Los Angeles (May 13, 1943) it would have been quite easy for any city desk or rewrite man to establish the following facts: no people of Japanese blood were within the city limits at all except those still confined to public institutions, a few soldiers on leave, and about twenty Japanese women who were married to Caucasians.

The Tolan Committee, a year before, had turned a deaf ear to the Issei and had heard only a few Nisei who necessarily had to go along with the plan for evacuation or be suspected as disloyal. The Dies Committee was equally restrictive and also improved the system. Its real hearings were held in advance for the press, and in the formal sessions the sensational testimony from smear witnesses always preceded the testimony from WRA officials. Newspapermen, out to beat a deadline, naturally covered the smear cases; the defense received little—and belated—publicity.

Martin Dies himself rode to a fall of sorts. A junior member of Congress, Representative John Costello of California, took over the West Coast hearings as chairman—and in no time at all the newspapers were calling it the "Costello Committee."

Carey McWilliams, in his excellent book *Prejudice, Japanese Americans, Symbol of Racial Intolerance* says that Mr. Costello "conducted not a hearing, but an inquisition."

But the whole thing was too palpably a farce and the Dies Committee or the Costello Committee—call it as you will— got pretty badly trounced in the American press. Representative Herman P. Eberharter, of Pennsylvania, who had fought valiantly for a fair hearing, delivered the minority report. "I cannot avoid the conclusion that the report of the majority is prejudiced and that most of its statements are not proven."

Having been frustrated to an extent by the Dies Committee investigations, the racist groups in California quickly rallied and began working on the state legislature, as well as on the public. A State Senate Committee was convened. Fred Howser, District Attorney of Los Angeles County, told this group "we are going to have large-scale massacres or we might say free murder or manslaughter" if any Japanese were allowed to return to the West Coast.[7]

A Gold Star Mother, Mrs. Benaphl, told the State Senate Committee:

"We want to keep the Japs out of California."
State Senator Slater: "For the duration?"
Mrs. Benaphl: "No, for all times."
State Senator Slater: "That's the stuff!"[8]

That was the stuff, indeed, of the incredible West Coast prejudice which persisted long after the heroic record of the all-Nisei 442nd Regimental Combat Team was well known.

Three Nisei boys from Sacramento were killed in one week in the Italian fighting. A friend clipped the news item about their deaths from a newspaper and mailed it to State Assemblyman Chester Gannon of Sacramento. Mr. Gannon was chairman of an Assembly Committee that was working to keep the Japanese from returning to the state.

On the postcard to which he pasted the news clipping, the friend wrote: "Here are three Japanese who will not be coming back to California."

The card came back in the mail. Written on it now was, "Glory! Hallelujah! Hallelujah! Hallelujah!"[9]

Fourteen

My American friends . . . no doubt must have wondered why I renounced my citizenship. This decision was not that of today or yesterday. It dates back the day when General DeWitt ordered evacuation. It was confirmed when he flatly refused to listen even to the voices of the former World War Veterans, and it was doubly confirmed when I entered Manzanar. We who had already proven our loyalty by serving in the last World War should have been spared. The veterans . . . had to evacuate like the rest of the Japanese people, as if they were aliens.

I did not expect this of the Army. When the Western Defense Command assumed the responsibilities of the West Coast, I expected that at least the Nisei would be allowed to remain. But to General DeWitt, we were all alike. "A Jap's a Jap. Once a Jap, always a Jap." I swore to become a Jap a hundred percent and never to do another day's work to help this country fight this war. My decision to renounce my citizenship there and then was absolute.

It is my sincere desire to get over there as soon as possible to help rebuild Japan politically and economically. The American Democracy with which I was infused in my childhood is still unshaken. My life is dedicated to Japan with Democracy my goal.

—Statement by Joe Kurihara.[1]

I

The thousands of evacuees who had chosen to go to Tule Lake were by no means all disloyal. They included "loyals" who wished to remain with their parents and some who gave lip-service to disloyalty to avoid resettlement; others had been told the big farming project at the segregated Center would provide them jobs for the duration and that Tule Lake probably would be a permanent community even after the war.

Their first view of Tule Lake was disheartening. A double fence, eight feet high and manproof, had been built around the entire area. The number of military police, barracked outside the fence, had been raised from about two hundred soldiers to full battalion strength, and a number of ominous-looking tanks stood where everybody could see them.[2]

Old residents of Tule Lake had all the better jobs, either through tenure or rapid promotion to fill vacancies left by the "loyals" who had been transferred to the other Centers. They also had the best living quarters. The people coming in found themselves scattered and separated from their friends. They were jammed into apartments that had been stripped of shelves and partitions by the previous occupants.

The transferees at once began to make trouble. Young

toughs, mostly Kibei, broke into the women's shower rooms shouting, "This is Japan, and here men and women bathe together!" [3] They broke up dances of the Nisei because the dances were not Japanese. Japanese language schools were established, and there were ten Buddhist priests but only one Christian minister conducting church services. Classes were formed to instruct girls in such niceties as sitting on the floor in proper Japanese style. So long as community self-government would prevail, Tule Lake was going to be "Japan," indeed: at a basketball game the toughs ordered the man in charge of the recorded music to stop playing American jazz and play only Japanese records. A number of the new arrivals refused to cross from the barracks area to the administrative center until the American flag—which had been hoisted there by Nisei Boy Scouts—was lowered. [4]

A voluntary curfew was imposed on young girls. Nisei girls who worked as typists in the Center's housing office were slapped and insulted, and one of them gave vent to her indignation in pure American:

Anything can happen in this dump! It's almost as bad as being in Germany. . . . No fooling, these guys have no respect for women, and, boy, do they believe in Gestapo methods! [5]

On October 13, three firemen were seriously hurt when a fire truck overturned. Two days later a farm truck carrying twenty-nine workers rolled over on the road. Everybody aboard was cut and bruised; five men, pinned beneath, were seriously injured. One, a man named Kashima, died. [6]

These were accidents, but the troublemakers seized upon them to charge the administration with negligence. Two small boys had been hurt in the farm truck, and a rumor spread that the driver was only sixteen. About eight hundred farm workers promptly pledged themselves to stay away from the fields and "make the problem Center-wide" until certain demands were met.

The strike imperiled a harvest of vegetables and grains

worth thousands of dollars. But Block Managers met and passed a resolution supporting the farm workers. "Because of this favorable opportunity," the resolution said in part, "we resolve to solve, in coöperation with all the residents, all important general problems pertaining to living conditions." [7]

The leadership of the young and active Kibei and other dissidents was beginning to show. Neither Raymond Best nor any other Project Director could have done much with the growing crisis. The mood of the disloyal transferees was such that they would not have been satisfied with the most luxurious living conditions. They had been looking for a weapon, and they found it. Block elections were held that night, and the old, conservative Tule Lake residents were defeated.

The newly elected officials showed their preference for things Japanese by calling themselves the *Daihyo Sha Kai,* which translates to "Representative Body." It was really not a representative group. It must be remembered that Tule Lake held a large number of older people who wanted only to stay in California. Raymond Best says, today, that the

strong arm, troublemaker group was never representative of all the Center residents . . . but it never ceased to terrify a majority of the peaceful citizens of Tule Lake.[8]

The *Daihyo Sha Kai* demanded a big public funeral for Kashima, the man killed in the truck accident. Mr. Best refused.

At this time, [he told the author recently] I must admit that my memory is rather hazy in connection with the exact details of the many and complicated events at Tule Lake. However, the refusal for a public funeral for Kashima was justified on many grounds probably mainly for security reasons.

A large crowd gathered, and the funeral services were held at an athletic field in direct defiance of Best's decision. It was reported that officials turned off the electric power for the entire Center while the services were going on, so that the public address system could not be used.[9] Mr. Best does not remember the power shut-off but recalls that the public address equipment had been forcibly taken from the Nisei who were charged with its custody and use.

II

The crop was still in the fields, and negotiations were not getting anywhere. Project Director Best harked back to Kashima's funeral and told the negotiating committee that he had refused permission for a public service because

> they didn't ask me, they demanded that I appear at the funeral and speak. They demanded that I transmit a letter of condolence to the widow. I do not recognize demands.[10]

He blamed Congress itself for the difficulties in Tule Lake—because:

> The Congress of the United States demanded and ordered segregation. The Tule Lake Center was selected as the place. . . . I don't want to blame you [the evacuees], and I don't want to take the blame. I guess the blame rests on Congress.[11]

Then he announced that he was going to find a buyer and sell the crop in order to save it. On October 26, Best wired the Poston and Topaz Centers asking that they recruit loyal workers to come and harvest the Tule Lake crop. Shortly after this, he had to make a trip to San Francisco. According to an article published in the Topaz *Times* on October 28, somebody on the staff at Tule Lake was not entirely truthful with his fellow WRA officials. The Topaz Project Director stated:

> In discussing the job I have been asked to find out if there is any trouble like a "strike" at Tule Lake. Last night I phoned to Tule Lake and received this information: "There is no strike or labor trouble in Tule Lake." The residents of Tule Lake have had meetings with their project director and have said they did not feel they should harvest crops that were going to the other centers.

Semantics? This may have been one of the precedents for the often used claim that a labor situation is a "work stoppage," and not a "strike." In either case, it was certainly "labor trouble."

Newspapers on October 29 reported that the workers from the other Centers were to be paid a dollar an hour. The farmers at Tule Lake were getting sixteen dollars a month. This, more than anything else, angered the people who were renouncing their citizenship: the difference between loyalty and disloyalty was now expressed in dollars and cents. The farmers asked that Raymond Best's strike termination order be retracted, and a spokesman said it was possible they would all return to work. But during Mr. Best's absence, the Assistant Project Director declared that he had no authority to retract the termination order and announced on October 30 that the subject would be discussed when the National Director, Dillon Myer, visited the Center on November 1.

The first contingent of workers from the other Centers arrived on October 30 and was billeted in tents outside the eight-foot wire. The anger of the Tule Lake residents flared up again when they learned that food supplies had been taken from the Center to feed these "outsiders."

Nobody was going hungry; this was just another incident that inflamed the rebellious mood of the evacuees. It may have been more basic than that. Many of the older Issei in the Center could remember rice famines in Japan. Some of them may have believed that any diversion of food supplies might threaten them with starvation.

Daihyo Sha Kai leaders met at the administration center early on Monday morning, talked to the Assistant Project Director, and tried to set up interviews with Dillon Myer. They were told that they would have to wait until the following day, but just before noon they learned that Mr. Myer was already in the building.

They fanned out to the Center mess halls and passed the word at lunch time. In a little while, a vast crowd surged into the administration area. At first the officials were alarmed, but when they saw many women and children in the throng they felt confident all would be peaceful.

Myer agreed to talk to the negotiation committee. A public address system was set up by the evacuees. Over in the Army compound, troops were readied, and tanks were warmed up, just in case.

But the trouble broke out in a different quarter. In the Center hospital, the chief medical officer, Dr. R. Pedicord, noticed that small groups of evacuees kept coming in and circulating among the hospital employees. The doctor assumed this was an attempt to induce the employees to join the crowd, which by this time was estimated to be somewhere between five and ten thousand people. (He used these figures in the official WRA Semi-Annual Report. But the same Report, farther on, said there was a steady stream of evacuees going in and out of one ward that was used for classrooms and that had restrooms. No other restrooms were available in the area.)

At any rate, Dr. Pedicord ordered the intruders to leave. They did, but a score of them remained outside on the steps, and then pushed their way into Dr. Pedicord's outer office.

His secretary screamed. The doctor stuck his head out of his private office to see what was going on, and somebody pulled off his eye glasses. Dr. Pedicord landed one good blow on this man before the others moved in. Five young men bore the doctor to the floor, kicking him in the face and body, and then dragging him out of the building. The leader of the group ordered the beating stopped, and the gang dispersed.[12]

A telephone message to the Project Director's office told what had happened. This interrupted the talk between Dillon Myer and George Kuratomi, a transferee from Jerome who was acting as spokesman for the negotiating committee. Kuratomi obviously knew nothing of what was going on at the hospital, but he sent some men "to stop it."

The discussion had got off to a bad start. Kuratomi said the *Daihyo Sha Kai* had voted to ask for the resignation of all Caucasian doctors and nurses at Tule Lake. Myer said he would have any specific complaints investigated. Kuratomi said the evacuees were "demanding" the removal of Caucasian hospital personnel.

Now Myer reinforced the stand the Project Director, Raymond Best, had previously taken, by stating: "I have never taken any action under threat or duress." [13]

Other issues were raised during the two-and-a-half-hour talk, but nothing of importance was settled. At the end of the interview, Myer made a brief address to the crowd. He said he had the utmost confidence in the Project Director and asked all the residents to coöperate with the Center administration.

That afternoon the Center officials set up a night patrol of the administration area. It was agreed, after a conference with the military police commander, that any of the Center's internal security officers was authorized to call in the troops. The Caucasian hospital staff was sent to its quarters.

Next day the Caucasian employees of the Center made demands of their own. They wanted another high fence—this one to protect the administrative area. This was constructed.

Meanwhile, several of the Caucasian staff members resigned; one of them later gave a somewhat lurid story to the *San Francisco Examiner,* which quoted him as saying: "I couldn't sleep. I kept waking up with the expectation of feeling a knife against my throat."

That sort of thing was manna to the growing movement to keep the Japanese from ever coming back to California. Probably not one reader in ten distinguished between the bad apples in Tule Lake and the good ones in all the nine other Relocation Centers.

III

The Kibei have largely been blamed for the troubles at Tule Lake, and certainly a share of the blame was justified. That a number of Kibei were involved and were young and hotheaded and extremely vociferous is undoubtedly true. A special meaning had been given the term "Kibei" by the Nisei:

anyone was a Kibei who acted "in a Japanesey manner." But even today there is a vast disagreement as to how many Kibei there were.

Robert H. Fouke, who represented the California Joint Immigration Committee (composed of the American Legion, the State Federation of Labor, the Native Sons of the Golden West, the California State Grange, and many individual members) had told the Tolan Congressional Committee that there were "about 50,000" Kibei in California and Hawaii. A previous estimate had been 40,000; Dorothy Thomas's sociological study later said that one out of every five Nisei was a Kibei who had studied in Japan.

Considering the economic status of Japanese Americans on the West Coast, these figures are extremely suspect. It took money to send children to Japan for school. Mike Masaoka insists that some zeroes were dropped in that latter estimate and that the figure should have been "one in every five hundred." WRA statistics showed that only two percent of the Nisei under fifteen had been in Japan for more than a year; 93 percent had never been there at all. Of those over the age of fifteen, yes—twenty percent had been in Japan for schooling. But of those up to twenty years of age, only 12.2 percent had had three or more years of schooling in Japan.

There were enough Kibei, at any rate, to swing the pendulum at Tule Lake over to violence.

Food again was the *cause célèbre*. On November 4, two days after National Director Myer had left the camp, a group of young men carrying clubs converged on the administrative offices with the avowed intention of preventing any transfer of food from the warehouses to the "loyal" volunteer workers at the farm. One Caucasian member of the internal security staff was injured in the altercation that followed. There were some shouts about getting the Project Director. The troops were called.

Floodlights were turned on at the watch towers. Tanks rumbled into Tule Lake, and jeeps buzzed about the Center. It was late at night, and in spite of the noise the majority of the residents did not know what was going on.

They woke on the morning of November 5 to find that the Army had taken control of Tule Lake. Martial law was declared eight days later. It was not until two months afterward that the period of Army control ended.[14]

Negotiations broke down because of resentment toward the military control. The evacuees charged that there was a shortage of coal, and they were cold; they said no children over seven months old were getting enough milk. The garbage collection service had broken down. The butcher-shop employees were reduced due to inability to meet Army clearances; only twenty-five of ninety-eight warehouse workers were cleared for reemployment.[15] Whatever anybody thought of it, Tule Lake actually was a community, a town, a suburb of sorts set up by Government policy: it had to have milk, garbage collection, and many other things. Too many of the services of this sort were not available.

The Spanish Consul came—twice within a week. As the representative of a neutral power, he had been asked by the Japanese government to investigate conditions in Tule Lake.

He found a number of young men, mostly Kibei, held in a stockade without formal charges or trial. He found that since the Project Reports Officer had left the camp after the troubles of November 4, there was no censorship at all: the camp newspaper, *The Tulean Dispatch,* printed articles stating boldly that Japan would protect the Japanese in Tule Lake. There were editorials headed "Mother Country That Has Not Forsaken Us."

As the boys shouted when they invaded the women's shower room: "This is Japan!"

To the shame of the WRA and the Army, Tule Lake really *was* a little bit of Japan for about two months. The mimeographed newspaper was suspended. Tensions, fears, and suspicions were rife; morale was low. The Army refused to deal with the original negotiating committee, members of which were now imprisoned in the stockade. There was talk of both a general strike and a hunger strike. The people were desperate.

The Spanish Consul made another visit and appealed to the negotiating committee to resign. By this time, more than two hundred people had been confined in the stockade. There was a hunger strike in the stockade that accomplished nothing, although it lasted "six days and two meals."

Strikes and partial strikes swept the Center, and there was a steady increase in human misery. The people who were not working had no income. Many children were without shoes. There was no clothing allowance. Under the Army, the camp necessarily took on a prisonlike atmosphere.

The Army's control was so complete after the November incident that the Washington headquarters of the WRA could not get reports from Tule Lake on which to base a statement that might have refuted some of the lurid charges that were being made and widely publicized in the West Coast press. A series of investigations had been started, both in the California State Legislature and in the U.S. Congress. But when a State Legislature committee headed by Hugh Donnelly went to the scene, they could talk only with some of the fomer Center employees who had proven "particularly unreliable during the crisis and had subsequently resigned"—and the talks were held not in the Center, but in the nearby town of Tule Lake.

U.S. Representative Clair Engle, whose California district included the Center, made a quick trip there in an attempt to get some first-hand information. It might be thought that a Congressman would outrank the commander of an army battalion, but Mr. Engle was not permitted to pass the MP's at the gate and had to get what data he could by sitting in on the Donnelly Committee sessions in the village.[16]

Almost two weeks passed before the Washington office of the WRA could release any factual statement on what had happened. During the interim one of those unforeseeable, un-

explainable, little things that plague Governments, corpora-
tions, and personages—but delight newspaper editors—happened.

WRA's press relations had fallen to a discouraging low.
Early in December, the Cleveland area office of WRA printed
a newsletter to be circulated in the Centers, pointing out with
the best intentions in the world that there were excellent opportunities for the evacuees to relocate in the farming areas of
the Middle West. It said the Japanese Americans might even
contribute a great deal to rural living in this area, since their
habits of cleanliness were well known, and since many midwestern farm homes did not even have bathtubs.

This did it. Within forty-eight hours the WRA was either
condemned or ridiculed by a dozen leading newspapers and
was being denounced by a score of midwest Congressmen. At
this remove there is some earthy, unwashed humor about the
whole affair, but at the time the WRA could find nothing
funny about it.[17]

In Tule Lake, a Nisei girl was writing, "There were no activities. Everything stopped. We had a curfew. Oh, it was a
miserable life . . . we got baloney for Thanksgiving."

Finally there was a ballot. The people were so resentful that
the decision to return to normal was carried by only 473
votes. Even in this there was a charge that the Army had
picked up a number of the *Daihyo Sha Kai* members to keep
them from voting. But after the ballot, the Army lifted martial
law, pulled most of the soldiers out of the Center, and retained
control only over approximately two hundred prisoners who
were still in the stockade.

Fifteen

Governments exist to protect the rights of minorities. The loved and the rich need no protection—they have many friends and few enemies.

—Wendell Phillips Speech, December 21, 1860.

I

The majority of the people at Tule Lake had indicated that they wanted to be Japanese citizens. On July 1, 1944, the President signed Public Law 405 of the Seventy-Eighth Congress, making it very easy for them to accomplish this. This law provided that "whenever the United States shall be in a state of war" any person could renounce his United States citizenship by making a written declaration.

During winter and spring of 1944 and 1945, the U.S. Attorney General received some 5,700 applications for renunciation of citizenship—most of them from the evacuees in Tule Lake. Many of the people who requested this were like Joe Kurihara—they resented the treatment they had received and had long before made up their minds to turn to Japan. Also, secretly-organized pressure groups were working, urging renunciation and advocating immediate repatriation. The most active of these were the *Hoshi-dan,* or parent organization, and the *Hokoku,* which was made up of young men. Members of the two organizations boasted that they were the only "true Japanese" in the United States.

Morale at Tule Lake had been extremely low for a long time, and the pressure groups helped to persuade a large number of the people. But travel to Japan was not immediately possible, and on December 17, 1944, two simultaneous announcements produced a reaction that indicated very quickly that many of the renunciants did not really want to become Japanese, after all.

The first was a decision by the Western Defense Command that rescinded the orders that had excluded Japanese Americans from the West Coast. Now they could go back to California, to Oregon, to Washington, to the only parts of America they had ever known.

The second was a statement from the War Relocation Authority that the evacuees would have to resettle, because all of the Centers would be closed within the next twelve months.

The latter announcement was a bitter blow to some of the older evacuees, who had lost their properties back home, and had come, gradually and under conditions which certainly were not calculated to inspire ambition, to regard the WRA Centers as security. In them, they were at least assured of food, shelter, and creature comforts. Many had put themselves on record as being "disloyal" because they feared being thrown out of the Centers. A common question was, "They can't force us out if we have signed for renunciation, can they?"

One Issei remarked:

Put it this way. If you're a Caucasian, you take this matter of your loyalty record seriously and would never say anything to soil it. But if you're a Japanese and nobody believes your loyalty in this country anyway, you'll think about your future and your family. We are going to have our children renounce citizenship just to stay here.

In the long run, America lost some people like Joe Kurihara, who had been described as having a genius IQ and who could have done much to bind the wounds of war and evacuation. In the longer run, we wound up with some 4,000 Nisei and Kibei renunciants who did not get to Japan, at all, but were left in America in a condition that had no precedent: they were *"aliens ineligible for citizenship in the land of their birth."*

It sounds impossible. When the older and more intelligent Issei heard about it, they exclaimed: *"Tondemonai!"* a very expressive Japanese word later to be loosely translated to the GI's in Japan as meaning: "Never happen!"

But it did happen. It was not until August 26, 1949, that a decision in the Federal Appellate Court for the Ninth District confirmed a lower court ruling that the benefits of citizenship can be renounced or waived only as a result of free and intelligent choice, and set aside the renunciations of three Nisei. The decision in the Court of Appeals was handed down by Judge William Denman, who made a hard and judicial swipe at "General DeWitt's doctrine of enemy racism inherited by blood strains."

Registration for leave clearance had been completed in most Centers in March, 1943. The "disloyal" had been segregated into Tule Lake by October. In the interim, 15,000 loyal evacuees had resettled in the Midwest and elsewhere, and another 20,000 left the camps before the end of December and were trying to establish themselves farther east. The move, made with coach fare and twenty-five dollars supplied each person by the WRA, took quite a bit of courage.

II

Tule Lake, being a community, had a crime rate. It was actually lower than the crime rate of average towns of the same size, but it included murder.

On May 24, 1944, Shoichi James Okamoto, 30, who was born in Garden Grove, California, and had never been to Japan, was driving a truck assigned to the Center's construction crew. He returned to the Center via Gate Four. Subsequent testimony never did clear up exactly what happened, but there was some sort of argument about passes with an Army sentry, Pvt. Bernard Goe, . . . who ordered Okamoto to step down to the ground, marched him to the rear of the truck, and shot him to death at close range.[1]

On June 21, a mentally deranged evacuee attacked his roommate and another elderly Issei with a hammer, nearly killing one of them.[2]

On July 2, Takeo Noma, who was the general manager of the Coöperative Enterprises of Tule Lake, was stabbed to death by assassins who were never known.[3]

Suspicion, distrust, fear, greed, and envy by now had held sway so long in the Center that Takeo Noma's death, far from being mourned, was actually hailed. As the Coöp manager, he had been listed as a "Number One Public *Inu*," and thousands of the residents were firmly convinced that anyone connected with the Coöp was taking graft and making a lot of money through outright theft. Others believed Noma had cheated fellow Japanese as an insurance agent before the war and that his killing was a grudge murder.

Joe Kurihara had been very vocal before transferring to Tule Lake but strangely quiet afterward. If he engaged in any political activity there, it was only in influencing some of the more radical groups. But now he made a statement:

The killing of T. Noma was a blessing to the residents. I have yet to see anyone who really feels sorry for him, other than those of his immediate family. Never have I seen such pleasant reactions to a murder in all my life. Several others are said to be in line for the grave, . . . and their deaths, violent as they may be, will be openly rejoiced by the residents.

The public sanction of T. Noma's murder will undoubtedly encourage the executioner to carry on his or their work. A good work. . . . Why do I approve it? Because there is no law here in this camp. . . . The administration has so far listened to the Rats (*inu*) and upon the strength of their flimsy charges it arrested and threw many into the stockade.[4]

Anonymous threats were made to the effect that all members of the Coöperative Board would be killed. The Board resigned, and so did the whole evacuee police force.[5] Some of the key officials were placed under protective custody. The people, expecting the canteens to be closed, swamped them to buy food supplies. A new Board of Directors was elected, and the Coöp survived, but panic gripped the Center for several weeks. The residents, living in crowded blocks, never knew when someone next to them might be beaten or killed; young girls had to stay off the streets at night or risk insult or attack; young men of the Hokoku made the morning air hideous with the noise of their bugling, their goose-stepping military drills, and their shouts of *"Banzai!"* Recalling this period, Mr. Best estimates that there were as many as five hundred bugles in the camp: the troublemakers, he explains, had bought them from mail-order houses.

The administration asked Modoc County officials to indict several men, who were in the stockade, for Takeo Noma's murder. But the evidence against them was too slender, and no true bill was ever returned. Actually, Noma's death was quickly forgotten, probably because it had been committed by resident Japanese. Private Goe's shooting of Okamoto was different—it became a *cause célèbre* for the reason that it had occurred outside the Center and could be laid to the U.S. Army.

Even Mr. Best went all out to commiserate with Okamoto's widow and lend his presence to a big public funeral, in contrast to his refusal to do either in the earlier case of the man killed by a WRA truck.[6] He says today that the strong-arm troublemaker group "was never representative of all the Center residents, and never ceased to terrify a majority of the peaceful citizens."

III

Fortunately, the black picture at Tule Lake was not representative of the other Wartime Relocation Centers, and the "incidents" that had occurred at Manzanar and Poston were minor by comparison.

Many Caucasian residents of the mountain and interior

states had begun to discover, as early as the fall of 1942, that the Nisei were not only good Americans but were excellent farm workers. Some constructive programs were going on in the Centers; one of the best was that which supplied manpower, in season, to save the sugar-beet crop. Center management still was an extremely complex and difficult task, and even the salvage of the sugar beets had unforeseen and inescapably bad results at Manzanar. The temporary absence of nearly a thousand young Nisei was enough to defeat a new plan for self-government in the Center.

The Topaz Center was living up to its humorous sobriquet as "the Jewel of the Desert," in a serious and worthwhile way. It had nearly 3,000 students in school, and eventually would turn out more than a thousand high-school diplomas. Half the teachers were evacuees, being paid $16 or $19 a month. The classrooms were heated by smoking coal stoves, the benches had severely straight backs, and nothing was as comfortable as the traditional Little Red Schoolhouse. But the students learned, and even a larger number of adults were going to school at Topaz, studying Americanization, English, and technical subjects that ranged from the delicately exquisite art of Japanese flower arrangement to the grease-smudged intricacies of automobile repair. Topaz had an excellent library where one could study art, mineralology, and many other subjects. The residents hunted arrowheads; they collected tiny shells from the ancient inland sea, and converted them into preciously wrought jewelry.[7]

They had things to do at Topaz, while at Tule Lake dissension was the main topic and the principal employment.

The individual ability to become adjusted, of course, was the key to the entire experience of Evacuation; and this applied regardless of such factors as age, education, and prior standing in civilian life. This was proven by the elderly Mr. H., who was keeping his Journal down in the Gila Center. Mr. H.'s path had not been one of roses. His wife had died in the Center; her death later was attributed to lobar pneumonia and a tragic lack of facilities, instead of to breast cancer. He had been working as a cook at $12 a month. One of his two daughters—the one who had completed three years at the University of California—was allowed to leave the Center to finish her education at a college in Denver, but she still had to work her way. She found a job for her younger sister in Denver and made plans to see that the younger girl also got a college education.

What about Mr. H., himself:

I have changed my job for the farming and continuously worked 8 months, but my chronic Neuralgia pains come back. I have to quit my job, and now I am selling 2 Japanese Language papers printed at Denver and Salt Lake City, calling loudly for the news with ached feet. I never dreamed I will be Newspaper boy at the age of sixty years, but job of Newspaperboy has a little more income than W.R.A. jobs pay. Little extra money will help daughters school expenses. I don't care what people will say.

Mr. H. did not care what people said, and yet he confided to his Journal that it hurt his conscience to be making so much money—several dollars a day—by selling newspapers. And he was a man wondrously human, and utterly honest:

I am getting old, but my interest in females are not declining. I should confess, there are plenty of widows at this Center some are pretty some are homely, and most of them act like man hater. And they are pretending they don't have any carnal desire at all, or they do not like to have any conversation with the mens folks. If I have not any moral virtue, I may induce one of those females to my own way very easily, but I could not do it for my daughters sake. My daughters are believe their father is a real gentleman.[8]

By March, 1943, 461 evacuees had gone out of Topaz. Nine were in Army uniform, 49 were on educational furlough, 173 were on permanent leave, and 230 were on short-term agricultural leave.

Still, there were the uncontrollable factors, and no Center entirely escaped trouble. In October, 1943, a gang of Caucasian boys drove past the Topaz Center three times, throwing rocks, and—at least on one of the three forays—firing shots into the community hall. Three persons were wounded. The boys were soon arrested and were sentenced to jail terms.

Where was the Army guard when this raid occurred? It had been on the job just six months before at Topaz, when old Mr. Wakasa got shot to death crossing the inner boundary fence. The impounded people had a right to expect that a guard would work both ways.

But the Topaz Relocation Center lived up to its name in that it relocated almost 2,000 evacuees throughout 98 different cities. The majority of these resettled in Chicago and caught on amazingly well there. It was generally believed at Topaz that the friendly and enlightened attitude of the Mormon Church of Utah was largely responsible for the placements.[9]

Still, most of the evacuees in Topaz and in all the other Centers really wanted only one thing—to go back to the homes they had loved in California and in other West Coast areas.

IV

Dillon Myer and other WRA officials were still practicing a "selective internment" policy in the relocation program; during 1943 they had pressed consistently for a revocation of the Army orders that prevented even a screened and selected few of the Japanese Americans from returning to the Coast.

The Army said no, even while it was recruiting volunteers for the 442nd Regimental Combat Team in the Centers. There were Nisei lads who wanted to join up, but they also wanted to know if joining up to fight for America would mean that they and their families could return freely to that particular portion of America they loved best. "Negative," said the War Department.

Assistant Secretary of War McCloy did try to get General

DeWitt to lift the ban on the Nisei soldiers, themselves. Although one would think that any man wearing the uniform of the United States Army should be permitted to travel anywhere in the United States and not just to ports of embarkation and combat areas overseas, and although McCloy's suggestion was a nudge from higher authority, DeWitt stubbornly refused and attempted to justify his stand in a memorandum to the Chiefs of Staff. This time, however, he was outflanked, outranked, and overruled. By direction from the War Department, on April 21, 1943, he issued his Public Proclamation No. 17, which suspended exclusion orders for Nisei in uniform. Except in extraordinary cases, however, it did not do the same for their wives.[10]

Selective Service induction for the Nisei became effective on January 20, 1944. Lieutenant General Delos C. Emmons had relieved DeWitt of the Western Defense Command in the previous September, when DeWitt's normal tour of duty ended. Emmons was in favor of doing two things: cutting down the size of the prohibited zone and opening it to individuals not actually or potentially dangerous.

A more tolerant officer than DeWitt and one convinced of Nisei loyalty by his experience in Hawaii, Emmons still had his regular Army, practical side. There was handwriting on the wall. Any time, now—and he so warned the War Department—there would be court actions that would undermine what authority the military exercised over civilians.[11]

Sixteen

The more I think of this problem of suddenly ending the orders excluding Japanese Americans from the West Coast, the more I think it would be a mistake to do anything drastic or sudden. As I said at Cabinet, I think the whole problem, for the sake of internal quiet, should be handled gradually, *i.e.*, I am thinking of two methods: (a) Seeing, with great discretion, how many Japanese families would be acceptable to public opinion in definite localities on the West Coast. (b) Seeking to extend greatly the distribution of other families in many parts of the United States. I have been talking to a number of people from the Coast and they are all in agreement that the Coast would be willing to receive back a portion of the Japanese who were formerly there—nothing sudden and not in too great quantities at any one time. Also, in talking to people from the Middle West, the East, and the South, I am sure that there would be no bitterness if they were distributed

—one or two families to each
county as a start. Dissemination
and distribution constitute a great
method of avoiding public out-
cry. Why not proceed along the
above line—for a while at least?

—Memorandum, President F. D. Roosevelt to Acting Secretary of State
Edward R. Stettinius, Jr.; copy to Secretary of the Interior Harold Ickes.
June 12, 1944.[1]

I

This was a tragically informal, inconclusive, and indecisive bit
of writing, in that it caused the evacuees to be held in the
camps overlong. "For the sake of internal quiet" seems to be
the key phrase; the rest is made up of "I am thinking," "I have
been talking," and "I am sure" construction. When he wrote it,
the Chief Executive obviously was not sure at all. He wanted
to move gradually—that much is clear—and the memorandum very effectively delayed any plans for a wholesale release
of the more than 100,000 evacuees who hoped to return to the
West Coast. But the War Department and the WRA held
widely divergent views as to exactly what the President
wanted, and apparently nobody dared go back to him for clarification. The Western Defense Command, however, began
formulating new policies to meet the probability that the mass
exclusion orders would be lifted.

As before, a strong statement from the White House likely
could have assured that "internal quiet" on the West Coast. If
Roosevelt had gone on the air with his masterful stage presence
and charming diction to say, "These people are Americans,
innocent of any traitorous or treasonable conduct and important to our economy and the successful prosecution of the
war . . ." it seems certain that the evacuees could have been
reestablished on the West Coast with less difficulty than was
finally encountered. The trouble was that nobody in high au-

thority ever spoke up in their behalf.

It was 1944—an election year. No one can say, authoritatively, how much of a role national politics played in the delay of releasing the Japanese Americans. Did the Administration fear the anti-Japanese vote on the West Coast in the November elections? In November 10, with the elections over, Secretary Ickes again brought up the matter. This time Roosevelt agreed to permit unconditional release of most of the evacuees, thus allowing them to return to the West Coast.

In the summer of 1944, with the tide of war running full flood in the Pacific for America, the President could have afforded to be more generous. His idea of sending a large number of the evacuees throughout the country—"one or two families to each county"—was a rather cruel philosophy. The people had been uprooted once, and this would have separated them from their friends and relatives. "Nothing sudden and not in too great quantities," Roosevelt said. But the Evacuation had been sudden and in great quantities, indeed.

II

What the WRA has mildly described as "the hardening of the West Coast opposition" went on for any months after the Nisei soldiers had shed their blood and won their laurels both in the Italian campaign and in the island-hopping battles of the Southwest Pacific. It increased in intensity and hatred after the Nisei began trickling back to their old West Coast homes "in not too great quantities." Again, word from the White House could have stopped much of it.

The well-organized campaign, waged by hate groups old and new, was based on racism and on color. It was directed only toward the Japanese. It was largely carried on in the state that had spawned the first vigilantes.

It should be remembered that as early as October 12, 1942, the U.S. Attorney General had freed Italian nationals from enemy alien restrictions, and that two months later General

DeWitt did the same thing for German nationals living on the West Coast. In January, 1943, a Gallup poll taken on the Coast showed that fifty-four percent of the sampling favored the return of the Japanese *after the war* . . . although some people qualified their answers to apply only to citizens.

But fifty-four percent of the intelligent and fair-minded citizens of California were not running the state in 1943 or at any other time. The pressure groups were active, and now there were more of them. During the summer of 1943, the following advertisement appeared several times in the columns of the *Sacramento Bee,* a McClatchy newspaper:

Out with the Japs. Men and women wanted to solicit membership in the Home Front Commandos, an organization whose objective is to deport the Japs after the war. Workers will be compensated for their time. Write for appointment, give references, age, and occupation, telephone number. Address Home Front Commandos, 1020 8th Street, Sacramento, California. Help organize a chapter in your county.[2]

The manner in which the West Coast public had begun to demand segregation of the "disloyal" Japanese, in some place like Tule Lake, carried at least an implication that the "loyal" should be rewarded by being released. But when the WRA started pushing its policy of getting all eligible evacuees out of the Centers, the West Coast—and particularly California— changed its tune.

Signs went up in store windows saying that the Japanese were not wanted; some stores refused to serve the returnees. Many who had returned to their old homes advised their friends still in the Centers to remain there. Pasadena, which had always been a fairly tolerant community, broke into two widely-divided camps of public opinion when a Nisei girl came home to re-enter a junior college, but the citizens remained calm.

There were night riders, in the rural districts. A rancher near Fresno admitted he had fired some shots at the home of a returned evacuee family. The court compounded this felony by giving him a light sentence—and suspending it. In November, 1944, an American Legion Post in Hood River, Oregon, demonstrated its Americanism by erasing the names of sixteen Nisei servicemen from its honor roll.[3]

It is difficult to say whether this action was stupid or merely due to an unawareness of what was going on. The newspapers had told, all during the previous month, how the Nisei of the 442nd Regimental Combat Team moved into the Vosges Mountains to rescue the Lost Texas Battalion, and Major General John E. Dahlquist, commanding the 36th Division, had just written about the 442nd: "The courage, steadfastness, and willingness of your officers and men were equal to any ever displayed by United States Troops." [4]

Some newspapers over the country—but only nine in California—were moved to editorial comment when Secretary Ickes denounced the light and suspended sentence in the Fresno shooting case. But even before this happened, there was another incident in Southern California.

A Nisei girl, Mary Masuda, had just returned to her home in Talbert, California, from the WRA Center at Gila. On the night of May 4, 1944, several men called on Mary Masuda and warned her that she might be physically injured if she tried to remain.

Mary Masuda's brother had recently been killed in the Italian fighting: he was Staff Sergeant Kazuo Masuda, the former truck gardener from Santa Ana, who improvised a mortar mount and turned back two Nazi attacks.

Mary Masuda, naturally frightened, left her home after the night riders' warning. Six months later Miss Masuda returned, and truth and justice triumphed. In December, 1944, it was announced that Sergeant Masuda had been posthumously awarded the Distinguished Service Cross. The WRA worked with the War Department to make the presentation of this award an occasion of some merit. General Joseph (Vinegar

Joe) Stilwell was chosen to make the award.

Vinegar Joe had already sounded off in no uncertain terms about Nisei fighting men:

The Nisei bought an awful big hunk of America with their blood. You're damn right those Nisei boys have a place in the American heart, now and forever. And I say we soldiers ought to form a pickax club to protect Japanese Americans who fought the war with us. Any time we see a barfly commando picking on these kids or discriminating against them, we ought to bang him over the head with a pickax. I'm willing to be a charter member. We cannot allow a single injustice to be done to the Nisei without defeating the purposes for which we fought.[5]

The award ceremony to Mary Masuda was best described by the *Los Angeles Times:*

Stilwell led the way to the front porch where members of the Masuda family were waiting. At the bottom of the steps he raised his hand in salute to the family, and PFC Masao Masuda, twenty-nine-year-old Fort Snelling soldier soon to go overseas, returned the gesture.

Then General Stilwell's aid read the citation. It told how Staff Sergeant Kazuo Masuda had walked through two hundred yards of enemy fire and single handed had set up an improvised mortar position to pour twenty rounds of ammunition into the enemy. It also told how he gave his own life to save the lives of men he was leading on a night patrol into heavily mined enemy territory.

"I've seen a good deal of the Nisei in service and never yet have I found one of them who didn't do his duty right up to the handle [Stilwell, addressing Mary Masuda]. The Distinguished Service Cross in itself is a small thing, but since it stands for gallantry in action, I hope you and your family will remember that Sergeant Masuda, in winning it, has also won the respect and admiration of all real Americans."

Then he pinned the medal on the soldier's thirty-four-year-old sister, who in turn gave it to her mother. "In accepting this distinction for my brother" [said Miss Masuda] "I know that he would want me to say that he was only doing his duty as a soldier of our beloved country." [6]

III

A purely chronological account of the anti-Japanese moves in California, during 1943 and 1944, is virtually impossible of presentation in relation to the larger history of those years. But during that time, intolerance and prejudice were being very cleverly manufactured by a number of organizations. Among them were:

The California Citizens Association of Santa Barbara, founded in February, 1943;

The Pacific Coast Japanese Problem League, 112 West Ninth Street, Los Angeles, formed July 13, 1943;

No Japs, Incorporated, established in San Diego, August 16, 1943;

The California Citizens Council, organized in Los Angeles, October 11, 1943;

The Salinas Chamber of Commerce, active through Fred S. McCargar, Chamber Secretary and top hand in the annual Salinas Rodeo;

The Home Front Commandos, of Sacramento, already mentioned;

In Los Angeles, also a group known as Americanism Educational League.

In addition, there were the old stand-bys: the California Joint Immigration Committee, the Native Sons of the Golden West, the not-so-American American Legion, the Associated Farmers, the State Grange, and—early in the game—the State Federation of Labor.[7]

The Home Front Commandos, Inc., 607 Nicolaus Building, Sacramento, were headed by an attorney, J. A. Harder. In addition to their newspaper advertisement in the *Sacramento Bee,* they struck off a handbill:

Come and hear the facts—Lend your help to Deport the Japs— If you can't trust a Jap, you won't want him as a neighbor—Any good man can become an American citizen, but a Jap is and always will be a Stabber-in-the-Back gangster; rebel. After the war, ship them back to their Rising Sun Empire.

There was another pamphlet that stated "No Jap Is Fit to Associate with Human Beings." This was circulated under the heading of "Slap the Jap Rat." Carey McWilliams, in his *Prejudice, Japanese Americans, Symbol of Racial Intolerance,* named C. M. Goethe of Sacramento as the financier of the Home Front Commandos. Mr. Goethe, a wealthy man, was not listed as a sponsor. He was extremely active in the Northern California Council of Churches and did good works. He was also treasurer of the California Joint Immigration Committee.

Mr. Goethe, additionally, was director of the Eugenics Society of Northern California. This group was so concerned with racial integrity that it reportedly admired Hitler's tactics in holding trials to determine the fitness of German citizens for parenthood.

The executive director of the Pacific Coast Japanese Problem League, Dr. John Carruthers, was a graduate of Princeton and a Presbyterian minister. Before the California State Senate on October 19, 1943, he said: "It is our Christian duty to keep the Japanese out of this western world of Christian civilization." As the result of prayer, he said, he would urge "the deportation, if possible, by every means possible, of all the Japanese from the American continent." [8]

Heights—or depths—of absurdity were reached. Just when the Army and the Navy were desperately trying to find Japanese interpreters, only to discover that Japanese language schools had not really taught anybody at all, the California State Supervisors Association came out with a resolution advocating that the teaching of Japanese should be forever barred in this country. Just when the Army was recruiting and organizing the famous 442nd Regimental Combat Team, the Native Sons of the Golden West and the California State Grange opposed the entire idea of Japanese in uniform. Along with the Hood River, Oregon, Legion Post, the California town of Gardena took the names of seventeen Japanese service men from the municipal honor roll.[9]

The American Legion in Portland, Oregon, actively fought against any care for the local Japanese cemetery.[10] In Salinas, California, where vigilante groups were being organized to prevent return of any Japanese, the citizenry went Portland's Legionnaires one better.

A Nisei dentist, Dr. Harry Y. Kita, told the story in 1954 when the Japanese American Evacuation claims were being heard. He was from Salinas and was a University of California graduate. His father and mother were buried in a small Japanese cemetery in Salinas. The cemetery had been established in 1912, and by the 1940's its cherry trees and lawns were flourishing. But when Dr. Kita came back from a Relocation Center, the grass was dead, goats were feeding on the cherry trees, and vandals had knocked over more than thirty of the headstones.

The Yamato Cemetery Association filed a damage claim of $4,000. Dr. Kita was informed at the official hearing that this could not be legally paid since only an individual and not an association or charitable organization could claim damages. . . .[11]

IV

When evacuees were being resettled in the Midwest, the California Federation of Women's Clubs expressed great concern for the physical safety of Caucasian women where the Japanese might go—a strange attitude in view of the fact that no Japanese had been charged with molesting a white woman in California.

Everybody—and especially the press—was having a field day. The Hearst press assigned one of its best trained seals, Ray Richards, to cover an inspection tour of the WRA Centers by Senator Albert B. Chandler of Kentucky. The WRA was under fire (in 1943) and Chandler's tour had to do with a proposal that the Centers be transferred to control of the War Department.

Senator Chandler promised "an almost sensational report" a promise that must have sounded oddly cautionary at the time. But it was borne out by his news releases, none of which were authenticated in any way and all of which were brief. Ray Richards was hard put to evolve any real propaganda material from this, but where there is a Hearst, there's a way.

California opposition to the return of the Japanese began to spread like a disease. Governor Osborn of Arizona took alarm at California's attitude and feared that at the end of the war his state would have a disproportionate number of Japanese within its borders.[12] Congressman Karl Mundt of South Dakota was moved to ask a question which was never answered.

If the Japanese were, in fact, a menace to the defense industries of the West Coast and were removed for this reason, why aren't they an equal menace in Omaha, Nebraska, or Kansas City, Missouri? [13]

The press in California kept sounding off. Now it was reporting anti-Japanese activities by the California Society of the Sons of the American Revolution, the San Jose Knights of the Round Table, the Grand Court of California of the Foresters of America, and many other organizations.

On December 4, 1943, the *Los Angeles Times* headlined a wire service story: "Four Hundred and Fifty Cases of Whisky to Go to Tule Lake." Next day, it said, "Whisky Flow to Tule Lake Under Inquiry," and in an editorial it wondered if there was a connection between the Tule Lake riots and whisky. This was extremely poor journalism or what has been called in the newspaper profession "editing with your wrist." A belated follow-up check with the Tule Lake WRA officials revealed that no liquor at all was permitted in the Wartime Relocation Centers and that the shipment of whisky had not been sent to the Center, at all, but to the adjacent town of Tule Lake.

That story can stand for a dozen others that would show that the cards were stacked and that the Japanese Americans could not win.

In Martinez, California, a woman named Mrs. Horton Terry, a Japanese, married to a Caucasian defense worker, was threatened by her neighbors, and "No Japs Wanted Here" appeared on signs posted outside her apartment. She had a brother serving in the 442nd Regimental Combat Team, and when there was a threat of evicting her from the community, many people in California wrote letters in her defense.[14] She stuck it out.

Pearl Buck faced a Town Hall audience in Los Angeles, on November 1, 1943, and made a remarkably prescient speech. She told California,

In a curious fashion you are—or soon will be—the leader of the nation. The people in our Eastern states are already looking toward you as these great questions arise of how to deal with the people of Asia and South America. "What does the West Coast say?"—I hear that question asked every day, and wherever a policy is about to be shaped. The Eastern states are far more sensitive to your opinions today than they ever have been before. Imperceptibly the center of gravity in our country is moving westward. I say confidently that the future foreign policies of our government will be primarily decided by you, looking out over the Pacific, and not by those who face the Atlantic. The reason is that the center of the world has moved from Europe to Asia.[15]

Seventeen

She thinks that even up in heaven
Her class lies late and snores,
While poor black cherubs rise at
seven
To do celestial chores.

—Countee Cullen, *Epitaph: A Lady I Know*

I

A sense of humor and an attitude of tolerance very often go hand in hand. Some of the anti-Japanese pressure groups in California—especially the Native Sons and Daughters of the Golden West—were singularly lacking in both.

In 1943, the Native Sons organization went to court in an attempt to breathe legal life into one of their old but not very cogent arguments. But for its tragic intent, the basis of their claim might almost have seemed ludicrous. Essentially, it was this:

Some of the Issei (who could neither become citizens nor own land) had allegedly entered this country in violation of the Oriental Exclusion Act. Therefore, reasoned the Native Sons, the children of these Issei *were not "legally present" at their own birth.*

Any one absent legally from his own birth, the argument continued, could not be a citizen of the United States.[1]

The Grizzly Bear, official organ of the Native Sons and Daughters, had first been published in 1907,[2] and for more than thirty-five years had been hammering editorially on the racist theme of keeping California "the white man's paradise." In the issue for March, 1942, the editorial exhorted:

Regardless of the United States' anticipated and hoped for complete victory over the Japs in the struggle now raging, California, as well as the other Pacific Coast states, will in time be lost to the

220

White race unless all Japs now here, alien and native-born, be permanently routed from these shores. . . .

Want to preserve California as a White man's paradise? Speechifying and resoluting will not do it. So, organize and prosecute a campaign along the course here suggested.[3]

(*Author's note:* In this extract, the upper-case, upper-class, superior capital "W" has *not* been superimposed.)

Several Parlors (or chapters) of the Native Daughters, around that time, had urged separate camps for Japanese men and women, so they could not multiply during their time of internment. This proposal was in keeping with the organization's general policy of attacking the Japanese principally on *biological* grounds, to a much greater degree than did other pressure groups. Members of the various Parlors, descended from pioneer families in many instances, were rather secure from an economical standpoint. But many of the leaders had reached an age of diminishing returns in the biological aspects of life, and their endless obsession with the allegedly prolific breeding habits of the Japanese suggests a shade of purely Freudian envy.

II

The suit seeking to cut off native born citizenship with the severing of the umbilical cord was filed by John T. Regan, grand secretary of the Native Sons of the Golden West, against Cameron King, who was Registrar of voters in San Francisco. It was aimed as a wedge toward ultimately rescinding the citizenship of the Nisei and not merely as a challenge to their right to vote. The West Coast Nisei were not casting any absentee ballots that year; they were not given the opportunity to do so, and even if they had been—according to Dr. Joseph D. Sasaki, the former Fresno JACL leader previously quoted—most of them had been forced to sell or abandon their homes and so had no residency.

Mr. Regan was represented and guided by Ulysses S. Webb,

former Attorney General of the State of California, and one of the authors of the 1913 Alien Land Law. Mr. Webb had plainly put things on a racial basis that year (1913) when he told the Commonwealth Club of San Francisco:

> The fundamental basis of all legislation upon this subject, State and Federal, has been, and is, race undesirability. It is unimportant and foreign to the question under discussion whether a particular race is inferior. The simple and single question is, is the race desirable. . . . [The law] seeks to limit their presence by curtailing their privileges which they may enjoy here; for they will not come in large numbers and long abide with us if they may not acquire land.[4]

Thirty years had not mellowed Webb when he pushed the Regan suit in 1943—and now he was out not merely to "curtail their privileges" but to get rid of the Japanese entirely. In the Regan suit his thesis strongly resembled that of pro-slavery factions in the period before the Civil War. The American government, he said, was of and for and by the people all right, provided they were "white people." The Declaration of Independence had been made by white people; the people mentioned in the Preamble to the Constitution were white people. As far as the Fourteenth Amendment was concerned,

> not only its main purpose but its only purpose was to citizenize the Negro because of the effect that such status might have upon the election returns of the States which had seceded. [It was] repellent [Webb said, to think that] it was intended to achieve the citizenship of all other peoples of color born in the United States.[5]

Except, perhaps, for the Joint Immigration Committee's "Exhibit E" before the Tolan Committee, the anti-Japanese groups on the West Coast had largely pussyfooted around the color question and especially any mention of the Negro problem. Webb's brief to the court ended with the statement,

> The status of the Negro is in no way involved in this case. Neither the citizenship of the Negro nor his eligibility to naturalization is questioned.

The tail-end position of this disclaimer makes it open to the suspicion that it may have been somewhat hastily appended when Webb discovered that two of the attorneys for the Japanese American Citizens League, which presented a brief in the role of Amicus Curiae, "friend of the court," were Negroes. They were Hugh E. MacBeth and Thomas L. Griffin, of Los Angeles. Counsel also included A. L. Wirin, of Los Angeles—and two Nisei, Walter T. Tsukomoto of Tule Lake Relocation Center (formerly of Sacramento); and Saburo Kido of Poston Relocation Center (formerly of San Francisco).

Saburo Kido was the wartime president of the Japanese American Citizens League. Walter Tsukomoto, then an Army Reserve captain, has been previously mentioned in connection with his fight to be called up to active duty.[6]

Counsel for the "friend of the court" shot U. S. Webb's arguments full of holes. As far as that piece of nonsense about a person's being not legally present in the country at the time of his own birth, counsel cited a delightfully extreme case from the writing of Richard W. Flournoy, Professor of International Law at the National University Law School:

"But," one may ask, "if a Chinese merchant and his wife are returning from Europe to China via the United States, and a child is born to the woman in San Francisco the day before they sail, is such child, by the mere accident of having first seen the light in this country, a citizen of the United States?" Absurd as it may seem, the child is indeed a citizen of the United States under the law of this country, although it is also a Chinese citizen under the law of China. Although it is unfortunate that such cases are possible, there is, on the other hand, much practical advantage in a system in which mere proof of birth in the United States is sufficient proof of citizenship.[7]

The *San Francisco Chronicle* editorially slapped Mr. Webb while the case was being heard in the U.S. District Court.

It is true, as Mr. Webb says, that the Declaration, and the Constitution for that matter, was written by white men. It is not true that it was exclusively "for" white men. These charters are for human, not race principles, and to suggest otherwise now is to furnish excuse for unjustified accusation that America is not true to its principles.[8]

Attorney U. S. Webb, Appellant John T. Regan, the Native Sons and Daughters, the Joint Immigration Committee, and all others seeking to take citizenship away from the Nisei lost this round hands down. Higher courts dismissed the case without certiorari—they did not summon the records of the trial for review.

The case was significant only in one way. Mr. Webb's denial that the status of the Negro was involved somewhat plainly put him in the category of protesting too much: any nonwhite, including Chinese and Filipinos, had only to follow the trial in the newspapers to realize the depth of his personal involvement. And the American Japanese and American Negro—probably for the first time—were clearly put into the same basic camp for the still-continuing struggle for civil rights.

III

In America, the John Joneses can criticize the Supreme Court with impunity, and the John Birchers can scream for the impeachment of the Chief Justice. But the U.S. Supreme Court decisions usually stand once they have been announced, and no amount of piety or wit can cancel half a line.

The high court's ruling in the case of a Nisei named Gordon K. Hirabayashi—handed down unanimously—was important to the Japanese evacuees. Another decision, in the case of Fred Toyosaburo Korematsu, set a precedent later on which even today hangs like a menacing shadow over all minorities, or, for that matter, all Americans.

The Korematsu decision upheld the constitutionality of the Evacuation.

In each case, some of the same attorneys who had represented the Japanese American Citizens League in the Regan action, again submitted briefs of *amicus curiae*. Saburo Kido and A. L. Wirin especially had a busy year. . . .

Gordon Hirabayashi, a Nisei of the Quaker faith, had never been to Japan; he was a senior at the University of Washington. In 1942 he was arrested by Federal authorities and was convicted in a lower court of having violated both the Army's curfew and its exclusion (*i.e.,* Evacuation) orders. He was sentenced to three months' imprisonment on each count—the sentences to run concurrently.[9] In making them concurrent, the trial judge no doubt felt he was being kind. And he was— to Hirabayashi. But, in the long run, this merciful ruling backfired on all the evacuees.

Hirabayashi's counsel appealed. The Ninth Circuit Court was unsure of its ground, because it knew "of no decision in which citizens residing in areas *not subject to martial law*" had been subjected to curfew and exclusion by military order. There was, in other words, no precedent. The Ninth Circuit Court certified a question to the higher bench. Was DeWitt's exclusion order "a constitutional exercise of the war power of the President derived from the Constitution and statutes of the United States?" [10]

If Hirabayashi's sentences had been consecutive, rather than concurrent, perhaps the Supreme Court would have felt obliged to deal with the constitutional validity of the Evacuation, then and there. As it was, the Court dealt only with the military curfew. Reviewing the case in 1943, the Court considered the military situation on the West Coast during the spring of 1942 and decided that

reasonably prudent men charged with the responsibility of our national defense had ample ground for concluding that they must face the danger of invasion.

It studied the evidence (certainly consisting of estimates and opinions, not facts) purporting to show that the unrestricted presence of Japanese Americans constituted a special danger. Chief Justice Stone said:

> We cannot reject as unfounded the judgment of the military authorities and of Congress that there were disloyal members of that population, whose number and strength could not be precisely and quickly ascertained.[11]

Whose judgment? That of Congress? Did this include the testimony of anti-Japanese spokesmen before the Tolan Committee? The wild-eyed reports of Dies and Chandler? Or the racism of the West Coast Congressional delegation which asked the President to make it possible to move the Japanese? Did the Court rely on such unreliable statistics as those given to Congress on February 17, 1942, by California Senator Hiram Johnson when he stated: "we have 130,000 Japanese, 30,000 of whom are citizens"? [12]

The Supreme Court need not have done so, in the latter case, because the error was plainly pointed out in the brief *amicus curiae*.

Mr. Justice Douglas said:

> We must credit the military with as much good faith . . . as we would any other public official acting pursuant to his duties. . . . We cannot sit in judgment on the military requirements of that hour.

To be fair, the Court indeed was passing upon the constitutionality of an action taken at "that hour" and based upon the conditions then prevailing.

It found, unanimously, that the curfew was constitutional. It refrained from taking any action on the Evacuation.

Ten Broek (*Prejudice, War and the Constitution*) charges that the Supreme Court's review of the Hirabayashi case failed to apply the time-honored "substantial basis" test to the conclusions the Army had reached about the Japanese Americans, that the Court of its own initiative established no facts upon which those conclusions were founded . . . but simply referred to facts and circumstances of "public notoriety;" to facts which were "generally believed," or which had "been deemed" to exist, or which "may well' have existed.[13]

The same sort of judicial procedure was applied in the much farther-reaching Korematsu case, which tested the constitutionality of the Evacuation.

Korematsu, a native of Oakland, was a high-school graduate; he was not a dual citizen; he could read and write only English and had never been out of this country. Because he was suffering from stomach ulcers, he had been classified as 4-F. He worked as a shipyard welder until the attack on Pearl Harbor—after that he was expelled by the Boilermakers' Union because he was Japanese. He had fallen in love with a Caucasian girl and wanted to avoid evacuation. He hoped to have plastic surgery to alter his nose, change his name, and stay in Oakland to marry. The FBI caught up with him.[14]

The American Civil Liberties Union made bail for him. But (according to the American Civil Liberties Union News) the jailer, instead of releasing Korematsu, phoned the military police, who took him to the Tanforan Assembly Center. In a short time he was back in the county jail.

At his trial, he was found guilty of violating the exclusion order but was given a suspended sentence and put on probation for five years. His loyalty to America had not been attacked, but probation presented a rather interesting situation: a lone Japanese American at large by virtue of court authority. The Army would not have it: military police seized Korematsu again and threw him in the Assembly Center. Finally, his case began its move through the courts as a test instituted by the Japanese American Citizens League.

The Ninth Circuit Court of Appeals was of the opinion that the Supreme Court had already disposed of the constitutionality of the Evacuation, when, as a matter of fact, that august body had only ignored it insofar as the Hirabayashi case was concerned.

The Supreme Court Justices proceeded to split a few hairs. Korematsu, they said, had not been excluded from the military area because of hostility to him or his race. He was excluded

because we are at war with the Japanese Empire, . . . because [the Army] decided that the military urgency of the situation demanded that all citizens of Japanese ancestry be segregated from the West Coast temporarily.[15]

Justice Black recalled that the Court had upheld the curfew order, and said, "The Hirabayashi conviction and this one rest on the same 1942 Congressional Act and the same basic and military orders."

Justice Jackson dissented. "The Court," he pointed out, "is now saying that in Hirabayashi we did decide the very thing we there said we were not deciding."

Justice Roberts dissented. He felt that a hypothetical case had been substituted for the case actually before the Court, and that the process involved dividing what was "single and indivisible."

Justice Murphy dissented. He said the Evacuation fell "into the ugly abyss of racism." [16]

Unanimity had been broken, but the majority ruled.

Thus, the arbitrary removal of more than 110,000 persons from their homes, and their detention, without a hearing, behind barbed wire, was held to be in accordance with the Constitution of the United States.

It remains thus sanctified today, although for years, now, the official U.S. Army History has in effect acknowledged that the cloak of "military necessity" was an extremely thin and shoddy garment.

The New York Times Magazine of January 9, 1966, carried an excellent article by William Petersen, professor of sociology at the University of California, entitled: "Success Story, Japanese American Style." I quote the ultimate paragraph:

The Chinese in California, I am told, read the newspapers these days with a particular apprehension. They wonder whether it could happen here—again.

IV

The court cases involving the evacuated people are not being related here, necessarily, either in strict chronological order or according to the measure of their importance. At the time they were tried, more significance understandably was attached to the immediate impact the court decisions had upon the evacuees.

James Purcell is an honored name among the Japanese Americans. As a young attorney in San Francisco, Mr. Purcell had become acquainted with the Nisei and the Japanese American Citizens League through a friendship with Saburo Kido. After the Pearl Harbor attack, Purcell quickly saw the injustices being visited upon Japanese Americans. He protested against the Evacuation, and represented without fee State civil service employees who were discharged purely because of race.

Finally, Jim Purcell, a fighting Irish Catholic,[17] decided to challenge the whole constitutionality of the Evacuation. In doing this, he moved shrewdly and displayed great generalship. It took a long and painstaking search to find precisely the former California State employee he wanted for a test case. She was Mitsuye Endo, who had been dismissed from civil service. She had never attended a Japanese language school and could neither read nor write Japanese. She was not a dual citizen. She had a brother serving in the United States Army. Her family did not even subscribe to a Japanese language newspaper.[18]

Purcell filed a writ of habeas corpus on behalf of Miss Endo, contending that the War Relocation Authority had no right to detain a loyal American citizen who was innocent of all the various allegations the Army had used to justify evacuation.

Purcell remembers, now, that when the case came to trial the Army put on a considerable display of uniformed rank in the courtroom, as if seeking to emphasize the importance of the Evacuation orders to the national security. But this had no effect. Purcell lost in the lower courts or at least found them reluctant to rule. He fought the case on up through the Appellate Court and into the United States Supreme Court, personally arguing the issues, personally defraying printing and other costs.

He won his battle on December 18, 1944. The Supreme Court ruled that Mitsuye Endo "should be given her liberty."

Mr. Justice Douglas said:

Loyalty is a matter of the heart and mind, not of race, creed or color. . . . Whatever power the War Relocation Authority may have to detain other classes of citizens, it has no authority to subject citizens who are concededly loyal to its leave procedure.

Mr. Justice Murphy said:

I am of the view that detention in Relocation Centers of persons of Japanese ancestry regardless of loyalty is not only unauthorized by Congress or the Executive, but is another example of the unconstitutional resort to racism inherent in the entire evacuation program . . . racial discrimination of this nature bears no reasonable relation to military necessity and is utterly foreign to the ideals and traditions of the American people.

All nine of the Supreme Court Justices agreed that the WRA had no right to detain loyal American citizens in the Relocation Centers.[19]

This broke the dam. Within forty-eight hours Major General H. C. Pratt, now commanding the Western Defense Command, announced that the West Coast mass exclusion orders would be revoked, effective on January 2, 1945. With the exception of certain individuals, the Japanese Americans were free to go home again.

V

What had begun with a bang was ending, now, with a long and drawn-out whimper. A very confusing situation developed, and the evacuees were neither out of the woods nor out of the Relocation Centers.

On the day following the Army's announcement, WRA Director Myer served notice that all Relocation Centers would be closed before the end of 1945, and that the entire program would be terminated by June 30, 1946. The Jerome, Arkansas, Center—last to open—was the first to shut down; it had been closed on June 30, 1944, after about half of its population had resettled in the midwest and eastern states, and the remainder of some 5,700 residents were transferred to other Centers. At the time the mass exclusion orders were revoked, 35,000 evacuees had left the Centers on indefinite leave. These included the Nisei who had gone into the Army.

Closing of the Centers was definitely a blow to many of the older Issei. There were 30,000 of these noncitizens. The ones who had sons in U.S. uniforms, of course, had a bigger stake in America and a greater desire to go home. Others would be returning to places that suddenly seemed far away and unfamiliar, to an existence that was barely remembered. And from all they had heard, there were perils waiting.

The Western Defense Command was lifting the mass exclusion orders, but it was being Army to the last; it had refused to accept leave clearance judgments reached by the WRA and insisted upon makings its own tests. It would be hard to find a more unjustified example of unnecessarily duplicated man hours and paper work while a war was on, even in a Government notorious for such waste. By December 17, 1944, the Japanese Americans had been sorted and filed and card indexed into three groups:

Nearly 109,000 of them were cleared to go anywhere in the United States after January 20, 1945.

To be kept in the Centers were 4,963 males, most of them segregants at Tule Lake.

To be excluded from the West Coast were another 4,810 males, most of whom had asked for expatriation to Japan.

WRA Director Dillon Myer was doing everything possible to step up the movement of the people out of the Centers, by providing travel grants and transportation of household goods. The latter assistance must have evoked some wry humor: what kind of household goods could anyone, starting from scratch, have accumulated in the tar-paper barracks? Center schools were closed; farm projects were shut down.

Still, by July, 1945, only 16,000 of more than 60,000 evacuees remaining in the Centers had moved out.[20] Meanwhile, the Department of Justice had found cause both for suspicion and alarm in the number of applications for renunciation of American citizenship that came out of Tule Lake. There were more than 600 in mid-December, 1944, double that by January, and 3,400 by the end of January, 1945. A thousand more were added in February. By April 18, 1945, the total exceeded 6,000.[21]

Considering the way the war was going and the fact that the West Coast was once more being opened to the Japanese Americans, these figures were startling and incomprehensible. John L. Burling, of the Department of Justice, went out to California for a look, and the Justice Department began trying—perhaps belatedly—to break up the nationalistic Japanese groups in Tule Lake. This effort mainly took the form of removing the leaders of such groups. The citizenship renunciations of these malcontents were speedily approved, and in increments that ranged from 70 to 650, they were moved out of Tule Lake and into the Department of Justice Internment Camp at Santa Fe. A total of 1,416—1,098 renunciants and 318 aliens—were put in one internment camp or another.[22]

A little later, the Department of Justice held hearings at Tule Lake on more than 6,000 renunciation requests and did its best to insure that the applications were not due to coercion. It approved more than 5,500 of these, from persons older than seventeen and a half years of age. Eight of these were later found to be mentally defective.[23]

When exclusion was lifted and the West Coast was once more open to the evacuees, renunciation of citizenship lost a great deal of its charm and turned out to have been sought in anger or in resentment of treatment and not at all as the result of considered judgment. So, requests came in to cancel the applications.

The wheels ground slowly. The Department of Justice quite understandably, planned to send all renunciants to Japan. What else? The status of American citizenship is not a thing to be lightly considered.

Court action followed. The American Civil Liberties Union got busy, and one of its attorneys, Wayne Collins—a good friend of the Nisei—sued on November 5, 1945, to have certain renunciations canceled. He had 987 plaintiffs then, but the number rose to more than 4,000 within a short time.[24]

Renunciation was a thing brought on by pressures and conditions beyond anybody's control. In the long run, not everybody wanted to go to Japan at all.

Even after Japan surrendered, Tule Lake had difficulty in closing down. The Army freed all the special and individual cases it had been holding. The Center, on August 1, 1945, still had 17,341 residents; on January 1, 1946, it had 7,269. By January 31, these had been reduced to 5,045 people.[25]

As had been said, "This is a town. You can't close a town."

The WRA set up field offices all over the West Coast and gave the returning evacuees an immeasurable amount of assistance in getting resettled. Housing was a problem. There were still escheat suits against evacuees' property and boycotts against their goods. As late as January 8, 1945, there was an attempt to dynamite and burn the packing shed of a returned evacuee in Placer County, California. Violence persisted until—and after—Secretary Ickes denounced it on May 14,

1944.

Ickes said that there had been 24 incidents of violence—15 shooting attacks, 1 attempted dynamiting, 3 arson cases, and 5 threatening visits. After sounding off on West Coast hoodlumism in general, the Secretary declared:

Many of the evacuees' Nisei sons are fighting the Japanese enemy in the Philippines, at Okinawa, and in other Pacific combat areas. They are far more in the American tradition than the race-baiters fighting a private war safely at home.[26]

Perhaps Californians did not listen to Ickes. In 1945, when there was no doubt at all about the outcome of the war, Captain Daniel K. Inouye reached San Francisco on his way back to Hawaii from the Italian campaign. He had a little time to kill before he boarded ship for Honolulu; he thought a haircut would be a good idea. And so he went into a San Francisco barber shop.

"What are you?" the barber asked.

"I am an American," Inouye said.

"Yeah . . . I know, but I mean who were your ancestors? Chinese?"

"Japanese," said Inouye.

"Sorry," the barber said. "We don't serve Japs here."

At the moment, Captain Inouye was in army uniform, with a number of ribbons for bravery on his tunic, including the Purple Heart. If this was not enough, he had an empty sleeve for the arm he had lost in Italy.

If the barber is still extant, he should know that he lost the chance to cut the hair of the present United States Senator Daniel K. Inouye, from the State of Hawaii.

Eighteen

"The injustice done to the Japanese Americans will remain forever a stain on American history. There is some comfort, however, in the general acknowledgment of this injustice and in the conscientious effort that has been made to provide restitution for the property losses suffered by the evacuated citizens. . . . Restitution or reparation of this sort is always, of course, pitifully inadequate. . . .And there is no way, obviously, to make amends for the loss of liberty and of dignity and of faith in American principles. The best that can be hoped for from this tragic story is an understanding by Americans that it must never happen again—that men are never to be judged in categories or by the color of their skin or the slant of their eyes. Loyalty to the United States is loyality to an ideal; and an indispensable part of that ideal is recognition of individual guilt and individual responsibility."

—*Washington Post,* October 9, 1965.

235

I

The government and the taxpayers were still paying the bill for the Evacuation in the fall of 1965, but not very much. Payments for property losses suffered by the evacuees were still being made seventeen years after legislation was passed authorizing the U.S. Attorney General to receive and adjudicate such claims. The average rate of the settlement was 10 percent of the amounts asked, based on the value of the 1941 dollar.

Nobody was ever paid a cent for losses due to death or personal injury, personal inconvenience, physical or mental hardships, or suffering. Neither was anyone ever compensated for the money he might reasonably have been expected to earn from business profits or gainful employment during the period of detention.[1]

In 1942, the Federal Reserve Bank of San Francisco estimated that the total loss to the evacuees would approximate $400,000,000. How closely the 10 percent rate of settlement followed this estimate is shown by the fact that when the last claim was adjudicated on October 1, 1965, the Govenment had authorized payment of $38,000,000 to 26,560 claimants.[2]

Thirty-eight million dollars is a modest sum when viewed in the light of Lyndon B. Johnson's $112.8 billion budget for the fiscal year of 1966. But the total cost of the Evacuation was far from being modest.

As for the separation of the loyal from the disloyal [says Leonard J. Arrington, Professor of Economics at Utah State University], no one could possibly have believed that it would have cost more to have had the FBI individually investigate them and segregate the potentially disloyal than it cost the government to feed, clothe, house and guard all 110,000 of them in detention camps for the duration of the war.

It is estimated that the cost of constructing the assembly centers and ten relocation centers was approximately $70,000,000, with virtually no salvage value. The estimated cost of maintaining the evacuees during the three years of detention was $150,000,000. The direct entire cost of the Evacuation, not counting the loss to the evacuees or the loss to the country of the productive activities in which they would otherwise have engaged, was on the order of $350,000,000.[3]

There have been other costs, not included in any of the above figures. They are smaller sums, but of a nature that tends to make a taxpayer's blood boil. For example:

In adjudicating the Evacuation claims during the single year of 1950, the Government spent $211,567 in administrative expenses. The average cost of adjudicating a single claim was more than $1,500. The average award per claim was only $440.[4]

II

The Japanese American Citizens League can take much of the credit for the fact that evacuees were ever paid anything at all. In 1946, the National Council of the JACL voted to memorialize Congress to enact some sort of program to compensate evacuees for their losses. The War Relocation Authority drafted a bill, and the JACL lobbied for it vigorously in the Eightieth Congress. President Truman signed it into law on July 2, 1948. January 3, 1950, was set as a deadline for the filing of claims.

More than 24,000 claims were filed before the deadline, but the procedure was bogged down in administrative and technical difficulties. In 1950, the JACL suggested an amendment that would start the wheels turning by authorizing compromise settlements. The Department of Justice agreed and proposed that the Attorney General be allowed to compromise and settle claims "up to $2,500 or up to three-quarters of the amount of the claim, whichever was less." [5]

This was a pitifully low rate. Even before the 1948 law had

been passed, an American Federation of Labor union official, Elmer J. Hewitt, told a Congressional committee that a claims survey had been conducted in Seabrook, New Jersey, where 300 evacuee families were resettled. Each family, Mr. Hewitt said, had lost an average of $6,000.[6]

The $2,500 compromise amendment became law, and by 1955 more than 20,000 claimants had settled for that amount or less. There was another amendment, sponsored by the JACL, in 1956, and the last of the compromise settlements was made two years later.

The really big claims had been put off until the last, and a number of the claimants died before their cases were ever settled. Eight claims were for a million dollars or more—and nearly $37,000,000 had already been paid out.

Attorneys were getting ten percent of the awards.

Many people living in the eastern and midwestern sections of the United States probably were both startled and suspicious when they read about million-dollar claims being filed by Japanese American evacuees. They had long been accustomed to thinking of the West Coast Japanese as living in the "Little Tokyos" of Los Angeles and other cities or on small truck and berry farms in the interior valleys. They had never heard of old Keisaburo Koda, who emigrated to this country in 1908 at the age of twenty-seven and was of the stuff of which Horatio Alger legends are made.

Keisaburo Koda had come to the United States before the Exclusion Act of 1924. He operated one of the first fish canneries on Terminal Island, ran fishing boats, and even drilled for oil. But where he really struck it rich was in the San Joaquin Valley in Merced County, at South Dos Palos, fifty miles northwest of Fresno. In the troubled spring of 1942 the Koda family owned 5,000 acres of land there—in the names of the two Nisei sons, William and Edward—and leased another 4,000 acres. Keisaburo Koda was then sixty-one and had long been known as the "Rice King." He deserved all he had. Among other things, he had pioneered the planting of rice from low-flying airplanes.[7]

Koda and his sons were sole owners of the stock in the State Farming Company, a California corporation. Their land had been acquired, mainly on the installment plan, from the famous pioneer cattle ranching firm of Miller and Lux. They grew and milled rice, engaged in general farming, and raised hogs. Profits were considerable—$52,373.58 for the year 1941 alone. The Kodas were thrifty and had plowed the profits back into the land. They finished paying off their Miller and Lux contracts only seven months before Pearl Harbor.[8]

They had an attorney—a Caucasian—on retainer to their corporation, but he resigned early in 1942 because of the increasing anti-Japanese feeling. The Kodas correctly foresaw that they would be evacuated and entered into a lease agreement with a prominent San Francisco rice broker, to whom they gave power of attorney. A board of directors was set up, and—by deliberate intent—on May 12 the people running the business were all Caucasian. This fact did not stop the State of California from filing an escheat proceeding, charging that Keisaburo Koda was violating the alien land law by operating through his sons. Under this action, the land could be reverted to the state.

It may seem curious that William and Edward Koda, American citizens by birth, would not be entitled to the ownership of land in California—*even if it had been given to them by their alien father*. But escheat actions were brought against many West Coast Japanese, under the alien land law, regardless of citizenship rights.

In May, 1942, after the escheat action had been filed, the Kodas had to stand the cost of planting a new rice crop which they would never harvest. The cost was $114,941.[9]

In the Merced Assembly Center in May, and in the Relocation Center at Granada, Colorado, in September, the Kodas at least were allowed to consult with directors of the State Farming Company and with its attorneys. It was a big business, and they still held most of the stock.

California's Attorney General, Earl Warren, was running for Governor. Robert Kenney was running for Attorney General. The escheat proceedings against the Kodas were being "continued by stipulation of counsel."

According to a statement made years later in behalf of the Kodas, before a Congressional group investigating the Japanese American Evacuation Claims, a lawyer connected with the farm's board of directors persuaded the Kodas that a substantial donation to Mr. Kenney's campaign might be "good if Mr. Kenney were elected." The Kodas paid the donation directly to this attorney.[10]

While they were behind barbed wire in the Granada Relocation Center the Kodas were told that the escheat proceedings very likely could be "compromised" if the stock they held were transferred to a company with persons of non-Japanese ancestry.

What could the Kodas do? They agreed to a sale of all the assets of the State Farming Company to a new outfit known as Mill Farms. The escheat program went on, and established the figure of $200,000 as a basis for compromise settlement to satisfy the State of California. In the long run, the compromise was set at $100,000. And financing had to be arranged to cover that sum.[11]

Little or no money came in to the Kodas from May, 1942, until they were released from the Granada Relocation Center on September 10, 1945.[12]

During late 1943 and early 1944, the Kodas heard that portions of their real estate were being sold. They could do nothing about this. When they protested to the Evacuation Center officials, they were told, "If you can't trust your attorney, whom can you trust?" [13]

The answer seems to have been that they couldn't trust anybody.

III

When the Kodas came home after the war, they found the mill, the machinery, and some 4,000 acres of the land had been sold—and not for a very good price. They started all over again. Finally, the California Supreme Court held the Alien Land Law to be unconstitutional, and later Keisaburo Koda was able to become a naturalized American citizen.

He filed suit against the United States in the Court of Claims for $2,497,500, and said, "I have every bit of faith in American democracy . . . in American justice." His faith was sorely tried. The case was argued for fifteen years. Keisaburo Koda died at the age of eighty-three while visiting Japan late in 1964; his son William had died in 1961. Two attorneys and an accountant who had worked on the case also failed to live long enough to see its dubiously successful termination on October 1, 1965.[14]

On that day, and probably with a prodigious sigh of relief, the Justice Department closed the books on the Evacuation claims. It had opened them officially on December 16, 1949, when it paid the first check—in the amount of $303.36—to Tokuji Tokimasa for books and office fixtures he had been forced to leave behind in Los Angeles when he was evacuated.

The Koda claim was not only the last, but the largest. The Court offered a $362,500 settlement to Edward Koda and Mrs. Jean Koda, William's widow, . . . and the long litigation was ended.

Ed Koda is not bitter; he says the Evacuation "was just something that happened." In saying that, he is being much more philosophical than most other Americans could ever be. He did not make any money out of the $362,500 compromise, either: his figures show that the Kodas spent nearly that much to prosecute their claims. But he started all over again with only 1,000 acres and is now farming three times that much. Through increasingly scientific practices, he is producing more rice on 3,000 acres than the bigger tract produced in 1941.

Still, Ed Koda can look across a field and see the tall rice mill his father once owned, now standing on a neighbor's property. The neighbor once farmed fewer acres than the

Kodas. He farms 20,000 acres, now, "because he didn't have to leave his business, and start over." [15]

When it came to settling the Evacuation Claims, the big operators and the people who were called the "pots and pans" claimants suffered alike: none of their claims was allowed to take into consideration the inflationary prices that followed the war. All compensation was based upon the values of 1941 and 1942.

Neither was any evacuee ever recompensed for the money he might have earned in shipyards, in other defense work, or in private industry, had he been at liberty. The loss to the impounded people, therefore, was doubled and tripled.

One of the former Justice Department attorneys has called the dime-to-the-dollar payments

almost a noble effort by the government to try to compensate, . . . at least in part. It showed these people there was some recognition [that] a mistake had been made.

The modifying word "almost," in that, is significant. In plain fact, the effort fell far short of nobility.

Mike Masaoka, who sparked the JACL's fight for the claims legislation, says:

While the Congress is to be thanked for enacting this legislation and appropriating the funds to pay the approved claims, it should be kept in mind that this was neither a generous program nor an expeditious one. . . . Nevertheless [it] represents a major triumph not only for JACL but also for the American way [and attests] to the ability of our system to correct, in part, our mistakes and blunders.

This raises a question. *Whose* blunder was it that the property of the evacuees was not adequately safeguarded?

Congressman Tolan, chairman of the Tolan Committee, repeatedly expressed concern during the Feburary, 1942, hearings, because no proper custodial arrangements had been made. The Evacuation was then in the planning stage; there was time in which to attempt, at least, to make such arrangements. But, as the War Relocation Authority says in its final report, "the Federal government was slow to set up the machinery for safeguarding the property of the people who were to be evacuated."

The Army, of course, was very busy handling a formidable job. Under military rules, however, that was no excuse. Actually, General DeWitt's Western Defense Command had been explicitly assigned the responsibility on February 20, 1942, the day before the Tolan Committee met. Paragraph fourteen of a long "Outline Memorandum" sent to DeWitt by Assistant Secretary of War John J. McCloy said:

It will, of course, be necessary that your plans include provision for protection of the property, particularly the physical property, of evacuees. All reasonable measures should be taken through publicity and other means, to encourage evacuees to take steps to protect their own property. Where evacuees are unable to do this prior to the time when it is necessary for them to comply with the exclusion orders, there is always danger that unscrupulous persons will take undue advantage or that physical property unavoidably left behind will be pillaged by lawless elements. The protection of physical property from theft or other harm is primarily the responsibility of state and local law-enforcement agencies, and you will doubtless call upon them for the maximum assistance in this connection. *Where they are unable to protect physical property left behind in military areas, the responsibility will be yours, to provide reasonable protection, either through the use of troops or through other appropriate measures.* The appointment by you of a property custodian and the creation by him of an organization to deal with such property in military areas may become necessary. The provisions of the Executive Order and the necessity in each given instance are such that you have authority to take such action, either directly or through another federal agency. [Italics supplied.] [16]

The Federal Reserve Bank of San Francisco was named and took over the problem of arranging warehouse storage for the household goods of evacuees; several agencies undertook to interview the evacuees to determine what property protection they would need. The plan looks good on paper. But it was too slow in being started, and if there was any real effort to put on a publicity program advising the Japanese that their possessions would be protected, it failed miserably. In 1954, before the Congressional Committee investigating the Evacuation claims, Congressman Edgar A. Jonas of Illinois said:

The evacuation orders, in many instances, gave the people affected desperately little time in which to settle their affairs. The governmental safeguards which were designed to prevent undue loss were somewhat tardily instituted, were not at once effectively publicized among the evacuees, and were never entirely successful.[17]

Besides, when the Evacuation began to roll in the spring of 1942, there had already been a precedent. No property custodian had been named at all when the Japanese residents of Terminal Island were given forty-eight hours to get out. It would have taken a vast number of trucks to transfer the household effects of those five hundred families within forty-eight hours. In this case, most of the people lost everything they had.

The human equation also entered the picture. In Los Angeles, the Nicheren Buddhist Church on East First Street was designated for use as a warehouse, and the adjacent parsonage was rented to a woman who—like Keisaburo Koda's farm manager—was given power of attorney. A year later an inspection party found the woman caretaker gone, and with her all the washing machines, stoves, refrigerators, and other accessories that were difficult to obtain in wartime. The trunks had been broken open and pillaged. It is not of record that this woman was ever brought to book.[18]

It should be borne in mind that among the more than 26,000 Evacuation claims, only a dozen or so were big ones: the majority were small, and had mainly to do with household goods that had been lost. Even so, when the people finally left the Relocation Centers, where the head of the family had been lucky to earn as much as $16 a month, it was hard to set up housekeeping again.

Nineteen

The freedom of which we boast
is not lost in shattered Dunkirks
and blazing Pearl Harbours, . . .
such events call forth the utmost
resistance. Freedom is lost little
by little in noiseless theft, a frag-
ment of concession to expediency
here, a morsel of "what does it
matter?" there. Then, shockingly,
we find that freedom has disap-
peared in the regimentation of not
only our daily doings but our
eternal ambitions.

—The Royal Bank of Canada Monthly Letter, January, 1966.

I

The barbed wire that surrounded the desert Relocation Centers has rusted and broken now—which makes it all the more
dangerous. The tar-paper barracks have fallen into slab-sided
ruin; the buzzards and desert coyotes reign supreme over the
desolate wastes where thousands of people lived for an enforced while, laughed, made love, dreamed, and died. The
desert, reclaiming its own in a dry and dusty and immutable
way, does not remember.

No American can really afford to forget.

The people who were interned in those Centers are, by and
large, doing extremely well today. The Nisei, mostly coming
of age during the war years, have produced thousands of educators, lawyers, doctors, dentists, judges, and other professional men, including many scientists. In these fields, they far
outrank any other American group of similar numerical
strength.

245

It should be remembered that as a minority group they achieved full and sovereign status *not* by demonstrations or sit-ins, not by parading with placards, not by resistance and riots. They shed no blood but their own, given in unstinted measure on the battlefields of Europe and in the jungles of the Southwest Pacific. The odds were against most of them, but they showed in a quiet, patient and capable way that they were true Americans.

But the rusty barbed wire and the things that brought about the barbed wire are still dangerous.

Today, twenty-four years after the fact, nearly everybody agrees that the mass removal of the Japanese Americans from the West Coast was militarily unnecessary, that it was a tragic and expensive blunder, and that it accomplished little more than an all-around waste of manpower and gave the Axis Powers excellent, ready-made propaganda material that proved Democracy did not always work.

Today, on the other hand, many of the people who were involved insist that the Evacuation was a "helpful catastrophe."

There was never a more strange wedding of words. Certainly the Evacuation was a catastrophe to some 110,000 persons. The belief that it was "helpful" is based on the fact that it gave the Nisei a chance to prove themselves the hard way, in the 442nd Regimental Combat Team, while those left at home amply demonstrated their willingness to go along with law and order.

Too many of the Japanese Americans who were in those desert concentration camps are willing to believe it is all finished business. They are glad to be where they are today and ready to let bygones be bygones, and nobody could blame them for this.

But every American should give some thought to the opinion of Justice Robert M. Jackson, of the Supreme Court, when he dissented in the case of Korematsu vs. the United States:

A military order, however unconstitutional, is not apt to last longer than the military emergency. . . . But once a judicial opinion rationalizes such an order to show that it conforms to the Constitution . . . the Court for all time has validated the principle of racial discrimination in criminal procedure and of transplanting American citizens. *The principle then lies about like a loaded weapon ready for the hand of any authority that can bring forward a plausible claim of an urgent need* [italics supplied].[1]

II

Today it is neither profitable nor possible to fix the blame for the Evacuation on any one individual or any one organization. We have shown that discrimination against West Coast Japanese did not begin with Pearl Harbor, but long preceded that attack. A large number of pressure groups and politicians were active in seeking the Evacuation—and yet it is debatable whether these *led* the West Coast citizens or merely followed them.

Nothing is to be gained now by pinpointing General DeWitt as the principal villain or chief author of the plan. He had a job to do, and it should be charitably assumed that he did the job as best he could, according to his lights. He lived out his last days in the Washington, D.C. area, perhaps aware or unaware of the fact that if he ever went back to California the Japanese American Citizens League planned to hit him with a million dollar libel suit. Although he refused to give ten Broek and his co-authors an interview or make any statement for their book, he actually joined the Japan-America Society of Washington and was active in that organization until his death. He once told Mike Masaoka that if history portrayed him as an enemy of the Japanese Americans it would be incorrect. The fact was, he said, that he had been wrongfully advised and misled by his staff.[2]

That was an extremely curious observation for any military commander to make. The man with the stars on his shoulders also carries the full weight of responsibility there; he can pass along rewards or punishments, but in the final analysis most of the glory of success or the risk of failure will be his alone. De-

Witt's much quoted "A Jap's a Jap, and giving him a scrap of paper does not make any difference" hardly sounded like staff work. It had the ring of impetuous spontaneity, and certainly most staff officers would have advised against it.

In blaming his staff, General DeWitt could have showed some others how to get out from under the onus of the Evacuation, if they had still been around.

Had Franklin Delano Roosevelt been wrongfully advised and misled by Secretary of War Stimson and by West Coast Congressmen when he issued Executive Order No. 9066?

Was the Supreme Court ill-advised when it upheld the Evacuation as a constitutional act, thus elevating it forever from the status of a military mistake committed in hysteria and creating an extremely dangerous precedent?

Was California's Attorney General Earl Warren poorly advised and misled by the State's law enforcement officers when he uttered such damning testimony against the Japanese Americans before the Tolan Committee, or was he just about to run for the office of Governor?

Warren made a good Governor of California, and Japanese Americans credit him with doing much, as the war ended, to help them resettle in the state. But there has been an indication, both on his part and that of General DeWitt, that certain episodes of history will simply go away if you do not mention them—and this is most curious.

On March 7, 1966, a courteous letter was sent to Chief Justice Earl Warren, informing him that a portion of this book would quote extensively from his testimony before the Tolan Congressional Committee in 1942. The letter paid tribute to the Chief Justice's record in the civil rights field, and requested that he make a statement for inclusion in the book, or comment in any way on the wartime Evacuation program.[3]

On March 30, an assistant to the Chief Justice wrote that because of the pressure of his official duties, Mr. Warren would not be able to comply with the request.[4]

It is entirely understandable that such a policy may be mandatory, because if any exception is made to the rule of judicial silence, the Chief Justice's office could well be swamped with requests for articles, statements, interviews, and comments on scores of subjects. The author, therefore, has no quarrel with Mr. Warren's 1966 decision, much as he may disagree with certain attitudes and statements on Mr. Warren's part in 1942. In the intervening twenty-four years, a lot of political water has flowed over the dam, and many opinions have been changed.

III

The Japanese American Citizens League fought for thirty-five years to eliminate the principle and the practice of racial discrimination in the American immigration code. It deserved much of the credit for what took place on Sunday afternoon, October 3, 1965.

On that day, in the highly symbolical shadow of the Statue of Liberty, President Lyndon B. Johnson signed into law the new immigration bill. This measure cast aside for all time the "national origins" system and will permit 350,000 persons to enter the United States every year. They will not come, now, on the basis of creed, color, or nationality, but on a fair and equal judgment of their skills and their relationships to émigrés already here.

For the first time, people of Asiatic ancestry will be given a fair shake as against those from Europe. In view of the record of more than 70,000 Nisei in this country, it was high time that this was done.

When the ceremonies were held on Ellis Island—the entry point for millions of emigrants over the years—the White House was not lacking in the amenities. It invited Mike Masaoka, Washington representative of the Japanese American Citizens League, to attend.[5] Mike Masaoka, first volunteer for the 442nd Regimental Combat Team and prominent in many other ways, might well qualify for the national title of Mr.

Nisei—except for one thing. Mike would rather be known, and deservedly so, as plain "Mr. American."

Which brings up a point. It is time now that all of us dropped the term "Japanese Americans," unhyphenated or not, in favor of just "Americans." Guests at this same ceremony included Senator Daniel K. Inouye, and his fellow Hawaiians, Congressman Spark Matsunaga (who served in the 100th Infantry Battalion and the Military Intelligence Language School at Camp Snelling, and who came out of the war with a Purple Heart) and Congresswoman Patsy Takemoto Mink. Mrs. Mink is undoubtedly the most charming member to grace the halls of Congress since that institution was established, and Senator Inouye has come a long and shining way since that time when the San Francisco barber would not cut his hair. . . .

IV

The Nisei are doing extremely well, indeed. Some 10,000 of them today are in civil service. A number have been graduated from Annapolis and West Point. About 20,000 live and are thriving in Chicago, which had only about three hundred persons of Japanese ancestry before World War II.

And they still insist that the Evacuation was a "helpful catastrophe" in that it supplied the vehicle which enabled them to prove their patriotism, their Americanism, and their individual worth. They are not bitter about the experience of the Evacuation. Their main concern, now, has to do with gaps in culture and heritage.

Remember that the Issei were the first settlers, and the Nisei were the second generation. The Nisei at least were exposed to Japanese speech, although many never really learned it; they had some knowledge of old country culture, legends, folkways, and other things that help people in this nation of immigrants to identify themselves with blood lines and with the past. But then came the Sansei, or third generation, arriving mostly after the war, and at a time when their parents were trying to prove that they were good Americans and were all too ready to dismiss the whole idea of Japanese culture and heritage.

The Sansei have been growing up as purely American as mustard on a hot dog, very few of them able to speak more than a few words of Japanese. Play a *kabuki* recording for them and they yawn and want some of the latest music that, heaven forfend, passes for American.

This is problem enough, but now we even have some small, cute, button-eyed and lovable kids who are Yonsei—fourth generation!

There is, of course, no answer to this problem. Other groups of immigrants tried hard to keep the ties of the old country alive: we had the *Turnvereins* and many such things and, while some still exist, their nationalistic significance has long vanished. But there is nothing wrong with the idea that origins should be perpetuated and honored, and any Japanese judo groups or flower-arrangement clubs certainly should be encouraged today. Any language schools should be doubly encouraged: it has been proved in time of emergency that we never have enough linguists.

As this was being written, that sprightly journal, the *Saturday Review,* came out with a humorous and still disturbing comment in Jerome Beatty, Jr's. "Trade Winds" column:

An unconfirmed rumor has come to my attention that our FBI is well prepared for a World War III in which our major enemy will be China. Detention camps have been secretly prepared in which will be "relocated" all the Chinese in the United States so that they may be screened, and prevented from sabotaging the war effort and from signaling Peking with short-wave radios.[6]

Tongue-in-cheek or not, Mr. Beatty is not really joking here, in the very least. There is a precedent, and at the hour that Peking becomes the target, the Chinese in this country could well become the victims.

This is essentially absurd. It was proved so before. It would require the expensive and inhumane roundup of thousands of little people such as your Chinese laundryman or your restaurateur who knows how to turn out egg foo yung but doesn't give a damn about Chinese politics. Let us hope and expect that FBI and Naval Intelligence will still know—as they did in 1942—the real spies and the real enemy agents.

And let us pray that, the next time, some strong and authoritative voice can keep hysteria in check.

V

Justice Jackson's "loaded weapon" is bad enough to have on the books. But there is still another such meance, all too little known.

As an American citizen, of whatever origins, you—the reader—probably consider yourself secure. This is not necessarily so, because laws have provided for future Evacuations, not on the basis of race or color but on the far broader and more dangerous ground of *thought* itself.

The McCarran Act (the Internal Security Act of 1950) provides in Section 104 (a) that in time of emergency the Attorney General or his representative is authorized to issue:

> *a warrant for the apprehension of each person as to whom there is reasonable ground to believe that such person probably will engage in, or probably will conspire with others to engage in, acts of espionage or sabotage.*[7]

When it comes to loaded weapons lying around, this one is double barreled. All it requires is to have your neighbor dislike you, or vice versa.

When this book was nearing completion, the author asked the Japanese American Citizens League if anything is being done toward getting the United States Supreme Court to revoke its decision that the Evacuation was a constitutional act. The answer is yes, but not very much. For years, the Japanese

American Citizens League has been seeking just the right test case to start on its way through the courts. For years, too, it has been deterred by two things: first, such a court case would cost a tremendous amount of money, and, second, all the Japanese Americans are doing wonderfully well today and are happy to forget the past.

Dr. Eugene V. Rostow, Dean of the Yale Law School and the foremost authority on constitutional law in America, has said he would like to see the constitutionality of the Evacuation revoked.[8] He does not think, however, that any and all minority groups are in danger so long as the decisions remain on the books—in other words, he minimizes the threat of Justice Jackson's "loaded gun." This would only happen, he points out, in a time of emergency.

To a layman who knows nothing of the law, constitutional or otherwise, that is not a very reassuring statement. And to anybody who reads the news about Viet Nam, the time of emergency may be tomorrow.

Chronology of the Evacuation and the WRA Program

1942

January 29: U.S. Attorney General Francis Biddle issues first of a series of orders establishing limited strategic areas on Pacific Coast and requiring removal of all enemy aliens from such areas.

February 13: West Coast congressional delegation writes President Roosevelt urging "immediate evacuation of all persons of Japanese lineage . . . aliens and citizens alike" from "entire strategic area" of California, Oregon, and Washington.

February 14: General John L. DeWitt, commanding Western Defense Command, sends memorandum to Secretary of War Henry L. Stimson advocating evacuation of "Japanese and other subversive persons" from West Coast area.

February 19: President Roosevelt signs Executive Order No. 9066 authorizing Secretary of War or any military commander designated by the Secretary to establish "military areas" and to exclude from them "any or all persons."

February 20: Stimson designates DeWitt as military commander authorized to carry out evacuation under Executive Order No. 9066.

March 2: DeWitt's Public Proclamation No. 1 sets up western half of three West Coast states and southern third of Arizona as military area, from which all persons of Japanese blood are eventually to be removed.

March 11: DeWitt creates Wartime Civil Control Administration to handle evacuation program; names Colonel Karl R. Bendetsen as its Director.

March 18: Roosevelt's Executive Order No. 9102 establishes the War Relocation Authority to aid people evacuated under

Executive Order No. 9066; names Milton S. Eisenhower as Director.

March 22: First big contingent of Japanese, aliens and citizens, moved from Los Angeles to Manzanar Assembly Center.

March 23: DeWitt's Civilian Exclusion Order No. 1 calls for all people of Japanese descent living on Bainbridge Island, Puget Sound, to be removed to the Puyallup Assembly Center within seven days.

March 27: DeWitt's Public Proclamation No. 4 halts all voluntary migration of Japanese from the military areas.

April 7: Governors and other officials from ten western states confer at Salt Lake City with Colonel Bendetsen and WRA Director Eisenhower. Most officials strongly protest unrestricted resettlement of Japanese in their states.

May 8: First evacuees reach Gila River Relocation Center near Parker, Arizona.

May 27: First evacuees reach Tule Lake Relocation Center in Northern California.

June 1: Manzanar Assembly Center transferred from Army's Jurisdiction to that of WRA, becomes Manzanar Relocation Center.

June 2: DeWitt's Public Proclamation No. 6 halts voluntary migration of Japanese from eastern half of California; announces that they will be removed to WRA Centers.

June 17: Dillon S. Myer succeeds Milton Eisenhower (resigned) as Director, WRA.

August 7: DeWitt announces that 110,000 people of Japanese blood have been removed from their homes.

November 3: Final contingent of evacuees from Fresno Assembly Center arrives at Jerome (Arkansas) Relocation Center. This completes transfer of control from Army to WRA.

November 14: Trouble begins with demonstration in Gila River Center protesting arrest of two evacuees charged with beating a third.

November 23: Troubles at Poston Center settled by an agreement.

December 6: Military Police temporarily take over control of Manzanar Center to stop demonstrations.

1943

January 28: Stimson reveals plan to organize a Japanese American Army Combat Team.

February 8: "Loyalty" registration both for Army enlistment and leave clearance begins in WRA Centers.

March 11: Director Myer writes Stimson urging relaxation of West Coast exclusion orders against Japanese. (Stimson rejects this on May 10.)

April 8: U.S. Senator A. B. Chandler of Kentucky, who has been head of a subcommittee investigating WRA, writes to Director Myer recommending that "disloyal" evacuees be segregated from other residents of the Centers.

June 25: Director Myer writes Assistant Secretary of War John J. McCloy on plans for a segregation program and selection of Tule Lake as the segregation Center.

October 11: Final contingent of "disloyal" evacuees reaches Tule Lake.

November 1: Tule Lake's troubles begin with mass demonstration.

November 4: Riots at Tule Lake. Army takes over control of Center.

1944

January 14: Military control ends at Tule Lake.

January 20: Stimson announces Japanese Americans hereafter will be drafted for military service.

June 30: Jerome Relocation Center, last to open, is the first to close, with 5,000 remaining residents transferred to other Centers.

July 1: Roosevelt signs Public Law 405 (Seventy-Eighth Congress) permitting American citizens to renounce citizenship in time of war.

December 17: War Department announces that, effective on January 2, 1945, the West Coast exclusion orders against Japanese will be revoked.

December 18: Director Myer announces closing of all Centers before the end of 1945 and liquidation of entire WRA program by June 30, 1946. His decision follows U.S. Supreme Court rulings.

1945

January 8: Returnees' many troubles begin with attempt to burn and dynamite packing shed of a Japanese in Placer County, California.

April 30: Director Myer officially estimated that on June 30 the Centers will still hold 44,000 "relocatable" evacuees.

May 14: Secretary of the Interior Harold L. Ickes strongly denounces the continuing West Coast terrorism against returnees.

August 15: VJ Day.

September 4: Western Defense Command revokes all individual exclusion orders and all military restrictions against Japanese.

1946

March 20: Tule Lake Segregation Center is officially closed.

June 30: War Relocation Authority program officially ends.

—Compiled, for the most part, from *WRA, a Story of Human Conservation.*
U.S. Department of the Interior. Government Printing Office.
Washington, D.C.

Bibliography

Primary Sources

Interviews with Japanese Americans who were in the Evacuation Camps.

Written recollections and journals kept by "Mr. H.," Dr. Joseph D. Sasaki, Marge Shimomoto, and others.

Correspondence and/or interviews with:
Colonel Karl R. Bendetsen, U.S. Army (ret.); Raymond R. Best, Carmichael, California; James Kipling Cooper, Yokahama, Japan; Admiral Arthur H. McCollum, U.S. Navy (ret.), Arlington, Va.; Mike Masaoka, Japanese American Citizens League, Washington, D.C.; Judge K. E. Morrison, Santa Ana, California; Admiral Rufus Taylor, U.S. Navy, Washington, D.C.; Mary Francis Stewart, Sacramento, California; Richard and Alice Winn, Sacramento, California; Roy Westmoreland, Imperial, California. Interviews with many members of the Japanese American Citizens League.

Personal recollections of some thirteen years as a newspaperman and an officer in Naval Reserve Intelligence in San Diego, Los Angeles, and San Francisco, and of twenty years of active duty with the Navy, including nearly six years as a captain in Japan and Korea.

Secondary Sources

ARRINGTON, Leonard J., *The Price of Prejudice* (Logan, Utah: The Faculty Association, Utah State University, 1962).

BANCROFT, Hubert Howe, *Works, Vol. XXV. California Inter Pocula* (San Francisco: The History Company, 1882–1890).

BLOOM, Leonard, and Ruth Riemer, *Removal and Return* (Berkeley: University of California Press, 1949).

BROOM, Leonard, and John I. Kitsuse, *The Managed Casualty* (Berkeley: University of California Press, 1956).

COOLIDGE, Mary E. B., *Chinese Immigration* (New York: Henry Holt, 1909).

EATON, Allen H., *Beauty Behind Barbed Wire* (New York: Harper & Bros., 1952).

GRODZINS, Morton, *Americans Betrayed* (Chicago: University of Chicago Press, 1949).

MCWILLIAMS, Carey, *Prejudice; Japanese Americans: Symbol of Racial Intolerance* (Boston: Little, Brown, 1944).

MIERS, Earl Schenck, *Freedom* (New York: Grosset and Dunlap, 1965).

MORIN, Relman, *East Wind Rising* (New York: Alfred A. Knopf, 1960).

MURPHY, Thomas D., *Ambassadors in Arms* (Honolulu: University of Hawaii Press, 1955).

OKUBO, Miné, *Citizen 13660* (New York: Columbia University Press, 1946).

POTTER, John Deane, *Yamamoto* (New York: The Viking Press, 1965).

POURADE, Richard F., *History of San Diego: The Explorers* (San Diego: Union-Tribune Publishing Company, 1961).

RICE, Richard Brewer, *The Manzanar War Relocation Center.* Thesis. (Berkeley: University of California Library, 1947).

ROSTOW, Eugene V., *The Sovereign Prerogative: the Supreme Court and the Quest for Law* (New Haven: Yale University Press, 1962).

SASAKI, Dr. Joseph D., *Unpublished Ms.*

SHIREY, Orville C., *Americans: the Story of the 442nd Combat Team* (Washington: Infantry Journal Press, 1946).

SMITH, Bradford, *Americans from Japan* (Lippincott, 1948).

SWANBERG, W. A., *Citizen Hearst* (New York: Scribners, 1961).

TEN BROEK, Jacobus, with Edward N. Barnhart and Floyd W. Matson, *Prejudice, War and the Constitution* (Berkeley: University of California Press, 1954).

THOMAS, Dorothy Swaine and Richard Nishimoto, *The Spoilage* (Berkeley: University of California Press, 1946).

THOMAS, Dorothy Swaine, with Charles Kikuchi and James Sakoda, *The Salvage* (Berkeley: University of California Press, 1952).

U.S. ARMY. Final Report (Washington: Government Printing Office, 1943).

U.S. ARMY. *Command Decisions* (Washington: Government

Printing Office, 1960).

U.S. ARMY. *The Western Hemisphere; Guarding the United States and Its Outposts* (Washington: Government Printing Office, 1961).

U.S. CONGRESS. *National Defense Migration. Hearings before the Select Committee Investigating National Defense Migration. House of Representatives, 77th Congress* (Washington: Government Printing Office, parts 29, 30, and 31, 1942).

JAPANESE AMERICAN EVACUATION CLAIMS. *Hearings before Subcommittee No. 5 of the Committee on the Judiciary, House of Representatives, 83rd Congress.* Serial No. 23 (Washington: Government Printing Office, 1954).

REVISION OF IMMIGRATION, NATURALIZATION AND NATIONALITY LAWS. *Joint Hearings before the Subcommittee of the Committees on the Judiciary. Congress of the United States.* Eighty-second Congress, 1951.

U.S. WAR RELOCATION AUTHORITY. Washington: Government Printing Office, 1943–1946. Publications include:
Wartime Exile. The Exclusion of the Japanese Americans From the West Coast.
The Evacuated People.
The Wartime Handling of Evacuee Property.
Token Shipment: the Story of America's War Refugee Shelter.
Legal and Constitutional Phases of the WRA Program.
Community Government in War Relocation Centers.
Administrative Highlights of the WRA Program.
People in Motion; the post-War Adjustment of the Evacuated Japanese Americans.

I have drawn, also, upon an M.A. thesis by John Y. Yoshino, dealing with the Evacuation Claims Act.

Periodicals and Newspapers

These sources, credited in the chapter notes, are too many and varied to be listed here with any degree of accuracy. They include publications of the American Academy of Political Science; the *American Mercury;* the *Chicago Tribune;* the *San Diego Union;* the San Francisco *Chronicle;* the *San Francisco Examiner;* the San Francisco *Call Bulletin;* the Los Angeles *Examiner* and the

Los Angeles *Times,* and *The New York Times.* They take in the Chicago *Tribune,* the *New Leader, Newsweek,* the *Pacific Citizen, Time, The Nation, Christian Century,* the *New Republic,* and others.

Notes

CHAPTER ONE

1. Blake Clark, and Oland R. Russell, "Japanese American Soldiers Make Good," *The American Mercury,* June, 1945.
2. John Lardner, *Newsweek,* November 8, 1943.
3. Shirey, Orville C., *Americans: The Story of the 442nd Combat Team* (Washington: Infantry Journal Press, 1946), Cf. later figures released by Adjutant General's Department of the Army.
4. Allen H. Okamoto to author.
5. Shirey, *op cit.,* and *The American Mercury, op cit.*
6. Selective Service System reports on "Special Groups," p. 142.
7. *The New Leader,* Editorial, March 3, 1945.
8. *The American Mercury, op. cit.*

CHAPTER TWO

1. Richard F. Pourade, *History of San Diego: The Explorers* (San Diego: Union-Tribune Publishing Co., 1961).
2. Arthur Walworth, *Black Ships off Japan* (New York: Alfred A. Knopf, 1946). Cf., Rear Admiral George Henry Preble, *The Opening of Japan,* edited by Boleslaw Szczesniak (Norman: University of Oklahoma Press, 1952), p. 6.
3. *Pacific Citizen* files. (The *Pacific Citizen* is the official weekly newspaper of the Japanese American Citizens League.)
4. *Ibid.*   5. *Ibid.*
6. The sharp increase in immigration for 1900 resulted when ships carrying Japanese settlers to Hawaii were diverted to the West Coast because of bubonic plague in the Islands. See Dorothy Swaine Thomas, *The Salvage* (Berkeley: University of California Press, 1952), p. 6.
7. Quoted by Jacobus ten Broek with Edward N. Barnhart and Floyd W. Matson, *Prejudice, War and the Constitution* (Berkeley: University of California Press, 1954).
8. *Ibid.*   9. *Ibid.*

10. Hubert Howe Bancroft, *Works, Vol. XXV. California Inter Pocula* (San Francisco: The History Co., 1882–1890).
11. *Pacific Citizen* files. 12. *Ibid.* 13. *Ibid.*
14. ten Broek, *op. cit.* Quoting 1900 editorial of Organized Labor.
15. *Ibid.*
16. Carey McWilliams, *Prejudice; Japanese Americans: Symbol of Racial Intolerance* (Boston: Little, Brown, 1945).
17. John S. Chambers, *The Japanese Invasion,* Annals of the American Academy of Political and Social Science, January 1921, p. 36.
18. Cf. McWilliams, *op cit.,* p. 72, p. 298, for a critical estimate of Gulick's abilities.
19. Theodore Roosevelt to his son, Kermit. Cited in Morton Grodzins, *Americans Betrayed* (Chicago: University of Chicago Press, 1949), p. 6.
20. *Ibid.* Citing Syngman Rhee. *Japan Inside Out.*

CHAPTER THREE

1. Field notes. 2. *Ibid.* 3. *Ibid.*
4. CBS, "The Twentieth Century." Produced 1965.
5. Field notes. 6. *Ibid.*
7. *Japanese American Evacuation Claims: Hearings Before Subcommittee No. 5 of the Committee on the Judiciary, House of Representatives, Eighty-Third Congress.* (Washington: Government Printing Office, 1954).
8. Department of Justice press release. December 6, 1942.
9. *Ibid.* 10. *Pacific Citizen,* June 11, 1942.
11. Brief, *Amicus Curiae,* Hirabayashi vs. United States (Japanese American Citizens League), p. 62.
12. Los Angeles *Daily News,* August 26, 1942.
13. *Ibid.,* August 22, 1942.
14. *New York Times,* August 4, 1942.
15. Los Angeles *Daily News,* August 22, 1942.
16. San Francisco *Chronicle,* August 2, 1944.
17. Chicago *Tribune,* June 15, 1943.
18. *Pacific Citizen* files.
19. Tolan Committee Hearings Transcript.
20. *Japanese American Evacuation Claims, op. cit.*

21. Field notes.
22. CBS, "The Twentieth Century," *op cit.* Also Mike Masaoka to the author.

CHAPTER FOUR

1. ten Broek, *op cit.,* notes, p. 348. Cf. Grodzins, *op cit.,* p. 380.
2. Quoted in *Japanese American Review,* August 23, 1941.
3. *Ibid.,* September 26, 1941.   4. *Ibid.,* October 4, 1941.
5. Grodzins, *op cit.,* p 380.   6. *Ibid.,* p. 382.
7. *Ibid.,* p. 383.
8. Correspondence supplied by Dr. Joseph D. Sasaki: letters between Dr. Sasaki and Congressman Gearhart.
9. ten Broek. *op cit.,* pp. 95–96.
10. *U.S. Army in World War II; the Western Hemisphere* (Washington: Department of the Army, 1961).
11. Fly to Attorney General Biddle, April 4, 1944. Cited by Wartime Relocation Authority in Wartime Exile.
12. Fly to Biddle, January 9, 1942; apparently not made public until April 1, 1944. Cf. Grodzins, *op cit.,* note 51, p. 292.
13. Grodzins, *op cit.,* p. 386, note 28.
14. *Ibid.,* p. 66.
15. ten Broek, *op cit.* p. 77. Cf. McWilliams, *op cit.,* p. 263.
16. San Francisco *Examiner* files.
17. New York *Herald Tribune,* February 12, 1942.
18. ten Broek, *op cit.,* pp. 85–86. See Pegler's syndicated column, "Fair Enough," February 16, 1942.
19. Final Report by General DeWitt. Also *Command Decisions; Western Hemisphere*
20. *Command Decisions, op cit.*   21. Final Report, *op cit.*
22. Earl Schenck Miers, *Freedom* (New York: Grosset & Dunlap. 1965), p. 163 *et seq.*
23. Grodzins, *op cit.,* p. 183.
24. San Francisco *Examiner,* February 22, 1942.
25. Tolan Hearings, *op cit.*   26. *Ibid.*
27. Final Report, *op cit.,* p. 25.   28. Tolan Hearings, *op cit.*
29. *Pacific Citizen* files.   30. Tolan Hearings, *op cit.*
31. Grodzins, *op cit.* Citing State of California Attorney General's Opinion No. 1-NS4108, February 17, 1942.

32. *Ibid.,* State of California Attorney General's Opinion No. 1-NS4083, February 7, 1942.
33. *Ibid.,* Citing "Minutes," meeting of California Joint Immigration Committee, February 7, 1942.
34. Tolan Hearings, *op cit.*

CHAPTER FIVE

1. Final Report, *op cit.*   2. Tolan Hearings, *op cit.*
3. *Ibid.*   4. *Ibid.*   5. *Ibid.*   6. *Ibid.*   7. *Ibid.*
8. A Department of Justice press release on February 16, 1942, said 1,266 Japanese aliens had been arrested on the Pacific Coast. Some of these were released after questioning.
9. Tolan Hearings, *op cit.*
10. *Ibid.*   11. *Ibid.*   12. *Ibid.*   13. *Ibid.*
14. *Ibid.*   15. *Ibid.*   16. *Ibid.*   17. *Ibid.*
18. *Japanese American Evacuation Claims, op cit.*
19. *Pacific Citizen* files.
20. Tolan hearings, *op cit.*
21. WRA reports show that the demand for military interpreters with a knowledge of Japanese always exceeded the supply.
22. Associated Press.

CHAPTER SIX

1. *Time,* March 5, 1965, p. 41.
2. *Command Decisions, op cit.*
3. *Ibid.*   4. *Ibid.,* p. 129.   5. *Ibid.,* p. 127.
6. *The U.S. Army in World War II; the Western Hemisphere, op cit.,* p. 129, note 49.
7. Rear Admiral Arthur H. McCollum, U.S.N. (ret.) to author.
8. Final Report, *op cit.*
9. Wartime Exile, *op cit.,* p. 101.
10. *Ibid.,* p. 102.
11. *The U.S. Army in World War II; the Western Hemisphere, op cit.*
12. W. A. Swanberg, *Citizen Hearst* (New York: Scribner's, 1961), pp. 500–501.

13. Copy for Final Report was transmitted to the War Department on June 5, 1943.
14. *The U.S. Army in World War II; the Western Hemisphere, op cit.*
15. *Ibid.*
16. ten Broek, *op cit.* From typescript of Ringle report to the Chief of Naval Operations.
17. Galen M. Fisher, *Far Eastern Survey,* Vol. II, 1942.
18. *Ibid. The Drama of the Japanese Evacuation; a Touchstone of Democracy.* Council for Social Action of Congregational Christian Churches.
19. John Deane Potter, *Yamamoto, the Man Who Menaced America.* New York: Viking, 1965.
20. *Time,* June 23, 1941, p. 17.
21. Frederic Sondern, "The Many Faces of the FBI," *Reader's Digest,* Dec. 1965, p. 182.
22. Field notes. Gordon Shoemaker to author.
23. *Ibid.*   24. Field Notes. Margot Coley to author.
25. Field notes.

CHAPTER SEVEN

1. Final Report, *op cit.*
2. *Vital Speeches of the Day,* 1942.
3. Journal of Mr. H.   4. *Ibid.*   5. Field notes.
6. *Ibid.*
7. Miné Okubo, *Citizen 13660* (New York: Columbia University Press, 1946). Cf. CBS, "The Twentieth Century," *op cit.*
8. Journal of Mr. H. *op cit.*

CHAPTER EIGHT

1. Thomas D. Murphy, *Ambassadors in Arms* (Honolulu: University of Hawaii Press, 1955).
2. Letters, Sasaki to Gearhart. Also John Yoshino to author.

CHAPTER NINE

1. Letters, Sasaki, *op cit.*   2. Judge Morrison to author.
3. Joseph D. Sasaki, *op cit.* Unpublished Ms.
4. Journal of Mr. H., *op cit.*   5. Field notes.
6. *Ibid.*   7. Tolan Hearings, *op cit.*
8. Roy Westmoreland to author, enclosing Marge Shimomoto letter.
9. *Ibid.*   10. *Pacific Citizen.*
11. *Los Angeles Times,* August 18, 1942.

CHAPTER TEN

1. Richard Brewer Rice, *The Manzanar War Relocation Center* (University of California: Oct. 29, 1947. Unpublished thesis).
2. *Ibid.*   3. *Ibid.*   4. *Ibid.*   5. *Ibid.*
6. *Ibid.*   7. Journal of Mr. H., *op cit.*
8. Kurihara's manuscripts are quoted extensively in the Appendix of *The Spoilage* by Dorothy Swaine Thomas; Berkeley, University of California Press, 1946.
9. *Ibid.*

CHAPTER ELEVEN

1. Richard Brewer Rice, *op cit.*   2. *Ibid.*   3. *Ibid.*
4. *Ibid.*
5. WRA, *A Story of Human Conservation.* Of Richard Brewer Rice, *et alii.* Thomas, *The Spoilage, op cit.* (p. 49) uses a pseudonymn for Tayama, but in this case fails to adhere to her usual practice of italicizing pseudonymns.
6. Richard Brewer Rice, *op cit.*   7. *Ibid.*
8. Leonard J. Arrington, *The Price of Prejudice* (Logan: The Faculty Association, Utah State University, 1962).
9. *Ibid.*   10. *Ibid.*   11. *Pacific Citizen.*
12. WRA.   13. *Ibid.*

CHAPTER TWELVE

1. WRA, *The Impounded People,* p. 100.
2. WRA, *et alii.* Cf. Thomas, *The Spoilage,* p. 64 *et seq.*
3. *Los Angeles Times,* April 14 and April 19, 1943. Cf. McWilliams, *op cit.,* p. 251.
4. Thomas, *op cit., The Spoilage.* pp. 73–75.
5. *Ibid.* p. 79.   6. *Ibid.* p. 81.   7. *Ibid.* p. 82.
8. WRA
9. Bradford Smith, *Americans from Japan* (New York: Lippincott, 1948), p. 306.
10. ten Broek, *op cit.,* pp. 164–165.
11. Raymond R. Best to author
12. McWilliams, *op cit.,* p. 189.

CHAPTER THIRTEEN

1. Thomas D. Murphy, *op cit.*
2. *Ibid.*   3. Field Notes.
4. *Pacific Citizen,* February 18, 1943. Cf. McWilliams, p. 253.
5. Allan Hynd, *Betrayal From the East.* Cited by McWilliams, p. 255.
6. Los Angeles *Herald Express,* May 19, 1943. Cf. McWilliams, p. 253.
7. McWilliams, p. 257.   8. *Ibid.*
9. *Pacific Citizen* files.

CHAPTER FOURTEEN

1. Thomas, *The Spoilage, op cit.,* Appendix.
2. Thomas, *The Salvage, op cit.,* p. 94.
3. WRA, *Impounded People,* p. 136.
4. Thomas, *The Salvage, op cit.,* p. 111.
5. WRA, *Impounded People, op cit.,* p. 136.
6. Thomas, *The Spoilage, op cit.,* p. 114.
7. *Ibid.,* p. 116.   8. Raymond Best to author.
9. Thomas, *The Spoilage,* p. 123.   10. *Ibid.,* p. 122.
11. *Ibid.,* p. 126.

12. WRA, *Semi-Annual Report,* July 1 to December 31, 1943, p. 14.
13. Thomas, *The Spoilage,* p. 135.   14. *Ibid.,* p. 145.
15. *Ibid.,* pp. 149–150.
16. WRA, *A Story of Human Conservation,* pp. 118–119.
17. *Ibid.*

CHAPTER FIFTEEN

1. Thomas, *The Spoilage, op cit.,* p. 249 *et seq.*
2. *Ibid.,* p. 266.
3. Tule Lake Coöperator, July 3, 1943. Cf. Thomas, *The Spoilage,* p. 271, *et seq.*
4. Thomas, *The Spoilage, op cit.* p. 272.   5. *Ibid.* p. 273.
6. *Ibid.* p. 256.   7. Arrington, *op cit.*
8. Journal of Mr. H.   9. Arrington, *op cit.*
10. ten Broek, *op cit.,* pp. 168–169
11. *Ibid,* Citing WDC Memorandum, p. 172.

CHAPTER SIXTEEN

1. Papers of Franklin D. Roosevelt.
2. Cited by McWilliams, *op cit.*
3. Bradford Smith, *op cit.,* p. 237, *et alii.*
4. Shirey, *op cit.,* p. 72.
5. Bradford Smith, *op cit.,* p. 327.
6. *Los Angeles Times,* December 9, 1945.
7. McWilliams *et alii.*   8. *Ibid.,* p. 240.
9. *Ibid.,* p. 244.   10. *Ibid.*
11. *Japanese American Evacuation Claims.*
12. McWilliams, *op cit.,* p. 249.   13. *Ibid.,* p. 250.
14. *Ibid.,* pp. 271–272.   15. *Ibid.,* pp. 272–273.

CHAPTER SEVENTEEN

1. Los Angeles *Daily Journal,* April 14 and 18, 1942. See ten Broek, p. 312. Cf. Grodzins, p. 417, for similar argument by Native Sons of the Golden West.
2. Grodzins, *op cit.* Note, p. 7.   3. *Ibid,* p. 49.

4. Yamoto Ichihashi, *Japanese in the United States* (Palo Alto: Stanford University Press, 1934), p. 275.
5. ten Broek, p. 314. Citing *"Brief for Appellant,"* Regan vs. King. No. 10299. U.S. Circuit Court of Appeals for the Ninth Circuit.
6. Mike Masaoka to author.
7. Japanese American Citizens League. Brief *Amicus Curiae.*
8. *Ibid.*   9. ten Broek, pp. 233–234.
10. *Ibid.* p. 212.   11. *Ibid.,* pp. 290, 265.
12. *Congressional Record,* February 17, 1942, p. 1371.
13. ten Broek, p. 216.   14. *Ibid.,* p. 236.
15. *Ibid.,* p. 263.   16. *Ibid.,* p. 290.
17. *Pacific Citizen* files.   18. *Ibid.*
19. ten Broek, pp. 253–254. Cf. Japanese American Citizens League, Brief *Amicus Curiae,* Hirabayashi vs. United States, No. 870 in the Supreme Court, October 1942.
20. WRA.   21. *Ibid.*   22. *Ibid.*
23. *Ibid.*   24. ten Broek, p. 179.   25. WRA.
26. WRA, *A Story of Human Conservation.*

CHAPTER EIGHTEEN

1. John M. A. Yoshino, *Legislative History and Administrative Procedures of the Evacuation Claims Act* (Loyola University, thesis, 1953).
2. Mike Masaoka, *Pacific Citizen.*   3. Arrington, *op cit.*
4. Yoshino, *op cit.*
5. Mike Masaoka, *Pacific Citizen, op cit.*
6. Yoshino, *op cit.*
7. Jack Jones, *Los Angeles Times.* November 7–8, 1965.
8. *Japanese American Evacuation Claims.* Hearings before Subcommittee No. 5 of the Committee on the Judiciary, House of Representatives, San Francisco, August 30–31, 1954, pp. 95–96.
9. *Ibid.,* p. 94.   10. *Ibid.,* p. 98.   11. *Ibid.,* p. 99.
12. *Ibid.,* p. 99.   13. *Ibid.,* p. 99.
14. Jack Jones, *Los Angeles Times, op cit.*   15. *Ibid.*
16. Final Report, *op cit.,* p. 29.

17. *Japanese American Evacuation Claims, op cit.*
18. Jack Jones, *Los Angeles Times, op cit.*

CHAPTER NINETEEN

1. ten Broek, *op cit.,* p. 332.   2. Mike Masaoka to author.
3. W. W. Norton & Co. to author.   4. *Ibid.*
5. *Pacific Citizen.*   6. *Saturday Review,* May 7, 1966.
7. James Thurber, *Alarms and Diversions* (New York: Harper & Row, 1966), p. 51, quoting Henry Pratt Fairchild of N.Y. University.
8. Eugene V. Rostow to author.

Index

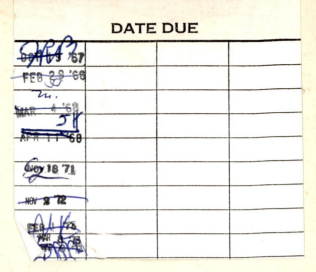